MW00612193

PARDON POWER

HOW THE PARDON SYSTEM WORKS — AND WHY

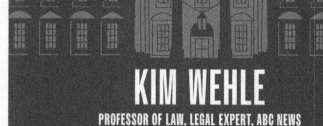

KIM WEHLE

PROFESSOR OF LAW, LEGAL EXPERT, ABC NEWS

"Is the quality of mercy strained? According to Kim Wehle, the answer is yes, at least in the context of today's political and legal landscape. Taking the reader on a fascinating historical journey from the ancient holy scriptures to January 6, Wehle highlights how an ecclesiastical instrument intended to correct for 'unfortunate guilt,' in the words of Alexander Hamilton, can (and has) become weaponized by occupiers of the Oval Office intent on subverting the rule of law. Wehle's analysis is a must-read for anyone who cares about creating transparency and accountability in one of the most awesome powers of the presidency, and bringing it back in alignment with the Framers' original vision."

—Asha Rangappa, Former FBI Agent, Former Associate Dean at Yale Law School, and Senior Lecturer at Yale University

"In *Pardon Power*, Kim Wehle debunks the orthodoxy that the President's pardon power has no limits and argues persuasively that its use for corruption has no place in our system of laws. A must-read for those who care about the fate of American democracy."

—Charlie Sykes, MSNBC contributor/columnist and author of *How the Right Lost Its Mind*

"Like all discretionary authority, the pardon power is only as virtuous as the person who controls it. Kimberly Wehle demonstrates that it can be a righteous tool to remedy wrongful convictions, reduce excessive sentences, and recognize extraordinary rehabilitation, but it also can be used to obstruct investigations, benefit political allies, and reward people for paying the President's friends. Professor Wehle's timely book illuminates a vast constitutional power likely to be debated during the 2024 presidential campaign and beyond."

—Rod Rosenstein, Deputy Attorney General, Trump Administration

"In sharp, accessible prose, Kim Wehle traces the President's pardon power from its historical origins to its looming implications for democracy today. This book is a vital contribution in a critical time where we must look to strengthen the guardrails against corruption."

—Mimi Rocah, former federal prosecutor and Division Chief, U.S. Attorney's Office, Southern District of New York

"The threat of Donald Trump pardoning the January 6th insurrectionists—and possibly even himself if he wins the White House again—puts Kim Wehle's remarkable new book at the center of the storm that could destroy American democracy. In compelling, readable prose, Kim lays out why the president is not a king—including when it comes to pardons. I have warned of a possible Trump 'pocket pardon' long before he was indicted for orchestrating an insurrection and stealing classified documents. Kim Wehle's new book answers all the questions about the president's power to pardon, and rejects self-pardons as unconstitutional. A compelling and important book that arrives at exactly the right time."

Glenn Kirschner, former career federal prosecutor, NBC News/MSNBC legal analyst, host of Justice Matters YouTube channel

PARDON POWER

HOW THE PARDON SYSTEM WORKS — AND WHY

KIM WEHLE

woodhall press

Woodhall Press | Norwalk, CT

woodhall press

Woodhall Press, Norwalk, CT 06855
WoodhallPress.com

Copyright © 2024 Kimberly Wehle

All rights reserved. No part of this book may be reproduced in any form or by any electronic or mechanical means, including information storage and retrieval systems, without written permission from the publisher, except by a reviewer who may quote passages for review.

Cover design: L.J. Mucci
Layout artist: L.J. Mucci

Library of Congress Cataloging-in-Publication Data available

ISBN 978-1-954907-50-8   (paper: alk paper)
ISBN 978-1-954907-51-5   (electronic)

First Edition
Distributed by Independent Publishers Group
(800) 888-4741

Printed in the United States of America

This is a work of nonfiction. It is designed to provide accurate and authoritative information in regard to the subject matter covered.

To the thousands of students who I've had the honor of working with for the past seventeen years: Thank you for constantly challenging my thinking. Education is for educators, too.

Table of Contents

Foreword by John W. Dean

On April 25, 2024, the U.S. Supreme Court heard oral arguments in *Donald J. Trump v. United States*, an appeal from an indictment charging the former president with four federal felonies arising from the January 6, 2021, insurrection at the U.S. Capitol. The story is well-known: A mob of Trump's supporters violently stormed the Capitol building to disrupt a joint session of Congress while counting the Electoral College votes to formalize the election of Joe Biden as president of the United States. The goal of the mob was to stop that process so their defeated candidate, Donald Trump, could illegitimately remain in the White House.

Trump's appeal to the High Court sought to stall this criminal case, as he had done with the three other criminal cases he faces, employing any and all tactics to delay conviction before the 2024 election, when he hopes he might find a way back to the White House and the temporary immunity enjoyed by all presidents during their time in office. Mostly as a political ploy, Trump's appeal claimed that he – and all presidents – should have permanent immunity from criminal charges, both while in office and after. In short, to tie up his case Trump was claiming what no other president had ever claimed: that presidents are above the law. Thus, the question before the Court is whether the indictment must be tossed out as a matter of constitutional law, after the lower federal trial court and Court of Appeals for the District of Columbia rejected this novel claim. That the U.S. Supreme Court did not summarily reject Trump's appeal, and is giving it serious attention, speaks to the radicalism that surrounds Trump, and to the fact that he nominated three of the justices who are now considering his call for criminal immunity. We await the answer as I write.

To date, over 1,200 people have been arrested and charged with offenses relating to the events of January 6, 2021. More than 460 have been sentenced to prison. Trump's argument that he—and he alone—should be immune from any legal accountability whatsoever for his role in the January 6th carnage, along with his multifaceted scheme to remain in office, were facts with which the conservative justices showed little interest. Rather, as Justice Neil Gorsuch stated during the argument, the controlling conservative majority appeared most interested in "writing a rule for the ages."

As Republicans have found it increasingly difficult to win electoral majorities, and consistently control Congress, they have focused on packing the federal courts with conservative judges and justices and expanding presidential powers. Trump has given the Supreme Court a case that should be used to strengthen democracy by checking presidential powers. Instead, the conservative majority appears to see it as an opportunity to vastly expand presidential power rather than constrain it, by placing the president above the law, both civil law (which Nixon accomplished in 1982, after his presidency, by prompting the Court to establish civil immunity for presidents in *Fitzgerald v. Nixon*) and now criminal law.

This potential landmark case is relevant because pardon power, the subject of this book, arose at least 13 times during the argument, and presidential immunity from criminal prosecution is closely associated with the unresolved matter of presidential self-pardons. (Trump claims he could have pardoned himself, notwithstanding the fact that no president has ever done so, nor save for Nixon needed to do so. Others never considered it, I suspect, because as Nixon was told, self-pardons are contrary to the reality that no one can fairly judge their own case.) The pardon power surely will influence the resolution of this presidential immunity case. Accordingly, the High Court had questions about the president for whom I served as White House counsel, Richard Nixon.

Justice Ketanji Brown Jackson asked Trump's lawyer: "What was up with the pardon for President Nixon? I mean if—if everybody thought that presidents couldn't be prosecuted, then what—what was that about?" He responded, incorrectly: "Well, he was under investigation for both private and public conduct at the time, official acts and private conduct."

The conservative justices showed great interest for the idea of creating a dividing line between "private" conduct by presidents that could be prosecuted, and "public" conduct that cannot—even though it's the public side that invites severe abuses of power. Justice Gorsuch noted in an exchange with Trump's attorney: "And then the question becomes, as we've been exploring here today a little bit, about how to segregate private from official conduct that may or may not enjoy some immunity . . . ." Nixon—like Trump—did bad things, this line of inquiry went. But only some of those bad things can give rise to criminal prosecution, even after a president becomes a private citizen.

By the time this book is published, we will have the Supreme Court's answer on criminal immunity for presidents. Questioning by the conservative justices suggested they may establish a radical new standard for the American presidency, making some criminal conduct by the U.S. commander-in-chief above the law. This will mean that by brazenly breaking the law, Trump will have managed to persuade these potential enablers to distort the Constitution to insulate not only his behavior, but that of future presidents, from legal accountability for lawbreaking. This is beyond ironic for me, not to mention a serious threat to our democracy.

As someone who served under Nixon from July 1970 until he fired me in April 1973, I can say with confidence that Trump's attorney is wrong about Nixon's abuses of power and the criminal conduct that forced his resignation. Everything Nixon did in connection with the so-called Watergate scandal would qualify as official presidential conduct that could now be immune from prosecution if the Court rules as some justices appeared inclined to do. As counsel for the government, Michael Dreeben, explained in response to a question from Justice Samuel Alito: "The Watergate smoking-gun tape involved President Nixon and [chief of staff] H.R. Haldeman talking about, and then deciding to use, the CIA to give a bogus story to the FBI to shut down a criminal investigation." Managing the Central Intelligence Agency—an entity lodged at the apex of Article II power to execute the law—is quintessentially official presidential conduct. Staving off its abuse is why we have legal and constitutional guardrails.

I understand this well. As the person who warned Nixon that his behavior was "a cancer on the presidency," and blew the whistle on his abuses of power, I know the criminal law is a powerful deterrent on the White House.

Justice Gorsuch raised a concern that the pardon power could be routinely abused by presidents if they aren't given criminal immunity. (Never mind that in our 236-year history, this problem has never materialized.) "What would happen if presidents were under fear—fear that their successors would criminally prosecute them for their acts in office?" Gorsuch asked. "It seems to me like one of the incentives that might be created is for presidents to try to pardon themselves." Without criminal immunity to keep them above the law, in other words, presidents would try to put themselves above the law "every four years from now on." So why not give presidents a permanent, preemptive pardon now, under the guise of criminal immunity? Justice Alito later raised the identical point.

Although the hypothetical is somewhat tortured, his concern that presidents can use the pardon power to commit or cover up crimes is a real one. To make the point: Nixon dangled pardons throughout Watergate as a means of accomplishing the cover-up on criminal activity, and the pages of this book illuminate other such situations.

It is high irony that Justices Gorsuch and Alito suggested the possibility of a self-pardon to justify immunizing presidents from accountability for crimes. As will be learned from the following pages, the pardon power is an arcane vestige of an unlimited monarchy, under which the divine right of kings—the belief that God selectively mandated the ruler's power and legitimacy—prevailed. Whether that view will retake hold in the 21st century—under a constitutional democracy established to reject that very model—may prove to be the greatest American political crisis of the age. Because of that sad reality, this book could hardly be timelier—or more important.

I was involved in one of the historic pardons recounted in this book, a pardon some believe was orchestrated by President Nixon as a quid-pro-quo for votes in the 1972 election. On December 23, 1971, Nixon commuted the sentence of Jimmy Hoffa, the former head of the International Brotherhood of Teamsters, who was serving an aggregate of 13 years for jury tampering, attempted bribery, conspiracy, and mail and wire fraud after two separate trials. When John F. Kennedy took office in 1961, his brother, Attorney General Robert Kennedy, made it a priority to pursue Hoffa–who was widely suspected of involvement in organized crime – and spearheaded what the press called the "Get Hoffa Squad" within the Justice Department.

The first Hoffa trial took place in Nashville, Tennessee, in 1962. The indictment alleged that Hoffa accepted $1 million from a trucking company to keep the peace among union members. That case ended in a hung jury. Two years later, Hoffa was tried and convicted in Chattanooga for tampering with the Nashville jury. And in June of 1963, he was indicted and convicted by a jury again, in federal court in Chicago, on charges of mail fraud, wire fraud and conspiracy stemming from a $25 million scheme to defraud a union pension fund.

Hoffa was barely five years into his 13-year sentence when Nixon pardoned him. The Teamsters subsequently endorsed Nixon in his re-election bid in 1972, despite its long record of supporting Democrats almost exclusively. Critics charged that Nixon pardoned Hoffa to win the union's favor and attract members to the Republican Party.

A *New York Times* story from March 17, 1974, declared that although the "political base upon which President Nixon built his landslide re-election victory in 1972 is melting away like a sand castle before an incoming tide . . . one block of his base, at least, has remained almost touchingly steadfast to the President—the International Brotherhood of Teamsters, the nation's biggest trade union, and its President, Frank E. Fitzsimmons." As this book explains, there's not much law constraining presidents' power to use pardons for personal gain. In 1974, like today, the public barely notices when presidents do abuse the pardon power, so it has increasingly become common practice.

Nixon's commutation of Hoffa came with a condition, however. To get out of prison, Hoffa could not "engage in the direct or indirect management of any labor organization" until March 6, 1980. There was speculation that Nixon made this conditional at the request of Frank Fitzsimmons, the new president of the Teamsters, in exchange for support in the election. Fitzsimmons denied it. After his release, Hoffa was determined to return to union leadership. He sued to invalidate the condition attached to the pardon, claiming it was unconstitutional and "formulated and imposed as the result of a conspiracy involving the President." (Hoffa lost the case, as described in the pages that follow.) Claiming that the condition was imposed in return for political favors from Fitzsimmons, Hoffa wanted the condition removed from his commutation. He also claimed that there was no historical precedent for attaching conditions to pardons. Not so.

I sat for a deposition in Hoffa's lawsuit, *Hoffa v. Saxbe*, because I came up with the idea of Hoffa's conditional pardon. Hoffa's lawyers subpoenaed documents related to the clemency decision, including memoranda by me to Nixon and his attorney general, John Mitchell, but the judge quashed the request on grounds of executive privilege. Although Hoffa appealed, the case became moot when he disappeared on July 30, 1975. He was later declared dead. To this day, it's widely believed that I drafted the conditional pardon at Nixon's direction—as part of his bid to get Fitzsimmons behind his re-election. That's not what happened, however.

A week or so before Hoffa's pardon, which was signed two days before Christmas in 1971, I was walking from the Executive Office building office to the West Wing of the White House, and ran into Mitchell, who had just come from a meeting with the president. Because pardons were processed through my office as a final review before going to the president after coming from the office of the pardon attorney in the Justice Department, Mitchell told me that they were going to pardon Hoffa. There had been newspaper speculation that Nixon might do this, so I was not totally surprised. But I was also aware that the Department of Justice was concerned about Hoffa's ties to organized crime.

When talking to Mitchell outside the West Wing that December 1971 afternoon, it occurred to me that the government might want to keep Hoffa out of the union business. I asked Mitchell, who had been my boss at the Justice Department before coming to the White House, if they were going to issue a conditional commutation. He had no idea what I was talking about or that Hoffa could be prevented from union activities in exchange for his release from prison. I explained that I had read that Abraham Lincoln, as president, had issued pardons after the Civil War that came with conditions. (When I recently shared this story with the author of this book, she reported that research revealed that on March 11, 1865, Lincoln offered a pardon to deserters of the Union army, "on condition that they return to their regiments and companies or to such other organizations as they may be assigned to and serve the remainder of their original terms of enlistment and in addition thereto a period equal to the time lost by desertion.") Anyway, Mitchell liked the idea and requested I draft some language and send it over to him, which was done.

I can still see the expression on Hoffa's face when he deposed me, and the disappointment also of his lawyers. They thought this was surely a sinister plot, long in the making, and not the happenstance that actually occurred. While I was White House counsel, in this instance, I had merely been a staff man making sure my superiors had what they needed – and in fact they did want to keep Hoffa out of union affairs, albeit out of prison for political reasons. I heard no talk of quid pro quo.

The Watergate scandal has been routinely resurrected during the Trump years, but looking back, there is no comparison of these men or their presidencies. Richard Nixon's abuses of power do not come close to those of Donald Trump, conduct which the Supreme Court appears poised to insulate, at least partially, from legal accountability. A few salient comparisons of these men: I am not known as a Nixon defender, but I cannot envision Richard Nixon having a sexual encounter with a porn star, nor an extended affair with a Playboy playmate. Nor did Nixon ever disrupt the transition of government power. When Nixon lost the 1960 presidential election to John Kennedy, notwithstanding serious irregularities in the Illinois returns, he conceded. Rather than put the nation through the agony of an impeachment trial for Watergate, he resigned. Nixon was an establishmentarian, not to mention a man with a conscience. Trump is neither. Let us hope we all are mistaken in interpreting the justices' questions, and they do not give Trump the pass he seeks.

Staging a coup to steal an election from a legitimate president is the essence of tyranny. Moreover, today there's a greater need to use the legal system to rein in presidential misconduct than in the 1970s, when Americans relied on trusted news sources for their information—outlets like *The New York Times*, *The Washington Post*, CBS, ABC and NBC. People made voting decisions based on a uniform set of facts. Nixon left office, at the Republican Party's insistence, because he had lost public trust. That's nearly impossible now. Nixon lost support – and his presidency – because the American people shared a common narrative that exposed him as a danger to the country. Today, while Trump piles on his endless lies, the modern Republican Party has redesigned itself to embrace his blatant dishonesty.

Donald Trump has made the pardon power an issue every American should understand. If he fails to win in November, he will be needing pardons for himself (both state and federal), for he will be convicted in one or more of the four cases (with 88 felonies total). But should he prevail, he will abuse the pardon power as no president ever has, an inescapable conclusion from his first term, and his very nature. From the pages that follow you can better appreciate how this will unravel our democracy.

May 2024

John W. Dean
Counsel to the President of the United States (1970-73)
The Nixon White House

Index of Notable Presidential Pardons Discussed

It is better that ten guilty persons escape than that one innocent suffer.
—William Blackstone

* * *

As has been stated by numerous legal scholars,
I have the absolute right to pardon myself, but why would I do that
when I have done nothing wrong?
—Donald J. Trump

I will tell you, I will look very, very favorably about full pardons [for
January 6, 2021]. If I decide to run and if I win, I will be looking very,
very strongly about pardons. Full pardons. We'll be looking very,
very seriously at full pardons because we can't let that happen . . .
And I mean full pardons with an apology to many.
—Donald J. Trump

* * *

It was an awesome, ultimate power over the lives of others that no
person or government should have, or crave.
—Pat Brown, former governor of California

Introduction

From 1959 to 1967, Edmund G. "Pat" Brown served two terms as governor of the State of California.[1] During that time, he received fifty-nine petitions from death row prisoners urging him to halt their executions and commute their death sentences to life in prison. In thirty-six cases, Brown denied the requests and the prisoners were put to death. The remaining twenty-three petitioners lived, at Brown's sole discretion.

By the time he moved into the California governor's office, Brown knew a few things about the criminal justice system. He had already served seven years as the San Francisco district attorney and eight years as California's attorney general. He understood that the public he served demanded victims' justice and public safety, and that the state legislature had enacted laws allowing for capital punishment. But he also knew that the criminal justice system is not a one-size-fits-all proposition. Each case is different. Death row inmates are mostly male, largely uneducated, and primarily Black or Hispanic. Many have personal and family histories of child abuse, mental health issues, and addiction.

In a book about his wrenching decisions to bestow life or compel death on what he called "the worst members of our society," Brown described his role as not the decider of guilt or innocence or of "the finer points of the law."[2] He was certain that everyone he considered for commutation was guilty of the brutal crimes involved. He instead sought "to look for some extraordinary reason why the defendant should not be executed"—a "legal or moral reason to go against the judgment of the court."

By Brown's account, he sometimes got the calculus right.

But he also got it wrong.

The story of John Russell Crooker Jr., who murdered his former lover with a kitchen knife in a crime of passion, ended well. Crooker confessed. He appealed his conviction all the way to the US Supreme Court but failed to persuade the justices that his confession was coerced. Governor Brown decided nonetheless to commute Crooker's death sentence to life in prison—after considering his psychological problems, difficult family history, the absence of premeditation or a concealed weapon, and his potential for rehabilitation. Crooker was eventually paroled and went on to lead a decent life.

Simon Wein's story ended differently. He was convicted of a series of sexual assaults, robberies, and kidnappings, and was sentenced to death. Wein had no prior felony convictions and was a docile inmate. Brown commuted his sentence to life. Wein was later paroled and went on to murder someone.

... AND WHY?
One pardoned prisoner lives a model life while another goes on to murder someone. Does this comparison say anything about the goals behind the power to pardon?

The contrast between Wein and Crooker is especially notable because they knew each other in prison. After Wein's release, Governor Brown met with Crooker. During the meeting, Crooker told the governor that he wished he had warned him not to commute Wein's sentence. The other prisoners knew Wein was dangerous. Brown later reflected on his conversation with Crooker:

> Crooker's comments stunned me into rare silence. The implications were at once obviously simple and subtly ironic. Here was a man whose life I had spared

2

at least in part because of his intelligence and future potential, now out of prison and leading a useful life, telling me that he and other prisoners turned out to be better judges of the inner nature of another man whose life I'd spared—better judges than a governor, several psychiatrists, and a host of other skilled professionals.

Yet commuting Wein's sentence was not Governor Brown's most regrettable clemency decision. His decision to deny Richard Arlen Lindsey's petition haunted him even more.

Lindsey was convicted of raping and murdering a small child and sentenced to death. Like the others, Lindsey had severe mental health issues and a troubled childhood. Governor Brown reported that he "couldn't for the life of me see how killing Lindsey would keep another madman from attacking another little girl somewhere down the road." He nonetheless denied Lindsey's petition—for political reasons. Brown was seeking to get a farm labor bill passed, and the deciding vote came from a legislator whose voters lived in the county where Lindsey committed his crime. The governor declined to spare Lindsey's life so he could get a minimum wage passed for farm workers.

In the American system of government—which hinges on a functioning representative democracy, and where politicians derive their power from the people and are accountable to the people—there is a gaping level of unconstrained power: the power to pardon. It is inherently inconsistent with democracy, vesting complete discretion and control in a single person to achieve fairness.[3] And in theory, the pardon power is somehow supposed to operate without undermining the message sent by the original conviction and sentence: "Don't try this, or you'll be held accountable, too."[4]

At the federal level, presidents can issue pardons for federal crimes. At the state level, some governors can pardon state-law crimes. Others share the power with boards or commissions. Governors pardon at much higher rates than presidents simply because there are many more state prosecutions than federal ones.[5]

Pardons also come in many varieties, spanning those that erase a criminal conviction altogether, to those that erase only part of it while retaining other sorts of penalties, to those that only shorten or alter a sentence—a form of clemency known as commutation. For purposes of this book, the term "pardon" is treated as one-size-fits-all, encompassing terms like "clemency" and "commutation," as well. The reason is that the technicalities regarding the *form* of pardon are less important to the aim of the book than the *ideas* behind the act itself: 1) that a single person, who is overwhelmingly White and male, is better positioned to make life-altering judgments about an individual's culpability for a crime than the legislators, judges, and juries that rendered the judgment in the first place; and 2) that such a person will exercise that power with fairness and integrity—rather than out of bigotry, laziness, callousness, or self-interest. Pardons really make sense only if *both* of these conditions are satisfied. As this book will show, the better argument appears to be that neither one is.

At their greatest height, pardons can wipe an individual's criminal record clean, unlock the prison doors, and put them back into society. In the normal course of the criminal justice system, in order for this to happen, that person would have to hire and pay lawyers to get them through months or years of fact-finding, legal analysis, hearings, trials, temporary incarceration, and appeals—all banking on the chance of an acquittal, a hung jury, a favorable plea, a shorter sentence, or some result that is less than the worst-case scenario. The criminal justice system is created, in theory, to make this process fair—not just to the individual involved and the victims, but to everyone else, including other criminal defendants and members of the public who feel invested in seeing justice done and having safety in the streets.

When it comes to pardons, much of this complex procedure and fact-gathering goes out the window. The president, or a governor, can function as lawyer, fact-finder, judge, and jury with the stroke of a pen, often without any explanation or record required and virtually no accountability—except theoretically through voters at the next election, who can only take steps to change the person in office, not the fate of any one individual, and that's only if the president or governor runs again. This is not how pardons operate throughout most of the world, and indeed in many American states, which have seemingly begun to reject a sovereign-like, unitary, unaccountable pardon power and the myriad dysfunctions associated with it.

. . . AND WHY?

**Pardon and commutations—also known as clemency—
interrupt and undermine the work of the criminal justice
system for a few, very lucky people. For what purpose?
If it's mercy, do pardons achieve that objective?
At what cost?**

Ideally, like Governor Brown, presidents and governors wielding this power strive to act fairly and with integrity, poring over applications with care and attempting to balance cases against each other to ensure that only the worthiest get a pardon. Or a president acting within his constitutional mandate might use it primarily, if not exclusively, to heal the public after a national trauma like a divisive war. Using the pardon this way, in theory, could move the goalposts of justice in American society closer to the Constitution's ideals of fairness, equality, and freedom.

But let's face it. The Framers of the US Constitution created a three-part system of government, instead of an unlimited monarchy, for a reason: They understood that it's not human nature to act with the purest character in every situation. Every state has its own constitution that separates the powers of government—judicial, legislative, and executive, as well—on the same theory: It's human nature to amass, entrench, and ultimately give in to the temptation to abuse power once people have it. There must be systems in place to push back on our worst instincts. Under the federal and states' constitutions, those systems mean that every branch has two other bosses—including presidents and governors, who must contend with legislatures and courts.

Given that our federal and state governments are built on the promise of accountability through frameworks of checks and balances, the massive power of the pardon is a strange rarity under US law. Consider how everyone else in government—and every other power exercised by them, including for presidents—is checked in multiple ways. Congress, for example, can constrain presidents' authority by passing laws that limit what the executive branch can do, or by holding hearings that bring to public light a president's bad decisions. Judges can also strike down presidential acts if they violate the Constitution. In 1803, the Supreme Court in *Marbury v. Madison* essentially gave itself that power by holding that the judiciary is the branch that reviews the constitutionality of the other branches' actions.[6] But as explained later in the book, the Court has oddly taken the position that the pardon power is mostly above the law—meaning that the federal courts can't do anything about corrupt pardons, even if they harm the public or violate the spirit of the Constitution.

Congress is also subject to systematic checks. Presidents can veto acts of Congress, and judges can strike down legislation that crosses a constitutional line. Courts are constrained, too. They can only hear cases brought before them by litigants—often prosecutors who answer to the president—under laws passed by Congress. If the Supreme Court interprets a law in a way that Congress doesn't like, it can change the law and essentially overrule the Court. (Not so for cases under the Constitution, but that's another issue.) And of course, presidents and Congress can be fired at the ballot box in the next election—and after two terms, the Constitution itself fires presidents. The overarching concept is that no single government actor or entity gets unlimited, unbridled, unaccountable power to make decisions that adversely impact the liberty of individuals without anybody overseeing them.

So what's constraining the president's power to pardon? That is a huge question, and a huge problem, that few people recognize, debate, or otherwise discuss. The answer is *not much*, if anything. And for the most part, the reason is that people just assume that the pardon power is absolute—like that of a king. But of course, the folks who fought the American Revolution and formed a government separate from England *rejected* the powers of a king. They wanted no part of that anymore.

So why does there exist such a strong mythology around the power of the pardon power? After all, as this book will explain, at the time the Constitution's pardon power language was drafted and ratified, King George III did not have the kind of unlimited power to pardon that nearly everyone seems to assume US presidents have today. It simply makes no logical or historical sense to treat the pardon power as monarch-like. That assumption must be wrong.

. . . AND WHY?
What are the checks on the president's power to pardon?
Answer: There aren't any to speak of.
Does this gap conflict with the spirit of the Constitution?

The question then becomes: What to do about this pesky pardon power? Can Congress pass a law outlining criteria that presidents must use before issuing pardons? And if Congress did that, would

7

the Supreme Court strike them down? If the answer to *that* question is yes, then do we need to amend the Constitution to get rid of the pardon power, or at least to limit presidents' obvious discretion to abuse it? These questions have been debated for hundreds of years and may ultimately be unanswerable. But they are surely important enough for voters to at least understand the basics of the pardon system—and the stakes.

* * *

The US president's pardon power derives from the English monarchy, originating between AD 668 and 725. At that time, the "law" as we understand it today—as a set of written rules that are supposed to apply to the general population evenhandedly—did not exist. The king or queen *was* the law. English rulers throughout the Middle Ages (1485 to 1603) acted pursuant to the "royal prerogative." The monarch—who obtained power hereditarily—was the boss of all bosses.[7] Because the king or queen was the ultimate boss, the idea of "justice" was administered according to the monarch's complete and unlimited discretion.[8] If an individual committed a transgression that might be considered a crime, their fate rested ultimately in the hands of the king or queen. Under such a legal regime, a pardon was a natural part of the sovereign's inherent, unconstrained power.

By the time of the American Revolutionary War (1775 to 1783), Britain was not a total monarchy. Instead, it had evolved into what's known as a *constitutional* monarchy.[9] King George III was on the throne, but his power had eroded over time. The government still acted in the name of "the Crown," but the king or queen's role had become subordinate to the legislative and ministerial body of Parliament and the courts. In 1690, Parliament enacted the Crown and Parliament Recognition Act of 1689, which made it *illegal* for the Crown to take certain actions without the consent of Parliament.[10]

In other words, the king did not have total and complete power when the Constitution was ratified and when the US president's power to pardon officially came about.

It may come as a surprise to many that the English monarchs did not have unlimited discretion to issue pardons when the pardon power was granted to US presidents in the US Constitution in 1788. Nonetheless, despite this historical context, the Constitution has since been construed to give an elected American president virtually *unlimited* authority to pardon federal offenses—greater than that of King George III, whose massive power was precisely what the revolutionaries fought and died to avoid.

. . . AND WHY?

Presidents today have greater powers to pardon than King George III did at the time of the American Revolution. Does that come as a surprise? Does it make sense?

Many of the rationales asserted by proponents of a broad pardon power remain the subject of debate in this text. When advocating for the Constitution as we know it today, positions differed over the reasons for giving the president the power to pardon, as well as the breadth of that power. Addressing the North Carolina convention on ratification, for example, James Iredell argued for including the pardon power in the future American president's job description on the rationale that "[t]here may be instances where, though a man offends against the letter of the law . . . peculiar circumstances in his case may entitle him to mercy."[11] Today, one of the primary rationales for the expansive pardon power is just that—the endowment of *mercy* on an individual. One question addressed in the pages of this book is whether the mercy rationale for the power to pardon still holds today.

Alexander Hamilton justified giving presidents the power to pardon (versus giving it to Congress or the courts) because "it is not to be doubted that a single man of prudence and good sense, is better fitted . . . to balance the motives, which may plead for or against the remission of the punishment, than any numerous body whatever." Hamilton thus assumed that individual men (only White males were envisioned for the presidency at that point in history) are better suited to make decisions about individual punishment than "numerous" bodies like legislatures, or perhaps even juries. According to Hamilton, "[h]umanity and good policy conspire to dictate, that the benign prerogative of pardoning should be as little as possible fettered or embarrassed."

If pardons are about mercy, Hamilton's theory goes, it's better to give the pardon power to a single president or governor than to legislatures or courts because politicians don't make it to the top executive branch post if they lack prudence and good sense. Furthermore, because "humanity" is served by merciful and compassionate leaders, he argued, that power should be virtually unlimited. A second question raised in this book is whether Hamilton's assumptions about the inherent nature of humans who hold lots of power still make sense today.

The Framers of the US Constitution accordingly adopted the English tradition of allowing the president to issue pardons for federal crimes, with only a single exception: Presidents cannot pardon convictions for impeachment (which, by the way, only apply to federal judges, members of a president's cabinet, vice presidents, and presidents themselves). The Constitution says nothing more about potentially unacceptable pardons; it doesn't even weigh in on pardons made for political gain, or to cover up a crime, or to amass a fortune, or to punish enemies, or to discriminate against "disfavored" races, genders, religions, or national origins. Yet all of these kinds of pardons *feel* wrong. These days, avoiding them comes down to an individual leader's integrity and good judgment.

Was Hamilton correct, then—that the president's pardon power should "be as little as possible fettered"? Or should the pardon power have limits? And if so, what should they be?

Suffice it to say that the overwhelming assumption that the president's pardon power is completely unlimited is likely overblown and analytically shallow. As we all know, the pardon power's use by presidents over the last century has raised numerous eyebrows. Most recently, it was President Donald Trump who grabbed headlines by pardoning a slew of political loyalists, including Roger Stone and Paul Manafort, in what appeared to be rewards for loyalty and possible obstruction of various investigations into Trump's actions as president, and before.[12] (Reportedly, a lawyer for Trump approached Manafort and Michael Flynn to offer pardons in the early stages of the federal investigations.) Trump also promised to pardon anyone who participated in the bloody events on January 6, 2021, at the US Capitol,[13] for which six sitting members of Congress—as well as Trump's lawyers Rudy Giuliani and John Eastman—reportedly sought pardons for their involvement.[14] Of course, Eastman and Giuliani were both indicted along with Trump in Fulton County, Georgia, over their alleged efforts to thwart the election results in that state. Trump was also indicted on four criminal counts in federal court in Washington, DC, for conspiracy and obstruction relating to the January 6th insurrection.

For supporters of Trump, January 6th pardons may feel utterly legitimate—done to counterbalance relentless and unfair investigatory probes that were perceived as motivated by politics, not facts. But Trump is not the only president who pulled the lever of "mercy" in ways that benefited him personally and politically. Presidents George H. W. Bush and Bill Clinton also issued dubious pardons on the way out of office, when all presidents no longer have to worry about political retribution at the presidential ballot box.[15]

There's no guarantee that every person who sits in the White House is someone you will like. But each president gets the same power to issue pardons as the last one. Sadly, it has become "just a given" that presidents will use that power at least in part to favor associates or cronies, and even to protect themselves. Meanwhile, over two million individuals—most of whom lack access to money and influence—are living in prisons in the United States.[16] All but a handful will not be pardoned, even if well-deserving, based to a large degree on elusive criteria with no pretense that they will be used in a way that strives for equality.[17] Many individuals who are pardoned receive that gift for entirely the wrong reasons, while others languish in prison or are put to death.

Still, with the exception of China, every contemporary government on the planet has within its charter some version of a pardon power.[18] The global assumption that it has value suggests that the pardon power serves some important purpose within a system of laws. In eighteenth-century England, when the king was most of the law, the pardon power evolved as a tool for establishing some system of rules in an otherwise lawless society. The criminal justice system did not really exist in the early days; crimes like robbery and murder were resolved between warring factions of private parties, not by the state on behalf of the people.[19] There were no police, so "justice" was the responsibility of local communities.[20] Until the jury trial was established in 1215, accused persons in England often underwent what was called an "ordeal"—by fire, which meant walking three paces holding a red-hot iron bar in their hands; by water, which meant being tied up and thrown into water; or by combat. If the accused survived, the verdict was "not guilty." In this harsh environment, the royal "prerogative of mercy" operated, at least in theory, to achieve justice for especially worthy individuals. The pardon functioned as a mechanism to shift criminal disputes from the people to the Crown.

Today, by contrast, there are well-developed criminal justice systems in the United States at the federal, state, and municipal levels. And over the past seven centuries, parole—which occurs when the government releases a prisoner early, with certain conditions—has become increasingly more common as a means of counteracting the harshness of sentencing.[21]

The pardon power appears in Article II of the original Constitution, which was ratified in 1788. Since then, the Constitution has been amended over two dozen times to add restraints on government.[22] The Bill of Rights was added in 1791 to make clear that individuals have particularized protections against their government—including the right to a jury trial on criminal charges, the right to confront one's accusers, and the right to be free of unreasonable searches and seizures of property by the police.[23] Later, with post–Civil War amendments, the right to due process of law by state governments was added, among other important provisions.[24] (This list of protections stands in stark contrast to the British "constitution," which, to this day, is not written down and does not specify individual rights.) Due process itself means, in its barest form, that the government cannot take a person's life, cannot put the person in jail, and cannot take the person's property without some form of hearing.[25] For criminal defendants, it means a full-blown trial by a jury of peers, with rules of evidence serving as a gatekeeper to ensure that the jury doesn't make decisions based on rumor or bogus allegations, but rather only on verifiable facts.

With the addition of these and other rights under the American Constitution, criminal defendants have had for a very long time many more protections against arbitrary government interference in liberty than those who lived in eighteenth-century England. The existence of due process and other protections for criminal defendants today thus raise some doubt regarding whether pardons as a measure of mercy are even necessary anymore.[26] If the criminal justice system is already designed to protect people from arbitrary injustices, why do we need presidents and governors as a stopgap measure? If the answer is that the criminal justice system doesn't work, why rely on the arbitrary judgment of individual politicians to address it? Maybe new laws are needed instead. And finally, if pardons are really supposed to be about showing mercy to counteract harsh treatment of the recipient, why have *posthumous* pardons at all, when it's too late for people to benefit from them?

One answer might be that there are many flaws in our criminal justice system—which systematically disadvantages low-income individuals, many of whom serve a full sentence before trial just because poverty makes it impossible to make bail—so the possibility of a pardon is needed as a last-ditch fix.[27] (So much for "innocent until proven guilty" if someone is low-income.) A Black person is five times more likely to be stopped by the police without valid justification than is a White person in America, and thus more likely to be caught up in the criminal justice system in the first place.[28] Once in, it can be difficult to get out, especially without the money to pay good lawyers.

Even so, it is hardly self-evident that the answer to the problems with the criminal justice system lies in unlimited pardon power. Perhaps Congress, state, or local legislatures could instead pass more laws protecting defendants, or prioritizing pardons for people who can't afford the kind of legal support that wealthy people get when they commit crimes. The courts could read the Constitution's relevant provisions more broadly to clamp down on the government's expansive power over individuals who are arrested and charged with crimes. Or maybe legislatures could create more pardon boards or commissions, put regular citizens on them, and articulate clear criteria and transparency requirements to ensure that pardons are issued fairly. A range of potential tools exists to address injustices without needing to empower a single person to exercise subjective discretion through the picking and choosing of "winners" in the pardon contest. The arbitrary exercise of power over individual liberty is, after all, the essence of tyranny.

Worse, as the pages of this book will explore, there are too many instances of presidents and governors—who wield the pardon power over state-law criminal defendants—using the pardon power politically, and even corruptly. Somewhat amazingly, the inherent temptation to abuse the pardon power for purposes of enhancing a leader's power—rather than for mercy's sake—has been at the center of debates over this power since the dawning of proverbial time. Even under an unlimited monarchy, England long ago put limits on the king's pardon power, but those did not make it into the US Constitution.

In the United States, the president's pardon power is treated as unlimited and sacrosanct, with virtually no debate or analysis as to why. Most people—even legal experts—have little if any grasp on why it exists, how it works, and whether it should endure in its current form. This book aims to begin to fill in those gaps for the lay reader, who might then engage in much-needed debate over the pardon power's role in American government and the criminal justice system. The book is divided into four parts.

Who? tells the stories of a few pardons. And they're pretty fascinating.

What? tells the history of the pardon power, from before England's monarchies to the US Constitution's ratification, and outlines how it works.

Why? explains and categorizes the pardon power into three major areas of use: mercy, amnesty, and politics.

Who Cares? puts the pardon power into perspective, asking why it matters for the separation of powers and issues of social justice. This section tries to answer the problems posed by the book with a handful of proposed reforms.

Spoiler alert: The book concludes that the reason the pardon power has endured for so long might have more to do with entrenching the power of the powerful than its original purpose as a counterforce to injustice. Thus, it may no longer serve its intended purposes, and can, in fact, create injustice and foster corruption.

On the other hand, access to the pardon power as a stopgap under extraordinary circumstances—such as the COVID-19 pandemic, which prompted the release of approximately 6 percent of the world's prison population in 2020[29]—may still justify a need for some measure of authority by heads of state to suspend or commute individual sentences. However, that power need not be exclusive to the president. For now, because the pardon power is in the text of the original Constitution, it's virtually set in stone. Unless the Supreme Court sees fit to interpret the pardon power to forbid corrupt pardons—which is entirely within the Court's power, but probably unlikely—altering the pardon power would require a constitutional amendment.

But Congress is not without options. It can pass legislation mandating transparency and accountability around pardons, so that the voting public at least knows what's going on—and the people can vote accordingly. That could make all the difference.

Part I
Who? Three Tales of the Pardon Power

The tale of the pardon power is really a story about people. Many, many people. The proper scope and use of the pardon power cannot be defined with a simple list of criteria or a balancing test. It depends on facts. Facts about the crime, the petitioner's life, and the mood of the country or the constituency that a president or governor is charged with serving. The question also invokes theoretical considerations like morals, ethics, policy, race, power dynamics—and even religion.

Although passed down from English law, and Roman legal traditions before that, pardons represent something bordering on the ethereal—ideas like redemption and second chances, which many Americans prize. Optimally, presidents and governors issue pardons to show mercy or grant amnesty to deserving people who were wrongly sentenced to prison or have reformed while incarcerated. Pardons may also go to individuals whom the president or governor feels have atoned for their crimes, or if there appears to be no further societal benefit for a person to remain imprisoned.

But being wrongfully convicted or showing signs of reformation are not requirements for pardons. Presidents do not have to explain *why* they choose to pardon an individual or a group,[30] and once the president grants or declines a pardon, that's it. There are no appeals, although some pardons are issued posthumously—often at the behest of their living relatives who want to clear their family member's good name. A single pardon can also forgive large groups of people for their crimes.[31]

17

One such pardon of a large group was issued by President James Buchanan to members of the Church of Jesus Christ of Latter-day Saints, also known as the Mormon Church or the "LDS Church."[32] It's a fascinating tale, which hits on many deeper policy issues embedded in the broader topic of whether presidential pardons are mostly good or bad, merciful, or corrupt—and how we should approach them today.

... AND WHY?
The Mormon pardons point to another primary justification for the pardon power, besides mercy: amnesty. Do presidents still need the power to pardon to address the political complexities of war?

The following story captures the two primary categories of pardons: amnesty on the one hand, and mercy for the individual on the other, and the various ethical and political considerations that often come into play for both. Mostly, it's a narrative of treason, trickery, demagoguery, and even murder—all of which were ultimately pardoned—and most of which occurred just before the Civil War, whose enormity probably eclipsed the retelling and impact of this Mormon story.

But as you read, consider again the central questions that opened this book: Was Alexander Hamilton right in urging that the president's pardon power should "be as little as possible fettered"? Should the pardon power instead have limits? And if so, what should they be?

18

1

Pardoning a Massacre: The Brigham Young Treason Pardons

Mormonism traces its roots back to Upstate New York in the 1830s, when founder Joseph Smith had a vision that led him to write the Book of Mormon.[33] Although based on Christian biblical teachings, Mormonism uses newer texts that religious adherents believe have more recent revelations from God and Jesus Christ. Mormons believe in the second coming of Jesus Christ to the Earth in the "latter days," so the religion is also known as the Church of Latter-day Saints (LDS).[34]

Joseph Smith Dies in Nauvoo City, Illinois: 1844

The Mormons faced intense religious persecution in the United States through the 1830s, as they moved west from Ohio to Missouri. After again being forcibly expelled from Missouri, they went to Illinois and began to settle peacefully in a town that they purchased in 1839. Joseph Smith became the mayor of the town, which they renamed Nauvoo City. Although almost totally abandoned when they arrived, by 1844, Nauvoo City had the highest population of any city in Illinois, overtaking even Chicago. Smith and his congregation had grown through locals and immigrants who had been converted by Mormon missionaries sent by the church to England and other parts of Europe.

In 1844, some non-Mormons and former Mormons who disagreed with Smith printed the first and only issue of the *Nauvoo Expositor* newspaper in Nauvoo City, in which they charged Smith with attempting to set up a theocracy in the town and practicing polygamy.[35] Smith had already been indicted on charges of polygamy, but was free while awaiting a trial the next year.[36] In response, Smith and the church-controlled city council declared that the *Expositor* was a public nuisance and ordered the printing press destroyed.[37] The press was demolished by a mob, which prompted the county to issue warrants for Smith and others for inciting a riot.

Smith escalated the conflict by declaring martial law in the City of Nauvoo, calling on three thousand members of the Nauvoo militia, which he controlled, for protection. He briefly fled the state but eventually returned and surrendered to face charges for inciting a riot. Once under arrest, in 1844, the Illinois governor charged Smith with treason for having declared martial law and calling up a militia—a charge for which bail was not available. Days after his surrender, and while he awaited trial, a mob killed Smith and his brother in an Illinois jail on June 27, 1844.

Smith was not only the leader of the LDS Church—he was also considered a prophet of the Mormon religion who wrote "the Book" on which Mormonism is based. Smith's death was transformational to members of the LDS Church because he was a larger-than-life figure. Mormons believe that Smith was able to communicate with God, and his writings were looked to as scripture. After his murder, it was unclear what should happen next and who would pick up Smith's mantle. The church membership split up, with some followers leaving for Texas and Michigan. Others, including Smith's family, stayed in Nauvoo City.[38]

Brigham Young Creates a Theocratic Governorship of the Utah Territory: 1847–1858

Most Mormons decided to follow a man named Brigham Young as their new prophet. Young led his followers west, becoming president of the "Quorum of the Twelve," a powerful position in church leadership. The group reached the Great Salt Lake in 1847, in what later became the Utah Territory. When their journey began, Mexico controlled the land,[39] which Brigham Young considered so far north of the rest of Mexico that there would be little opposition to him settling there and starting a type of theocratic state. Shortly after Young reached present-day Salt Lake City, the Mexicans admitted defeat in the Mexican-American War and signed over vast lands—including what is now Utah—to the United States in 1848.[40]

The suspicion that the LDS Church faced in Illinois followed Young to the Great Salt Lake. There was a general distrust of the Mormon religion, and their recent attempt to create a theocracy in Nauvoo City, Illinois, had put them on the national radar. But the fears went beyond the creation of a religious government, and many national politicians worried that separatism would grow out of the Utah Territory. This fear was not without cause.

In 1849, when the Mormon settlers in Utah Territory proposed to join the United States for the first time, they attempted to do so as the State of Deseret—a word that in the Book of Mormon means "honeybee." The US government denied their petition, and instead added the Utah Territory (named after the Utes, an Indigenous tribe from the Great Basin) as part of the Compromise of 1850, which aimed to maintain the existing balance of free and slave states when there was new American land to be divided following the Mexican-American War. The Utah Territory was a smaller area than had been proposed as the State of Deseret, but still made up all of present-day Utah, most of Nevada to the west, and some land to the east in present-day Colorado and Wyoming.[41] Because the area was a "Territory," the federal government would have more control and influence than if it had been granted statehood.[42] Territories had less autonomy than states because the governor was appointed by the federal Congress instead of through a citizen ballot.

In 1851, President Millard Fillmore appointed Brigham Young the first governor of the Utah Territory. Young had led the settlers to Utah and had already been the president of the LDS Church since 1847, a role he kept until his death in 1877. Fillmore's choice of Young turned out to be a fateful one.

Fillmore's selection was likely influenced by the petitions of Thomas L. Kane, an influential American attorney who had befriended the Mormons decades earlier and helped them in their previous negotiations with the US government.[43] Kane had worked to enlist a group of five hundred soldiers known as the "Mormon Battalion," which joined the United States in the Mexican-American War.[44] He managed to use his influence to secure refuge for the Mormons on Native American lands after they had been chased from their prior homes.[45] Kane gave an impassioned speech on behalf of the Mormons in 1850, which was reprinted widely prior to President Fillmore's appointment of Young. Fillmore felt Kane would be a great pick as territorial governor of Utah, but Kane deferred and recommended that Young be appointed governor of the Utah Territory instead. Fillmore took Kane's advice, appointing Young on September 28, 1850, scarcely three months after Fillmore took office.

On October 5, 1851, the territorial legislature of Utah passed a resolution establishing Millard County as part of the Territory of Utah, as well as the City of Fillmore, which became the territorial capitol.[46] The legislature was comprised of fourteen council members and twenty-seven members of the house of representatives. Some of these individuals were appointed, whereas others were elected.

Shortly thereafter, about thirty families left Salt Lake City for Millard County to establish a permanent White settlement. Utah's new government quickly implemented laws comporting with the views of the church, intertwining the church and the territorial government in kind of a democratic theocracy—a government ruled by religious authority. Bear in mind that while the Mormons were waiting on the federal government to approve Utah's territorial status, they created the Deseret government to act in the interim. Following the Territory of Utah's formation, it wasn't a far stretch for Utah's territorial legislature to implement the laws already on the books under the de facto Deseret government.

On February 8, 1851, for example, Governor Young signed an ordinance passed by the legislature entitled, "An ordinance incorporating the Church of Jesus Christ of Latter-day Saints."[47] Among other things, the ordinance allowed the church to sue and be sued, and to have a board of trustees represent it. The ordinance also gave the church the right "to worship God according to the dictates of conscience" and "to solemnize marriage compatible with the revelations of Jesus Christ."[48] Mormons believed that church founder Joseph Smith received such a revelation, and that "the possession of more than one wife was not only permissible, but actually necessary for complete salvation."[49] The ordinance went on:

> [I]t is also declared, that said church does, and shall possess, and enjoy continually, the power and authority, in and of itself, to originate, make, pass, and establish rules, regulations, ordinances, laws, customs, and criterions, for the good order, safety, government, conveniences, comfort, and control of said church, and for the punishment or forgiveness of all offenses.

Essentially, this "power and authority, in and of itself" language made the church's decisions regarding marriage and many other topics unquestionable by the US government.

Another early ordinance provided for the rejection of "common law"—or judge-made rules that are passed down over the years as case precedent—in court, instead favoring "equitable" principles of general fairness.[50] Under equitable principles, judges issued injunctions directing parties to do or not do something based on their own evaluation of the case as opposed to using juries under the common law system. Common law also allows parties to seek monetary damages as a remedy in a civil case. Since Mormons also controlled judges in Utah, the rejection of common law remedies and jury trials tilted the playing field against the plaintiffs and in favor of the Mormon-controlled government.[51] The Mormon judges could directly order that other parties do what was in the best interest of the church rather than put disputes before a jury of the parties' peers. In an effort to discourage lawsuits, the Utah legislature also passed an ordinance that denied lawyers the right to collect fees, making it less attractive to represent plaintiffs, many of whom might hire a lawyer with the understanding that they'd be able to retain a percentage of a money award as payment for pursuing a case. No money judgments meant no fees, and thus no lawyers willing to bring lawsuits.

Although Mormons were controlling all three branches of Utah's territorial government, Utah's entanglement with the Mormon religion wasn't limited to the government. Members of the LDS Church gave significant amounts of their property and power over to the church, too, and many would only do business with other Mormons. There was even a Mormon attempt to make their own thirty-eight-letter alphabet, but it didn't catch on.[52]

Most Americans outside the Mormon Church felt that the church-sanctioned practice of polygamy was particularly odious. In the minds of non-Mormons (or "Gentiles"), the practice (which was removed as an official LDS practice in 1890) also became intertwined with the secessionist attitude that was emanating from the Utah Territory. On the populated East Coast, the topic became a favorite of newspapers. As Mormons made their way across the East Coast from Europe on their way to Utah, they made for a strange and newsworthy spectacle. When a riverboat with two hundred Mormons tied up at a wharf to resupply, one Pennsylvania journalist noted:

> One of the chief saints on board had *three* very pretty wives. He is evidently a mere beginner in the practice of polygamy, yet he most assuredly rendered himself liable to a criminal suit in our courts. If not bigamy, most assuredly he is guilty of *trigamy*.[53]

Another piece, printed in a Portland, Maine, newspaper in 1854, recounted stories that Utah Mormons had shared with Chicago-based reporters about their experience. Preceding one story was this introduction from the Portland paper:

> MORMON LIFE.—The Chicago papers contain some amusing letters from the new "saints" of Utah. One happy brother writes in high praise of the institution of polygamy. He congratulated himself upon the possession of the three wives, the latest of whom, a German, he married three months ago.[54]

Polygamy came to represent perceived problems with the Mormon-controlled territory overall, and it so fascinated Americans that newspapers as far away as Maine would reprint otherwise uninteresting commentary from a Chicago newspaper about otherwise ordinary Utahns.

While polygamy interested and disgusted many ordinary Americans, Young's power over the territory worried many in the federal government. Even though there were federally-appointed government officials in Utah, Young ruled with an iron fist. As the president of the church, he had advocated a "Mormon Reformation," seeking to spiritually reawaken church members and encouraging polygamy and rebaptism, which confirmed and tightened followers' commitment to the church, even though the church already controlled much of their lives.[55]

Young's power, and his tendency to use it to manipulate the legal process, became problematic for federal judges and other officials. As LDS Church president, Young used his influence to prevent people from testifying during trials. Federal agents, drastically outnumbered by the Mormons, feared making arrests over efforts to obstruct justice. Many judges had left their posts and reported the problems back to federal authorities in Washington, DC. The first of these incidents took place in 1851, when, only months after first arriving, two federal judges and a federal territorial secretary fled Utah, never to return.[56] Their positions remained vacant until 1853, and in the interim, the legislature allowed for the Mormon-controlled probate courts to have concurrent jurisdiction with the US federal courts—a significant power grab.

Later on, William Drummond, a justice on Utah's Supreme Court appointed by President Franklin Pierce in 1855, was placed under arrest by a Mormon-controlled probate judge. After leaving Utah in 1857, Drummond wrote about his experience under Brigham Young. He claimed that the Mormons "refused to submit to civil authority" and that they were loyal to their church before the US Constitution. One (unfortunately named) federal "Indian agent" reported to his superior in Washington, DC, that Young, who was also the Utah superintendent of Indian Affairs, "has been so much in the habit of exercising his will, which is supreme here, that no one will dare oppose anything he may say or do."

There are many stories of federal officials fleeing Utah, and they tend to follow a similar pattern. The officials would arrive and were generally welcomed by the Mormons at the outset. Then, there would be an incident—often they were rumored to have spoken negatively about the Mormons, but other times they were alleged to have visited a sex worker or committed another moral infraction—and the federal official's relationship with the Mormons would quickly deteriorate. Then the official would leave Utah permanently. Some of these officials were run out of town by the Mormons, but others that stayed were largely ineffective. Without the ability to compel witness testimony or even arrest suspects, these federal agents often had their hands tied by Young's near-dictatorial control over the territory.

Young Declares Martial Law and President Buchanan Declares Utah in Rebellion: 1857

Shortly after his inauguration in 1857, President James Buchanan declared Utah in rebellion, and sent three thousand troops—at the time, 20 percent of the American army—to Utah to remove Young from the governorship and install a new governor.[57] Word made it to Young that the federal government was coming to remove him, but little else was clear in Utah at the time. The Mormons had repeatedly faced religious persecution and they may have feared the worst. In September of 1857, Young sent the Nauvoo Legion—his Mormon militia—to block federal troops from entering the territory, declaring that the Mormons were "not in bondage to any government on God's footstool," and that "any nation's coming to destroy this people, GOD ALMIGHTY BEING MY HELPER, THEY CANNOT COME HERE." On September 13, 1857, Young officially declared martial law, with an order that "[forbade] all armed forces of every description from coming into this Territory, under any pretense whatever" and directed "That all the forces in said Territory hold themselves in readiness to march at a moment's notice, to repel any and all such invasion."[58]

Young and the Territory of Utah were at war with the United States.

... AND WHY?

Brigham Young controlled Utah and effectively declared war on the federal government in 1857. Was it treason? If the answer is yes, then why were Young and his rebel followers later pardoned?

The Mountain Meadows Massacre:
September 7–11, 1857

Shortly before Young declared martial law, his followers initiated the Mountain Meadows Massacre, which unfolded against a group of travelers from Arkansas over the course of a few days in September of 1857.

As American forces approached the Utah Territory, Young and his militia prepared for battle. The prospect of a new governor added to the already high tensions in Utah. In the years leading up to what would be called the Utah War, Young's rhetoric had become increasingly heated, as he had been advocating for a religious reformation, and a rededication to the church. Young was skeptical of outsiders, and this came through in his speeches, which became more inflammatory in response to the imprecise threat from the US government. Yet his declaration of martial law left many local officials unsure of how to implement the policy. This intense atmosphere was not limited to northern Utah, where Young and most of the Mormons lived; tensions among the southern Utahns also soared.

While the mood in the territory reached a boiling point, a wagon train of about 140 people from Arkansas on the way to California was passing through Utah. The group was made up of separate smaller wagon parties that had met on their way to California and were traveling together for safety. Some of the families on the wagon train were wealthy, with ample cattle and other supplies to make it to California. Others planned to join relatives that had already settled in California. In August of 1857, they stopped in Salt Lake City to purchase additional supplies. But Young had put Utah under martial law, so Utahns were prohibited from selling grain to the weary members of the wagon train, and rumors started to spread about them killing a Mormon, stealing grain, and creating an array of problems on their way through Utah. Much of this remains unconfirmed today.

30

The traveling Arkansans left Salt Lake City without provisions, and followed a known trail to southern Utah that would lead them to California. Still, the Nauvoo Legion leaders in southern Utah disagreed over what to do about the wagon train. Some felt they should leave the travelers alone. Others suggested an ambush of the wagon train while disguised as Native Americans. They decided to ask Young for guidance, but it would take six days to hear back from him in Salt Lake City, at the territory's northern end.

On September 7, Nauvoo militia members dressed up as Paiute Native Americans and started to shoot at the Arkansans, who had stopped in Mountain Meadows to let their cattle graze before continuing. Although some of the travelers died during this initial attack, the Arkansans managed to fight back for days from circled wagons. The militia's initial intent is not entirely clear. It may have been to raid the wagon train for resources, and then blame it on Natives. Also unclear is whether some Paiute Native Americans were persuaded by the Mormons to join in the attack, or if it was only the Nauvoo Legion dressed as Paiutes. Because the Arkansans were successful at holding off the Mormon militia, the Mormons were forced to get closer to the party. But they became worried that they would be identified as White, and not Native American, and that their disguises would be found out. Afraid of being reported to federal officials, they made another plan.

On September 11, 1857, two members of the Nauvoo militia came into the migrants' makeshift camp with a white flag raised, dressed as militiamen, not Paiutes. They told the travelers that they had negotiated a deal for them, and that in exchange for their livestock and other supplies, the Paiutes would let them return to the last town they had traveled through. The Mormons would escort them the thirty-five miles back, and they would leave their supplies and livestock for the Paiutes. After days under fire and unable to defend themselves much longer, the Arkansans agreed to the Mormons' offer of protection. More members of the militia came to the Arkansans, and the militiamen escorted the men out of their circled wagons, one Nauvoo militiaman next to each Arkansan.

On a signal, the militiamen each opened fire on the man that stood next to them, while other Nauvoo Legion members ambushed the women and children. The militia killed all of the adults and children above seven years old. They adopted the remaining seventeen children, who they felt were too young to relay the story. One girl, four at the time, later recalled seeing them kill a ten-year-old in front of the other children, after deciding she was old enough to tell. After the atrocity, the perpetrators swore themselves to secrecy.

The Mountain Meadows Massacre was first investigated by Brigham Young weeks after it happened in September of 1857. He reported to the federal government in 1858 that Native Americans had committed the massacre. Although Young and the Mormon higher-ups were able to cover it up initially, and although the federal government sent investigators soon after the end of the Utah War, the Civil War kept the federal government from prosecuting anyone until years later.

It's not clear if Young knew of the massacre plan beforehand or what his role was, but he had been aware of the wagon train, which had passed through Salt Lake City. Previously, he had tacitly encouraged actual Native Americans to raid passing wagon parties in the time leading up to the massacre, since Young believed that American migrants passing through Mormon and Native lands posed a threat to both peoples. (In addition to serving as governor, Young was responsible for Native affairs in the Utah Territory.) He had also spouted dangerous rhetoric about the migrants.

In response to the message that the Nauvoo Legion members in southern Utah sent to him, Young had also sent a letter to the militia instructing them to grant the wagon train safe passage through Utah, but the letter arrived two days after the massacre. Young later used this letter to bolster his claim that he was not at fault for the massacre. (There is much debate as to whether this note was sent solely to abdicate Young's responsibility for the event, and if he had actually ordered the massacre.)

...AND WHY?

Under Brigham Young's leadership, Mormons in Utah ambushed and massacred a group of innocent travelers from Arkansas. That nightmarish incident was pardoned, too. What did that accomplish? Mercy? National unity?

The personal papers of historic Mormons are fraught with forgeries, which leave recently "discovered" letters and journals from those accused in the massacre of questionable value.[59] Whether or not Young was directly or indirectly responsible for the massacre remains unclear. Once the events were discovered by the federal government, Young was integral in preventing prosecutions for the killings. Federal marshals refused to arrest the suspects without US military protection from the local citizens, who were largely controlled by Young through his role as church president. His cordial relationship with his replacement, Governor Cumming, also likely aided his efforts to thwart prosecution for the events. With the outbreak of the Civil War, the federal government also needed to focus further east, which allowed most of the perpetrators to avoid responsibility for the massacre of 120 people.

Meanwhile, Young continued his defense against what his declaration of martial law called an "inva[sion] by hostile forces, who are evidently assailing us to accomplish our overthrow and destruction," the federal government. Yet instead of directly confronting the American army, Young's Nauvoo Legion focused on blocking passages with fallen trees, setting fire to two American forts and dozens of supply wagons, freeing and taking livestock, and otherwise impeding the American troops. Like the Arkansas wagon train, the federal troops were unable to purchase more provisions as they moved west, and their supply chain was crippled by the unconventional tactics of the Nauvoo Legion. As the American territorial officials sent to replace Young traveled toward western forts—where they expected to wait out the rest of the winter on the way to the Utah Territory—they found their forts had been burned by the Nauvoo Legion.

Thinking it unwise to continue their journey in the winter, the federal envoys built "Ecklesville," a camp named after the new chief justice of Utah's Supreme Court, Justice Eckles, who was among the officials headed to Utah.[60] While wintering in Ecklesville, Justice Eckles empaneled a grand jury consisting of members of the army that had been traveling with the officials.[61] The grand jury indicted Young and others for treason against the United States of America, citing the burning of the forts and supply chains, theft of cattle, Young's declaration of martial law, and other acts of war against the United States.

Buchanan Removes Young, Then Pardons the Utah Mormons for Acts of War: 1858

In early 1858, after a cold winter of resisting the US Army, Young was finally removed as governor by the federal government. Many Mormons had fled Salt Lake City in anticipation of the army's arrival, and those that remained were prepared to burn their homes to the ground to prevent the US military from using them. Thomas L. Kane—who had recommended Young for governor to President Fillmore—was again involved in making peace between the Mormons and the federal government. Young may have felt he was running out of options, or may have given in for other reasons, but in the end the office of governor was peacefully transferred to Alfred Cumming, who was appointed by Buchanan and inherited Young's unusual powers over the local probate courts, among other things. But when Cumming arrived, Salt Lake City had mostly been abandoned, on Young's orders.

Soon after Cumming assumed the governorship, President Buchanan offered "a free and full pardon to all who will submit themselves to the just authority of the Federal Government."[62] Buchanan stated that the purpose of the Mormon pardons was "to save the effusion of blood and to avoid the indiscriminate punishment of a whole people for crimes of which it is not probable that all are equally guilty."

...AND WHY?

**Was President James Buchanan right to pardon the Utah
Mormons for "levying war against the United States" with
"military force"? He said he did it to "save the effusion of blood
and avoid indiscriminate punishment."
Is this a valid argument?**

In his pardon, Buchanan explicitly laid out the seriousness of
the crimes, explaining that the Mormons' "determination to oppose
the authority of the Government by military force has not only
been expressed in words, but manifested in overt acts of the most
unequivocal character." Buchanan cited the burning of resupply trains
as one of the acts of war committed by the Mormons. He continued:
"Fellow-citizens of Utah, this is rebellion against the Government to
which you owe allegiance; it is levying war against the United States
and involves you in the guilt of treason." The pardon also clarified
the federal government's position that the Utahns in rebellion were
not subject to religious persecution, stating: "Every intelligent man
among you knows very well that this Government has never, directly
or indirectly, sought to molest you in your worship, to control you in
your ecclesiastical affairs, or even to influence you in your religious
opinions." Buchanan called the Mormon plan to secede "absurd":

> The land you live upon was purchased by the United
> States and paid for out of their Treasury; the pro-
> prietary right and title to it is in them, and not in
> you. Utah is bounded on every side by States and
> Territories whose people are true to the Union. It is
> absurd to believe that they will or can permit you to
> erect in their very midst a government of your own,
> not only independent of the authority which they all
> acknowledge, but hostile to them and their interests.

36

Buchanan's words ring hollow, however. Brigham Young had declared martial law over the Utah Territory and told the United States government that it was not allowed to enter for any reason. President Buchanan declared the territory in rebellion and sent 20 percent of US troops there. Young's forces burned US forts. US troops were not supplied because Nauvoo militia members had stolen their livestock and burned their wagons. Young and others were charged with treason against the United States. And less than a year later, all of them were offered a blanket pardon, so long as they agreed to follow the rules going forward.

What made this dramatic swing possible?

Buchanan may have been trying to quietly end the conflict and focus his attention elsewhere. The press had begun to refer to the Utah War as "Buchanan's Blunder."[63] Looking back, historians acknowledge that Buchanan had to do something and could not let a territorial government openly defy the federal government at a time when the expedition to Utah was called into question by the media and others in the government. At first, Buchanan was not direct with Governor Young about being replaced, which perhaps needlessly escalated the situation. There were also questions about the timing of the expedition so close to winter, and the inability to resupply the troops. Overall, Buchanan appeared incompetent, and needed the issue to recede. Buchanan was also facing pressure from Congress to end the conflict quickly and peacefully. Buchanan did not want to upset the delicate balance between pro- and anti-slavery states and did his best to appease the situation. If Buchanan's goal was to get everyone to forget about the conflict, it seems he succeeded. The Utah War was quickly forgotten by many, overshadowed by the Civil War.[64]

In the months that followed, the US Army set up a fort near Salt Lake City to help control the territory. To convince the Mormons to come back into Salt Lake City after many had fled, the new governor, Alfred Cumming, extended the president's pardon, stating in June that "All criminal offenses associated with or growing out of the overt acts of sedition and treason are merged in them and are embraced in the 'full and free' pardon of the President."[65] In June of 1858, Young and many others involved signed their pardons, and in so doing tacitly agreed to follow the laws of the United States going forward. After the signing, Young said, "If a man comes from the moon and says he will pardon me for kicking him on the moon yesterday, I don't care about it. I'll accept his pardon."[66]

But Young did not take his pardon and slink into the background. Instead, he remained active and extremely influential in Utah territorial politics, albeit without holding public office. In chapter 14 of *Roughing It*, Mark Twain's semiautobiographical travel book written in 1870–71, Twain cites a travel companion as saying: "There is a batch of governors, and judges, and other officials here, shipped from Washington, and they maintain the semblance of a republican form of government—but the petrified truth is that Utah is an absolute monarchy and Brigham Young is king!"[67]

As for the Mountain Meadows Massacre, it took eighteen years before John D. Lee, the leader of the militia at the site, was convicted of first-degree murder in 1876. With the Civil War over, focus again turned to the Mormons, and the federal government wanted someone to be charged for the massacre. The conviction came in the second trial of Lee, after his first trial ended in a hung jury, with the Mormon jury members voting to acquit, and the non-Mormons voting to convict. In the first trial, Young and the Mormon establishment in Utah had made it so that a conviction was highly unlikely.

The second trial was different, and it seems likely Young made a deal with Sumner Howard, the new US Attorney of Utah. Howard thought that getting a unanimous jury to convict Lee would require the consent of Young. By 1876, Lee was an excommunicated Mormon, and someone that Young would not mind sacrificing as a scapegoat. Although unconfirmed, speculation about the second trial is that

Sumner Howard and Young made a deal. If Young would provide witnesses against Lee, and the all-Mormon jury would convict, then other Mormon officials would not be prosecuted for the massacre, and evidence implicating other Mormon officials would not be presented at the trial. Howard objected to this assertion and said that it was concocted by Lee's attorneys to gain sympathy for him.

Whether or not there was coordination, the trial went very poorly for Lee. He was made out to be both the unequivocal leader of the massacre and also to have committed many acts of violence himself. The witnesses did not testify to remembering other people that were involved, so the prosecution was only aimed at Lee. During the trial, Lee's attorney presented this theory:

> I claim that Brigham Young is the real criminal, and that John D. Lee was an instrument in his hands. That Brigham Young used John Lee, as the assassin uses the dagger to strike down his unsuspecting victim; as the assassin throws away the dagger, to avoid the bloody blade leading to his detection, so Brigham Young used John Lee to do his horrid work; and when the discovery becomes unavoidable, he hurls Lee from him . . . and casts him far out into the whirlpool of destruction.

Knowing that it was no use, Lee did not want his attorney to make a closing argument, and the lawyer said only: "The Mormon Church had resolved to sacrifice Lee, discarding him as of no further use." (Lee does appear to have been involved in the Mountain Meadows Massacre, but he was not the only one.) Lee was executed by firing squad.

The reflex to pardon Young and all of those involved in the acts of war and treason on the United States may nonetheless seem understandable when viewed in context. President Buchanan desperately felt the need to appease everyone and hold the nation together on the eve of the Civil War. Because of Young's cover-up, Buchanan was not aware that 120 civilians had been killed by the Nauvoo Legion, and that their corpses were left in shallow graves to be eaten by wolves. Eventually, this was discovered by a federal agent sent to investigate, but Buchanan issued pardons to the Mormons at practically the same time they allowed Alfred Cumming to enter Salt Lake City and take the office of governor. At the time, Buchanan was likely trying to keep peace, and the Utah War had been an otherwise relatively bloodless military action. However, his reactive pardon of everyone involved in treason against the United States may have been shortsighted.

Again, Buchanan stated that the pardon was issued "to avoid the indiscriminate punishment of a whole people for crimes of which it is not probable that all are equally guilty." But this distorts the facts. Not all of the Mormons in Utah had participated at the same level: While some had declared war on the United States, most had simply followed their spiritual and political leader's orders.

Undeniably, Brigham Young had done the most. He declared war on the United States, and the pardon empowered Young and other powerful church leaders to stay in power and continue their lawlessness because there were no consequences for their actions. Young became the "governor" of the shadow government of Deseret, which he and other Mormon officials revived from the time before Utah had been given territorial status by the United States.[68] Mormons believed that, as Prophet of the Church of Jesus Christ of Latter-day Saints, Young received revelations from Jesus and God. This spiritual link became a powerful tool that Young leveraged to influence how Mormons voted. The staggering Mormon population in Utah made Young a political force to be reckoned with, even after his ousting as governor.

After the US government fully investigated the massacre and buried the corpses, they installed a cairn—a mound of stones topped with a cross—as a monument at the site in 1859.[69] Young and sixty other Mormons visited the site in 1861, removed the cross, and dismantled the cairn.[70] Young reportedly mocked the inscription on the monument during the visit. It was rebuilt by the US government again but continued to face frequent vandalism. Brigham Young died in 1877, a year after Lee was tried. He had fifty-six children with fifty-five wives. He also was pro-slavery and banned Black men from holding the priesthood.

Today, the LDS Church acknowledges that they technically declared war on the United States and apologized for the Mountain Meadows Massacre in a ceremony at the site of the massacre, in 2007.[71] Still, the Mormons involved in the rebellion benefited immeasurably from presidential pardons. In 1896, the federal government granted Utah statehood.[72] Mormons currently hold nine out of every ten seats in the Utah legislature—a firm hold on political power in that state to this very day.[73]

2

The Polygamy Pardons and Utah's Quest for Statehood

Although punishable under the federal 1862 Morrill Anti-Bigamy Act, and loathed throughout the rest of the country, polygamy was rarely prosecuted at the federal level until 1887.[74] During President Abraham Lincoln's administration, which followed Buchanan's, polygamy had not been prosecuted at all, as Lincoln had a "let-them-be" approach toward the Mormons.[75] Lincoln ignored the polygamy, especially as Brigham Young and the rest of Utah did not intervene in the Civil War. When Young sent T. B. H. Stenhouse, an assistant editor at the *Deseret News* and an active member of the church, to Washington, DC, to find out Lincoln's plan for Utah during the Civil War, Lincoln reportedly shared this:

42

Stenhouse, when I was a boy on the farm in Illinois there was a great deal of timber on the farm which we had to clear away. Occasionally we would come to a log which had fallen down. It was too hard to split, too wet to burn, and too heavy to move, so we plowed around it. That's what I intend to do with the Mormons. You go back and tell Brigham Young that if he will let me alone I will let him alone.

Lincoln's "just-plow-around-them" approach was largely what the Mormons had wanted all along, so they were happy to stay out of the Civil War if it meant the federal government would ignore Utah.

. . . AND WHY?
Abraham Lincoln likened the Utah Mormon situation to a fallen log. "It was too hard to split, too wet to burn, and too heavy to move, so we plowed around it." Do presidents need the pardon power to "plow around" problems?

But the federal government's tacit acceptance of polygamy did not last forever. Many female authors who emerged in the 1850s wrote about the negative impacts of polygamy with firsthand accounts of life in a plural marriage household.[76] In 1857 article, the *New York Times* reported on cases of girls aged ten and eleven being married to old men, and noted that marriages of girls aged fourteen was "a very common occurrence."[77] However, historian Laurel Thatcher Ulrich argues in her book, *A House Full of Females: Plural Marriage and Women's Rights in Early Mormonism, 1835–1870*, that polygamy—or plural marriage—was simultaneously empowering for women, who had the right to vote in Utah before women did nationally.[78] They also had to consent before their husbands could add another wife to a marriage. Ulrich told NPR's Terry Gross in 2017:

> I think plural marriage empowered women in very complicated ways, and to put it most simply, it added to the complexity and the adversity they experienced. And we can argue that women who deal with tough things—or a man—develop certain strengths and aptitudes. It also reinforced an already well-developed community of women to share work, to share child-care, to share religious faith, to share care in childbirth and in illness, in some sense strengthened bonds that were already very much present in their lives.[79]

Ulrich explained the religious justification for polygamy this way: "Joseph Smith taught that one of the forms of preparation was to gather all of the faithful, all of those who had embraced the new gospel into families, and part of that process meant creating plural households."

The negative stories nonetheless continued to circulate, and anti-polygamy narratives became a more mainstream element of fiction writing.[80] An anti-polygamy storyline even made it into *A Study in Scarlet*, an 1887 Sherlock Holmes story by Arthur Conan Doyle. In 1874, Fanny Stenhouse published *Tell It All*, which explained her disagreements with Mormonism and polygamy in vivid detail to those outside of the LDS Church. Fanny and her husband, T. B. H. Stenhouse—who had earlier carried the communication from President Lincoln to Young—had since left the faith. Even though some of this writing was fiction, the stories of men taking dozens of wives and the marriage of young girls were very real and horrified other Americans.

Congress responded with the 1882 Edmunds Act, which made it easier to prove that a crime had been committed by plural marriage

44

families by changing the legal standard for polygamy from proof of a legal marriage to simply proving cohabitation. Proving that a marriage took place required some documentation, or at least a pastor confirming that they had performed the ceremony. In the past, pastors who had performed plural marriage weddings could conveniently "forget" when federal authorities asked about them. The new cohabitation standard that Congress introduced made these cases much easier to prove.

The Mormons challenged the statute as an unconstitutional "*ex post facto*" measure—meaning it unlawfully charged past behavior with a new law.[81] They lost in the Supreme Court, which held in 1890 that laws against polygamy were legal,[82] on the rationale that the government was punishing the continued cohabitation—not their past marriages.[83] Feeling as though their way of life was under attack, representatives of the church authored an 1885 "Declaration of Grievances and Protest" and delivered it to President Grover Cleveland during his first term in office (he served as the twenty-second and the twenty-fourth president).[84] Cleveland and the federal government did not take the Mormon grievances and protests very seriously. In reference to Utah, Cleveland said in his annual address to Congress: "There should be no relaxation in the firm but just execution of the law now in operation, and I should be glad to approve such further discreet legislation as will rid the country of this blot upon its fair fame."[85]

In 1887, the federal government did take "further discreet action," as Cleveland foretold.[86] It started to enforce the Edmunds Act by prosecuting men for unlawful cohabitation. Congress also amended the Edmunds Act with the Edmunds–Tucker Act, which disincorporated the LDS Church and confiscated all church property valued over $50,000, including Mormon temples. It also disenfranchised polygamists and banned them from jury service. Polygamy made Congress wary of granting Utah statehood, so Utah reinvigorated its statehood campaign with a new state constitution explicitly stating that bigamy and polygamy were "incompatible with a republican form of government" and criminalizing the acts as misdemeanors. Later, in July of 1887, the legal process of seizing church assets in excess of $50,000 began.

The Mormons fought the constitutionality of the taking of church property at the Supreme Court in a case called *Late Corp. of the Church of Jesus Christ of Latter-day Saints v. United States.*[87] The church lost, with the Supreme Court holding that because Utah is a territory, the United States had plenary—or broad, almost limitless—authority over what happened there. With the Edmunds–Tucker Act declared constitutional in May of 1890, the church leaders knew they needed to denounce polygamy. By that time, there was also an equal population of men and women in the state, making polygamy harder to sustain.[88] Then-president of the LDS Church, Wilford Woodruff, released the 1890 Manifesto, officially ending the performance of plural marriages in the church.[89] The Manifesto did not say that existing marriages had to be dissolved, and most polygamists continued to live with wives from their existing marriages even though this violated federal law. Some plural weddings were still performed in Mexico, Canada, and other places where the practice was mistakenly believed to be legal.

Even so, many people who had stopped participating in plural marriage wished to be pardoned for their past transgressions and began to petition President Benjamin Harrison, who succeeded Cleveland after his first term in 1889.[90]

Up until this point, Utah had two major political parties: the LDS-backed People's Party, and the anti-Mormon Liberal Party.[91] Neither was affiliated with the two major national political parties. In May of 1891, the People's Party disbanded because LDS leadership felt that Utah had a better chance at statehood if its citizens were members of the national political parties.[92] At first, the strategy was to have high-er-ranking LDS officials join the Republican Party, because they felt it would afford them the best opportunity for Utah to become a state. The Mormons also thought that registering high-ranking church officials as Republicans would help their cause as they petitioned Republican president Harrison for pardons of violations of cohabitation laws.

In January 1893, the tireless efforts of the Mormons paid off, and just weeks before he left office, Republican president Benjamin Harrison granted a blanket pardon to

> all persons liable to the penalties of said act by reason of unlawful cohabitation under the color of polyga- mous or plural marriage who have since November 1, 1890, abstained from such unlawful cohabitation, but upon the express condition that they shall in the future faithfully obey the laws of the United States hereinbefore named, and not otherwise.[93]

The pardon was thus conditional upon those accepting it and continuing to reject polygamy. Effectively, it pardoned those who had not been cohabitating after the Supreme Court upheld the Edmunds–Tucker Act as constitutional and after the Manifesto was handed down in 1890.

...AND WHY?
President Benjamin Harrison pardoned Utah Mormons who engaged in polygamy, too—but conditioned the pardon on allegiance to the laws of the United States. Was that mercy or amnesty?

Much like the 1858 pardon for treason, this proclamation came with an ultimatum: "Those who shall fail to avail themselves of the clemency hereby offered will be vigorously prosecuted." The text of the pardon specifically stated that the church "president issued a man- ifesto proclaiming the purpose of said church no longer to sanction the practice of polygamous marriages and calling upon all members and adherents of said church to obey the laws of the United States in reference to said subject-matter." Harrison also mentioned the "very large number of cases" of individual applicants that had been granted amnesty in the past two years for their past polygamy offenses. The timing of these pardons alongside the Mormon leadership's decision to register with the Republican Party raised suspicion.

Nonetheless, the next year, President Cleveland, a Democrat, took Harrison's pardon a step further, issuing Proclamation 369 on September 25, 1894.[94] The first two paragraphs of the pardon's text are identical to Harrison's, outlining the law against cohabitation and identifying the church's 1890 Manifesto and recent teachings against polygamy as the turning point in Mormon behavior. Cleveland's pardon was broader though, encompassing "the offenses of polygamy, bigamy, [and] adultery," too. Cleveland's pardon also restored the rights of those who were "convicted of violations of said acts, [and] are now suffering deprivations of civil rights in consequence of the same," so long as they had "complied with the conditions"—mainly that they had ceased cohabitation after 1890. The right to vote and the right to serve on a jury were among the civil rights restored by the pardon. Cleveland noted his satisfaction with the church's progress toward ending polygamy in the pardon, stating:

> Whereas upon the evidence now furnished me I am satisfied that the members and adherents of said church generally abstain from plural marriages and polygamous cohabitation and are now living in obedience to the laws, and that the time has now arrived when the interests of public justice and morality will be promoted by the granting of amnesty and pardon to all such offenders as have complied with the conditions of said proclamation, including such of said offenders as have been convicted under the provisions of said act.

In reality, many church officials had not mended their ways. Some LDS officials still performed plural marriages in violation of the 1890 Manifesto. Because of this, there was a Second Manifesto issued in 1904, which threatened excommunication to those who performed new plural marriages.[95] But for those who had given up cohabitation, Cleveland's pardon re-enfranchised them.

These consecutive pardons by presidents of competing political parties, which occurred in January of 1893 and September of 1984, cannot be divorced from the politics of the Utah statehood movement. Utah became a state in 1896, pursuant to an enabling act signed by President Cleveland in July of 1894. Cleveland extended his predecessor's pardon two months later. In the text of the pardon, Cleveland did not cite what "evidence" makes him "satisfied" that the Mormons are no longer violating the law. But he did say "that the time has now arrived" to restore the rights of those who had lost them. Maybe Cleveland had the sense that a critical mass of Mormons had renounced polygamy by this point. Or maybe Cleveland, a Democrat, sought to influence the soon-to-be state by countering the prior Republican president's pardon with one of his own. Cleveland was certainly aware, in his words, "that the time [had] arrived" for Utah to become a state.

Cleveland's actions over the course of his two, nonconsecutive terms were politically contradictory on the question of polygamy. Nearly a decade earlier, in 1885, during Cleveland's first term, he implored Congress to take further action against the LDS Church to rid Utah of polygamy, an effort that ultimately led to the passage of the Edmunds–Tucker Act.[96] A decade later, Cleveland issued a pardon restoring the franchise to powerful men in the LDS Church, even as other Mormons continued their existing plural marriages in public, with the consent of the church. The pardon seemed to undercut and contradict what Cleveland was advocating for during his first term.

So what was Cleveland's motivation for the pardon—amnesty or mercy? Or do these pardons belie something more nefarious, like an unabashed bid for political power? If these pardons were mostly political, did they nonetheless serve a broader public purpose? Where is the line between pardons in the public interest and those for abject personal and political gain? And finally, how do Buchanan and Harrison's pardons compare to those of California governor Pat Brown, who labored over clemency petitions in which individuals begged for life over death at the hands of the government?[97]

When presented with the clemency petition of Vernon Atchley, who killed his wife and was sentenced to death in the electric chair, Brown initially rejected it.[98] He then decided to order an electroencephalogram (EEG), a brain scan, which revealed that Atchley had significant brain damage. Brown changed his mind based on this information, commuted his sentence to life, and ordered EEGs for everyone on California's death row. At least three other times, state governors have commuted all death sentences in their states before leaving office—Toney Anaya of New Mexico in 1986, George Ryan of Illinois in 2003, and Martin O'Malley of Maryland in 2014.[99] Surely, these could be considered acts of mercy.

But is it acceptable for a single elected official to wipe out the work of judges, juries, and legislatures—all of whom apparently determined in some measure that the death sentences were warranted? If nothing else, the Mormon stories—the pardons for the rebellion against the federal government, the Meadows Massacre pardon, and the polygamy pardons—reveal that the pardon power deserves attention and cannot be whisked atop a pedestal on the blithe assumption that the Constitution (for presidents, at least) unequivocally says this power is acceptable.

3
The Trump Pardons:
A Short List of Notables

Over the course of American history, US presidents have issued as many as 3,687 pardons during their terms in office (President Franklin D. Roosevelt) to as few as 0 (presidents William Henry Harrison and James A. Garfield).[100] Here are some highlights:

o President John F. Kennedy pardoned everyone convicted for the first time under the Narcotics Control Act of 1956 as a signal to Congress that the law needed changes.

o President Gerald Ford preemptively pardoned Nixon for any federal crimes Nixon might have committed during the Watergate scandal, even though Nixon wasn't charged with or convicted of anything.[101]

o George H. W. Bush pardoned former defense secretary Caspar Weinberger and former CIA official Duane Clarridge in late 1992, before they were tried on Iran–Contra affair charges.[102]

o President Bill Clinton pardoned his own brother, Roger, who had served a one-year jail sentence on a drug conviction.[103]

o President Obama commuted the jail sentence for WikiLeaks figure Chelsea Manning.[104]

o President Ronald Reagan pardoned New York Yankees owner George Steinbrenner for charges related to illegal campaign contributions made to President Richard Nixon's presidential campaign.[105]

. . . AND WHY?

Presidents have issued upwards of 3,687 pardons since ratification of the US Constitution. But none were more disturbing than the Trump pardons, thrusting the pardon power onto center stage as a tool for corruption. Is the presidential pardon power still justified in its current form?

All of these pardons were newsworthy. But as with many aspects of his presidency, Donald J. Trump may have managed to push the pardon power beyond the limits of recent memory. President Trump issued a total of 143 pardons—116 right before he left office.[106] Some were quite evidently within any reasonable understanding of the proper parameters of the pardon power. Others were suspect. Either way, Trump's array of choices reflects all of the arbitrariness, inconsistencies, and temptations for corruption that the pardon power still presents.

Susan B. Anthony and Alice Johnson

First consider, for example, that on August 18, 2020, Trump issued a full pardon to Susan B. Anthony.[107] In 1872, Anthony went to her polling place on Election Day and cast a ballot.[108] At that time, women couldn't vote in the United States. A federal marshal showed up at her home later and arrested her for wrongfully and willfully voting. She was ultimately tried and fined $100 (approximately $3,000 today). Women were only granted a right to vote under the Nineteenth Amendment to the Constitution on August 18, 1920—one hundred years prior to the day of her pardon.[109] Trump's pardon of Anthony was nonetheless controversial.

These days, there are two competing groups who claim to honor Anthony's memory and life. The first is the Susan B. Anthony List, a nonprofit organization in her name that promotes anti-abortion politicians.[110] The other is called the National Susan B. Anthony Museum & House.[111] The Susan B. Anthony List was happy that Trump honored Anthony by pardoning her. But the National Susan B. Anthony Museum & House (along with many historians who read her letters and notes to Elizabeth Cady Stanton and other suffragettes of her time) stated that Anthony "would have been adamantly opposed to being pardoned" because "[t]o pardon her for it is to give validity to the trial."[112]

The museum said it was not consulted prior to the pardon announcement; otherwise, it would have informed Trump of its stance on her behalf. "I stand before you tonight, under indictment for the alleged crime of having voted at the last presidential election, without having a lawful right to vote," Anthony herself said in a speech before her trial. "It shall be my work this evening to prove to you that in thus voting, I not only committed no crime, but, instead, simply exercised my citizen's right, guaranteed to me and all United States citizens by the national Constitution, beyond the power of any state to deny."[113]

Trump did pardon a number of other apparently deserving petitioners, as well, including Alice Johnson, who in 1996 was convicted of drug trafficking and sentenced to life in prison in Memphis, Tennessee.[114] Johnson lost her job of over ten years at FedEx due to a gambling addiction, a divorce, and the death of her youngest son from a motorcycle accident. Johnson said she "felt like a failure . . . and out of desperation" made a bad decision "to make some quick money."[115] She claimed that her involvement in the crime was limited to relaying coded messages over the phone, and that she never brokered any deals or handled drugs. Ten of Johnson's co-defendants reportedly testified against her and the charges against them were dropped.[116] Despite no previous drug charges, Johnson did not get the same deal as her co-defendants; instead, she wound up with a life sentence.

Johnson's children petitioned for her release, claiming that their mother was a "model inmate" who had been active in "many programs, including working at the prison hospice." Johnson's support gained traction.[117] In 2014, an organization called CAN-DO Clemency began advocating for Johnson, collecting letters of support from wardens in Johnson's prison. During the Obama administration, Johnson submitted a clemency application three times, but it was rejected. Johnson's story spread on social media and came to the attention of celebrity influencer Kim Kardashian, who began advocating for Johnson by hiring her a brand-new legal team and speaking to President Trump to lobby for Johnson.

Trump commuted Johnson's sentence shortly thereafter. Kardashian had reached out to renowned celebrity attorney Shawn Holley, whose client list included O. J. Simpson, Michael Jackson, and Lindsay Lohan. Kardashian was also in constant communication with Jared Kushner, Trump's son-in-law-turned senior presidential advisor. When Kardashian finally met with Trump on May 30, 2018, it was Johnson's birthday, and Kardashian posted about it on Twitter (now known as X). Trump followed up with a Twitter post in which he thanked Kardashian for coming and talking about prison reform and sentencing. Following the grant of a commuted sentence, President Trump invited Johnson to attend and speak at several events, which included the 2019 State of the Union Address, the White House's 2019 Prison Reform Summit, and the 2020 Republican National Convention, to highlight the good work he did in commuting her sentence. These events were followed by Trump granting Johnson full clemency.

Alice Johnson used her newfound public platform to advocate for others in a similar situation, which resulted in many people being granted clemency. In granting these pardons Trump reportedly sought advice from his friends, lawmakers, lobbyists, and other influencers rather than turning to the Justice Department's pardon attorney for consultation on recommendations. Many of those who were granted presidential mercy under the Trump administration were selected despite not having filed applications with the DOJ or meeting the Justice Department's usual preconditions for clemency, such as an acknowledgment of their crimes and a showing of remorse.

Charles Kushner, Steve Bannon, Lil Wayne, Tommaso Buti

Jared Kushner similarly advocated for use of the pardon power in the Trump administration—but instead, for the purpose of helping the elite get out of trouble. As far as we know, Trump never issued a pardon for himself or any of his children, but he did pardon Kushner's father, Charles Kushner, a billionaire real estate developer.[118]

Charles Kushner had served two years in prison for $6 million in tax evasion and retaliation against a federal witness, William Schulder, who happened to be Charles Kushner's former employee and brother-in-law. The tax evasion scheme came under scrutiny when then New Jersey US Attorney Chris Christie launched an investigation into Kushner's activities in 2003, relating to making illegal campaign contributions. According to a report by NPR, the senior Kushner "hired a prostitute to sleep with Schulder, secretly videotaped the encounter, then mailed a tape of it to his own sister," Schulder's wife. Schulder and his wife turned the blackmail tape over to prosecutors. At the end of the case, which Christie called "one of the most loathsome, disgusting crimes" he had ever prosecuted, Kushner pled guilty to sixteen counts of tax evasion, retaliation against a federal witness, and lying to the Federal Election Commission.

Charles Kushner served his time, and when asked about his hopes at a presidential pardon back in 2018, he stated, "I would prefer not to have a pardon" because it would only trigger further publicity.[119] His son Jared Kushner reportedly worked on prison reform as part of the Trump administration because of his father's experience, saying (somewhat confusingly) in 2018: "When you're on the other side of the system, you feel so helpless. . . . I felt like I was on this side of the system, so how can I try to do whatever I can do to try to be helpful to the people who are going through it and deserve a second chance."[120] Jared Kushner wasn't the only one who felt his father deserved a second chance; the Trump White House stated that Kushner had a "record of reform and charity" that "overshadows" his conviction.

Trump also pardoned his former chief strategist, Steve Bannon, who was charged with defrauding hundreds of thousands of people who donated more than $25 million to construct a wall on the US–Mexico border.[121] The charges included wire fraud and money laundering. Although he pled not guilty, Bannon allegedly received over $1 million from the donation organization through a nonprofit he controls, and used it in part on personal expenses. Interestingly, Trump pardoned Bannon even though their relationship was strained. He ousted Bannon from the White House administration just eight months into the job. Bannon had a hand in some of the most controversial efforts to come out of the Trump administration, such as the Muslim immigration ban, which put him in the spotlight. After Bannon was on the cover of *Time* magazine, Trump reportedly claimed that it was Trump himself who deserved more credit, not his advisor. Nonetheless, Bannon may have saved his severed relationship with Trump when, during the first impeachment proceedings, he launched a podcast and radio show to vigorously defend the president.[122]

Unexpected and seemingly arbitrary pardons for influential or elite figures persisted throughout the Trump administration. Trump loved to tweet and retweet when people praised him—enough to overturn some convictions as a result. Rapper Lil Wayne, aka, Dwayne Carter Jr., pled guilty to illegally carrying a firearm despite a prior felony conviction, a crime that carried ten years in prison. Trump pardoned him, too.[123] Lil Wayne and Trump were no strangers to each other. In October 2020, Lil Wayne met with the president and went on Twitter to tweet a picture of the both of them with the caption:

> Just had a great meeting with @realdonaldtrump @potus besides what he's done so far with criminal reform, the platinum plan is going to give the

community real ownership. He listened to what
we had to say today and assured he will and can get
it done.[124]

When it came to justifying the pardon, the White House cited CEO
Brett Berish of Sovereign Brands, a wine and spirits company, who
described the rapper as "trustworthy, kind-hearted and generous."

Trump also pardoned his friend, Italian restaurateur Tommaso
Buti, who moved to the United States from Italy in the late 1980s.[125]
He founded a gourmet food delivery service called "Focaccia" whose
clientele in the mid-1990s included the corporate elites of Wall Street,
such as Merrill Lynch and fashion designer Donna Karan. Buti opened
Fashion Café in Rockefeller Center, which became a celebrity hotspot.
The IRS came after Buti in 1998 for unpaid taxes, the restaurant shut
down, and Buti was sued by his partners in the amount of $15 million.
The same year, Trump opened a modeling agency with Buti, stating publicly that Buti was a "terrific, unjustly accused guy" who "loves women,
and women love him back. He's a natural to run a modeling agency."

In 2000, Buti was arrested in Milan along with his brother, and
was acquitted after trial in Italy in 2007. Years later, he faced a fifty-
one-count federal indictment charging conspiracy, fraud, and money
laundering relating to the restaurant. Before he could be tried in the
United States, Buti was granted a full pardon by President Trump.
Again, the White House claimed to base the decision on Buti's
"charitable" history. The official statement read:

> Mr. Buti is an Italian citizen and a respected busi-
> nessman. He is the Chief Operating Officer of a large
> Italian company and has started a successful charita-
> ble initiative to raise funds for UNICEF. More than
> twenty years ago, Mr. Buti was charged with financial
> fraud involving a chain of restaurants. He has not,
> however, been convicted in the United States.[126]

Corrupt Politicians, an Israeli Spy, and Blackwater Contractors

President Trump promised to "drain the swamp"—a phrase dating back to the Reagan administration that refers to a culture of unscrupulousness among Washington, DC, insiders—but he didn't hesitate to pardon both Republicans and Democrats for corruption convictions. Former Detroit mayor Kwame Kilpatrick, a Democrat, was sentenced to twenty-eight years in prison on charges of "racketeering, conspiracy, fraud, extortion, and tax crimes."[127] Kilpatrick allegedly made a great deal of money from city contractors with "pay-to-play" kickbacks and bribes. He apologized for these actions but denied stealing from Detroit's citizens. Kilpatrick served more than seven years of his twenty-eight-year sentence before Trump commuted his sentence, prompting his release from federal prison.[128] In justifying the pardon, the White House noted Kilpatrick's support from prominent members of the Detroit community, including Fox News personalities Diamond and Silk, as well as his public speaking classes and leadership of Bible study groups with his fellow inmates. Although his sentence was reduced, a commutation (versus a full pardon) means that Kilpatrick's felony convictions still stand, so he still owes $195,000 to the IRS and $1.5 million to the city of Detroit.[129]

Trump did grant a full pardon to former Republican congressman Mark Siljander, who was charged with "acting as a foreign agent on behalf of an Islamic charity that hired him to lobby Congress to have its name removed from a list of alleged terrorist-supporting organizations."[130] To add fuel to the fire, Siljander allegedly used his own charities to hide his lobbying work. The US Attorney in Kansas City further asserted that the congressman repeatedly lied to the FBI when questioned. Eventually, the FBI raided his organization, shut it down, and designated it a terrorist organization for having financially supported terrorists like Osama bin Laden and groups like Hamas, the Palestinian group that later attacked Israel in October of 2023. High-profile Republicans, including former speaker of the House of Representatives Newt Gingrich and former Arkansas governor Mike Huckabee, came to the aid of Siljander, urging Trump to grant him a pardon. In issuing the pardon, the White House noted Siljander's commitment to anti-abortion causes, claiming he was "one of Congress's most stalwart defenders of pro-life principles."

Aviem Sella received another notable pardon. Sella was a retired Israeli air officer indicted for espionage in 1987 for having served as a double agent who worked against the Pentagon by selling military secrets to Israel. Sella had enlisted Jonathan Pollard, a US Navy intelligence analyst who worked at the Pentagon as a spy. Sella fled to Israel as soon as Pollard was arrested. Although charged with three counts of espionage against the United States, Sella was not extradited to the United States, having enlisted the support of Israeli prime minister Benjamin Netanyahu and both the American and Israeli ambassadors to Israel. When Sella's associate Pollard immigrated to Israel after serving thirty years in a US prison, he was welcomed on the tarmac by Netanyahu himself. Accompanying Sella's pardon was a White House statement that Israel had apologized and requested the pardon to close an "unfortunate chapter in U.S.–Israel relations."[131]

Trump also issued disturbing pardons related to a private military contractor called the Blackwater company, which was founded by Erik Prince, the brother of Trump's secretary of education, Betsy DeVos.[132] Four contractors working as guards for Blackwater—Nicholas Slatten, Paul Slough, Evan Liberty, and Dustin Heard—were involved in a 2007 massacre in Baghdad's Nisour Square. In 2014, all four were convicted of killing fourteen Iraqi civilians and wounding seventeen more. Military officials said the massacre was "a grossly excessive use of force" and "grossly inappropriate for an entity whose only job was to provide personal protection to somebody in an armored vehicle."[133] Speaking about the pardons, one victim in the attack, Hassan Salman, told NPR: "I'm really shocked . . . The American judiciary is fair and equitable. I had never imagined that Trump or any other politician would affect American justice."

The Blackwater pardons also prompted a statement by the UN Human Rights Office and Human Rights Watch expressing that it was "deeply concerned" that the pardons "show[ed] contempt for the rule of law." The White House responded that the pardons were "broadly supported by the public" and had the backing of a number of Republican lawmakers.[134] (Bear in mind that according to a *New York Times* report, Prince was hired in the summer of 2018 by Richard Seddon, a former British spy, to launch a venture that would use undercover agents to infiltrate progressive groups, Democratic candidates, and other individuals disfavored by Donald Trump.)[135]

The Mueller Investigation Pardons

No list of Trump pardons is complete without mentioning those in connection with the investigation of Special Counsel Robert Mueller into Russian interference in the 2016 presidential election.[136] Trump pardoned or commuted the sentences of a slew of people who pleaded guilty to lying and obstructing justice during a federal investigation, including:

o Michael Flynn, Trump's former national security advisor;

o George Papadopoulos, a foreign policy advisor;

o Alex van der Zwaan, Trump's former campaign chairman;

o Paul Manafort, who was convicted of committing financial fraud and conspiring to obstruct the investigation of his crimes;[137] and

o Roger Stone, whose conviction on seven felonies Trump denounced as the work of "overzealous prosecutors" who pursued "proceed-based charges" in the "Russia hoax" and the "witch hunts."[138]

Mike Flynn had twice pleaded guilty to lying to the FBI concerning his conversations with Russian diplomats. He was the only White House official convicted of a crime in connection with the Mueller investigation.[139] (All told, Mueller secured indictments, convictions, and guilty pleas from thirty-four people and three companies—including Russian spies and hackers.) As the case dragged on and Flynn couldn't get an appeals court to block the criminal process, Trump went ahead and issued a pardon for Flynn, tweeting: "It is my Great Honor to announce that General Michael T. Flynn has been granted a Full Pardon."[140] Given Trump's personal and political stake in the Russia investigation, it's impossible not to question his motives in pardoning Flynn and the others.

... AND WHY?

**Russia interfered in the 2016 US presidential election
to help put Donald Trump in power.
By later pardoning a slew of allies who were prosecuted
for related crimes, did Trump establish a
"new normal" for presidents?**

Yet perhaps the most controversial pardon around the Russia investigation belonged to Paul Manafort. Flynn and Papadopoulos cooperated with investigators. Manafort, who is believed to have especially close connections to Russia, refused.[141] Before joining the Trump campaign, he worked for a pro-Russian political force in Ukraine and also met with Russian lawyers in New York City's Trump Tower.[142] Manafort also worked closely with a Russian army trainee, Konstantin Kilimnik. According to Mueller's findings, Manafort shared Trump campaign polling data with Kilimnik in the lead-up to the 2016 presidential election, which Mueller ultimately concluded was infiltrated by Russia, to Trump's benefit.[143] Mueller described Kilimnik as having "ties to Russian intelligence," and Senate Republican reports referred to him as a "Russian intelligence officer" who was the "single most direct tie" between Russian intelligence and the Trump campaign.[144] According to the FBI's website, Kilimnik is wanted under a 2018 indictment from the Mueller grand jury for obstruction of justice and engaging in a conspiracy to obstruct justice. In pardoning Manafort, Trump lavished praise on him for refusing "to break" during the investigation.[145] The pardon released Manafort from serving the remainder of his seven-and-a-half-year sentence.

* * *

If nothing else, the Trump pardon stories lay bare the reality of the abusive power of the pardon. It can be a mechanism for mercy and fairness, addressing inadequacies in the criminal justice system for the lucky few who catch the eye of a president or governor. Or as the Mormon pardons revealed, sometimes presidents need access to the extraordinary remedy of mass pardons to address fragile political situations that traditional diplomacy or the rule of law cannot outpace. But given that only a tiny fraction of people embroiled in the criminal justice system get pardons, and given how rare—and controversial—presidential acts of amnesty are, it's hard to square those benefits with the pardon power's temptation for political abuse, corruption, and injustice.

The next part walks through how we got to this disturbing calculus, on a path that winds over many centuries.

Part II

What? The Historical and Legal Evolution of the Pardon Power

A pardon is an official act of forgiveness by the president or a governor for a crime committed.[146] Often called "clemency," executive pardons erase the punishment associated with a conviction and exist under the laws of every state in the nation and in virtually every country in the world. A pardon absolves a person of legal guilt—or at least lifts some or all of the legal consequences that come along with being convicted of a crime. In that way, pardons distinguish recipients from the rest of the population, who without a pardon must usually pay the full penalty for committing the same crime.

A pardon can also be "full" or absolute, enabling an offender to walk away as if nothing ever happened—no offense, no trial, no conviction, no sentence.[147] A "partial" or conditional pardon, by contrast, can erase part of the consequences for the crime, or attach some criteria to the pardon that the offender must satisfy in order to secure the pardon.[148] In rare instances, as with President Gerald Ford's pardon of his predecessor, Richard Nixon, a pardon can be prospective, attaching before an individual has even been charged with—let alone tried and convicted for—a crime.[149]

As we've seen, presidents can also issue group pardons to entire categories of offenders.[150] Known as "amnesty," presidents invoke this category of pardons to address national interests in a way that only they are positioned to do—such as pardoning a class of soldiers who deserted a military operation during an especially controversial conflict. Amnesty stands out as a distinct category of pardon from the individual ones, and arguably deserves separate treatment and analysis because it does not implicate the same flavors of favoritism, arbitrariness, or cronyism that individual pardons do. Amnesty also triggers greater political accountability because presidents are forced to explain their actions; public transparency and a national response naturally follow large policy decisions out of a White House, particularly around the topic of war. Unlike an individual pardon, which has its constitutional roots exclusively in the president's power to execute the laws, amnesty also derives from the commander-in-chief power and the president's implied powers over foreign policy.

In addition to pardons, clemency, and amnesty, two additional subcategories of pardons are worth mentioning:

- o *Reprieves* amount to extra time for a prisoner before a punishment takes effect—say, to give birth to a baby or to appeal a conviction.[151] Reprieves do not cut a sentence short or remove a conviction altogether.

- o *Commutations* swap out a lesser sentence for a more serious one, as happened in California under Governor Pat Brown: Life in prison with or without parole was substituted for the death penalty.[152] (Counterintuitively, in January of 2024, Alabama executed Kenneth Eugene Smith by nitrogen hypoxia, an untested method of suffocation, based on an elected judge's decision to strike the jury's sentence of life imprisonment and replace it with death.[153]) Or a governor could commute a life sentence for time already served, enabling a recipient to finish life in free society. If you think a commutation sounds a lot like parole, in which an incarcerated person is allowed to serve a shorter sentence due to good behavior while in prison or the like, you are not alone. The two are indeed similar, and are often determined by the same government body at the state level. The differences, perhaps, are that parole is a highly regulated process, and parolees continue to serve their sentence on parole, along with certain restrictions imposed as a result of the conviction.

All of these terms refer to different forms of a pardon, so when the book mentions pardons, it means a pardon in any form, because all of them warrant some measure of justification and scrutiny. Keep in mind that when it comes to the US president, none of these pardon variations are spelled out in the Constitution. The fact that the discretion to shape the pardon power lies exclusively, and unaccountably, with one person (or, to some degree, the people to whom that person delegates the job of sorting through pardon applications) only underscores the bizarre posture of the pardon in our governmental system—one that otherwise runs on checks and balances between the various sources of public power.

As a practical matter, although presidents have the power to pardon federal offenses under federal law with the aid of White House staff, the Justice Department's Office of the Pardon Attorney also plays a role. The DOJ is the domestic law enforcement arm of the federal government and includes agencies like the FBI under its mantle; it essentially functions as the federal government's criminal law enforcement team of police officers, investigators, and prosecutors. Viewed this way, it perhaps makes sense that the same agency that is charged with determining which members of the public should be criminally charged under federal law would likewise weigh in on which convicted individuals should be considered for a presidential pardon.[154]

The DOJ receives hundreds of petitions a year. Its pardon lawyers apply a set of criteria to each application and present their recommended pardons in batches to the sitting president.[155] Advocates for the rights of criminal defendants might argue that the same group of people who were responsible for sending a person to jail in the first place cannot be objective when it comes to deciding whether a criminal conviction and sentence should be obliterated. A pardon absolves the accused of the very accountability for their crimes that the law enforcement officials worked so hard to secure.

Inevitably, unelected people within the DOJ's ranks—and not the president—are responsible for deciding certain winners and losers in the pardon lottery. They do so based on criteria that are not found in the Constitution or in any federal law. As discussed below, those criteria are also highly subjective. Presidents are used to having piles of documents put before them for signature; pardons are, historically, no exception. Given the demands of the job, it's impossible for presidents to personally review and study every file, let alone every petition. Ultimately, only presidents can grant pardons, but other people deny hundreds by never bringing the requests to a president's attention in the first place.

Trump's pardons were notable in part because he bypassed the DOJ, handing out pardons with an unparalleled arbitrariness and subjectivity that undermined the legitimacy of the process.[156] Arguably, that's a good thing, because the Constitution lodges the pardon power with the president—not DOJ staff. But as a matter of common sense and fairness, pardons granted on a whim or out of pure self-interest are perhaps even more disturbing than pardons denied by people other than a president, based on a set of criteria that applies evenhandedly to everyone. Nonetheless, to this day, there's nothing stopping the presidential practice of bestowing arbitrary pardons for the wrong reasons—despite many hundreds of years of abuse and debate stretching back to Jesus of Nazareth, and before.

1

From Emperors to Kings

The first question to ask about the pardon power is *Why have it at all*? Justice means that if everything in the legal system is working as it should, the guilty are punished and the innocent are set free. By its very definition, therefore, pardoning necessarily implicates some miscarriage of justice, a subversion of the laws, as *it sets free the guilty*. Understood this way, the pardon power is double-faced. Sometimes the technically guilty *should* be set free in order to exert fairness or mercy, to promote peace, to help a country move on, or even to correct manifestly unjust laws. But on other occasions, the power can be abused—such as when pardons are given out for money or favors, wind up releasing murderers and war criminals, or are used to subvert the will of the legislature by freeing those who breaks its laws.

In America, the Constitution divides the power to punish between three branches of government, at both the state and federal levels. The legislature decides what acts are punishable and to what extent by passing laws and mandating the penalties for violating them. The executive branch, through prosecutors and law enforcement personnel, apprehends suspected perpetrators and mounts lawsuits against them. And the judicial branch holds trials for suspects during which judges interpret the laws of crime and punishment. Absent a plea deal, the final decision of guilt, innocence, and punishment is ultimately left to citizens themselves, in the form of juries. Even there, the ultimate choice whether or not to punish is given not to one individual, but spread between twelve (or fewer, depending on the case) who in many cases can only convict unanimously. If these divisions of power prove insufficient to protect defendants against abuses of the government's exclusive power to punish and deprive individuals of liberty, and even life, the Constitution contains further safeguards for people accused of crimes.

The awesome power to pardon is completely separate—and different—from the criminal justice system and the rule of law that governs it. Instead of being spread out between various diffuse sources of power, at the federal level the pardon power belongs entirely to one man (thus far)—the president. (State pardon systems vary, as described later in the book.) And unlike the power to punish—which is confined by the amendments to the Constitution (e.g., the First Amendment prohibits punishment for speech or the practice of religion)—courts and commentators generally treat the power to pardon as unrestricted. The Constitution suggests that the president can pardon *anyone, anytime,* for *anything* (with the exception of pardons for rare impeachments).[157] Because the government's power to punish can be used for good or ill, the Constitution divides it up so no single bad actor can abuse it. The power to pardon can also be

70

used for good or ill—and yet, the Constitution gives it to one person, whose actions cannot be second-guessed, appealed, or reversed.

...AND WHY?

The Framers modeled the president's pardon after the English monarchy, whose history is rife with debates over whether kings should have the unlimited power to pardon. If it's too dangerous for kings, why should presidents have limitless power to pardon?

The US president's power to pardon derives from that of the English king, who did have the power to pardon as sovereign.[158] So when the Founders met at the Constitutional Convention in Philadelphia in 1787, they had to answer two questions about the English monarch's pardon power.[159] Would the new Constitution include a pardon power, too? And if so, would it be given to one person, or spread around the political branches like the power to punish? They did not have to discuss these knotty issues in a complete vacuum. They had centuries of history to examine, as well as the opinions of some of the most brilliant politicians and philosophers of the age.

Before examining the choices the Framers made in Philadelphia, we need to look at the same history and theory they did. As they discovered, people had been asking the same hard questions about the pardon power for hundreds of years. It turns out that the two-faced nature of the pardon power—its potential for use and abuse—has been its defining characteristic for almost four thousand years of legal and political history.

The Qur'an, Jesus, the Greeks and Romans, and Early England: 1800 BC—AD 668

Pardons for crimes have existed as long as punishments for them. The Code of Hammurabi, the famous eighteenth-century BC Babylonian legal text, was one of the first examples in human history of a ruler imposing on his people laws and punishment for violations.[160] But alongside punishments, the Code also provided ways in which those punishments were limited. Some wrongdoers could earn clemency for their crimes. On accession to the throne, Babylonian kings would often declare a *misharum* for certain individuals, which amounted to a general discharge or amnesty from debts and crimes.[161]

The Qur'an recognizes acts of pardon several times.[162] Under Islamic Sharia law, *diya* "is the payment of 'blood money' to compensate for death or injury caused by a serious offense against a person and to provide [a person] relief from [punishment]."[163] There are three broad categories of crimes in classical Islamic jurisprudence: *hudud*, *tazir*, and *qisas*, which in turn are generally divided into two groups: homicides and bodily injuries.[164] The Qur'an allows for retaliation against those who commit a *qisas* crime, but favors forgiveness. Under Sharia law, homicides are punished either by death or a payment of *diya* by the perpetrator to the victim's family, the acceptance of which evades a death penalty. By choosing a money payment over execution, the family increases its standing in the afterlife. In Iran, the pardon power exists as a legal mechanism for mercy, but the victim's family must grant the pardon.[165]

Pardons also feature in Mosaic Law, which are the laws given by God to the Jewish people in the Hebrew Bible.[166] (*Torah*, the Hebrew word for the first five books of the Bible, literally means "law.")[167] In the Book of Samuel, for example, King David was urged by his advisors to execute his enemy, Shimei.[168] Shimei's crime involved insulting

King David and gloating that he defeated the king's rebellious son, Absalom, in battle. Later, David won the war against Absalom and the other rebels, but he did not punish Shimei. Instead, the king pardoned him and his companions, promising "to remit to all offenders their punishments." To Shimei himself, he said "Thou shalt not die." Thus, in this story, even though Shimei committed a crime against the king, the king chose mercy, pardoning him.

Perhaps the most famous pardon from the ancient epoch of the Abrahamic religions appears in the Bible's New Testament account of the crucifixion of Jesus of Nazareth.[169] Pontius Pilate was the fifth governor to rule over Judea under the Roman emperor Tiberius.[170] In a rather interesting legal twist, Pilate learned that Jesus was from Galilee, and declared he had no jurisdictional authority to decide his fate. (I discuss the notion of jurisdiction in my book, *How to Read the Constitution and Why*, and explain—in-part—that jurisdiction is the "government's general power to exercise authority over all persons and things within its territory.") Lacking jurisdiction, Pilate sent Jesus to Herod, who was the governor of Galilee but just happened to be in Jerusalem at the time.[171] Herod was elated to meet Jesus because of the many stories of miracles he had performed. He found no fault in Jesus, and instead mocked him and sent him back to Pilate. Pilate agreed with Herod that Jesus had not done anything warranting a death sentence and was willing to release Jesus. Against a growing and agitated crowd, Pilate made a political decision that quite literally changed the world.

Pilate had planned to release a prisoner as part of the Passover celebration. This traditional pardon, he believed, would be enough to quiet the crowds. He presented the people of Judea two options: Jesus or Barabbas—a notable criminal in prison for treason and murder. Pilate likely believed that the people would spare Jesus and demand accountability for the murderous Barabbas. Instead, instigated by the chief priests and elders, the crowds demanded that Barabbas receive the governor's pardon. Pilate succumbed to the pressure and will of the people who demanded Barabbas's release, pardoning him as though he had never committed his crimes. Against this backdrop, Pilate acknowledged the lack of evidence supporting the claims against Jesus, but still cast him to certain death. Jesus was crucified.

The story of Jesus's death is an example of the long-standing Jewish tradition of pardoning a criminal during the Passover feast, which predated the Roman conquest of the Holy Land. The "Paschal Pardon" operated by popular acclaim: One criminal, of the local people's choice, would be released every year. Scholars believe that these early pardons arose primarily as a means of controlling violence. As Daniel Pascoe notes, "Clemency was often dispensed in conjunction with local holidays, when the Romans were most interested in quieting crowds." Before the advent of criminal law and centralized societies, offenses against other persons were dealt with privately by the relatives or friends of the person harmed, which inevitably led to a never-ending cycle of revenges, blood feuds, and vendettas. Evidence of these feuds is all over the literature of ancient civilizations—not just in the Old Testament, but also in the myths and histories of the Ancient Greeks.

...AND WHY?

What's the oldest and most famous pardon of all? The pardon of a murderer named Barabbas instead of Jesus, who was sentenced to death and crucified. Does it surprise you to know that a pardon lies at the heart of this story?

The *Oresteia*, a trilogy from the fifth century BC by the Greek playwright Aeschylus, gives an account of the semi-mythical kings of Mycenae that illustrates how these cycles occurred in ancient society. King Atreus's wife, Aerope, committed adultery with the king's brother, Thyestes.[172] As revenge, King Atreus murdered Thyestes's sons, cooked them, and tricked his brother Thyestes into eating them. Thyestes subsequently sired another son, Aegisthus, who in his turn killed both Atreus and Atreus's son, Agamemnon. Agamemnon's own son, Orestes, then took revenge by murdering Aegisthus. Shades of this violence appear in the more modern story of the Hatfield and McCoy families, and their similarly bloody feud that played out in an Appalachian Mountain society that was almost as lawless as Ancient Greece.

In an effort to forestall these cycles among their own families and the families of their supporters, the rulers of early societies began to impose the rule of law upon their subjects, ordaining that, for certain especially bad offenses (homicide, theft, rape, arson, etc.), the offenses were not against the victim, or the vengeful family of the victim, but against the king himself. It thus became the king's decision, and not that of the vengeful family or friends, as to whether the offender should be punished or forgiven. In the Old Testament, King David admitted granting Shimei clemency not because he felt sorry for him, but to prevent "[raising] new troubles and seditions among us, now the former are over."[173] Essentially, he pardoned Shimei not out of mercy, but because if he executed Shimei, Shimei's relatives would be entitled to take revenge on him, thus continuing the cycle of violence and preventing peace.

Another example of this phenomenon appears in early Anglo-Saxon England, when society was still organized along tribal lines and men were honor-bound to avenge the deaths of kinsmen.[174] The story of Earl Uhtred in the eleventh century AD bears a bloody resemblance to the Greeks' *Oresteia*.[175] Uhtred, a powerful lord in the north of England, was murdered by a local rival named Thurbrand. Uhtred had been traveling to meet the king, and was taken completely by surprise when Thurbrand's men ambushed him in a banquet hall by hiding behind the wall hangings. Uhtred's son,

Ealdred, then murdered Thurbrand in revenge. Then Thurbrand's son, Carl, killed Ealdred. Ealdred's grandson, Waltheof, therefore did the natural thing and surprised Carl's sons and grandsons while they were at dinner and slaughtered them all. The modern television series *Game of Thrones* enthralled millions with similar fictional plots of family revenge warfare.

As an alternative to such cycles of violence, a wrongdoer in Anglo-Saxon England could pay a fixed *wergild*—or private fine—to the family of the injured. Failure to pay the *wergild* "[exposed] the slayer to the vengeance of the slain man's kin."[176] Perhaps unsurprisingly, this option only led to highly inconsistent punishment, as well as additional violence and division between families like those of Uhtred and Thurbrand. Beginning with Wihtred of Kent in the seventh century AD, rulers gradually began superseding the *wergild* system with criminal laws they enforced against the perpetrators as sovereign rather than leaving it up to the families of victims. These laws also gave the king a corresponding power to remit sentences, so with the advent of these criminal laws arose a commensurate policy of forgiveness for violating them.

Unlike other early legal innovations designed to impose order on society, the pardon power has always been characterized by a religious or magical component as well. Objects, people, or practices considered divine or pure could bestow pardons on criminals. The classical period and early Middle Ages saw a variety of esoteric procedures that societies thought would miraculously cleanse perpetrators of crimes, sometimes because they signified divine intervention in the criminal's favor or lent him a kind of transferable purity or innocence.

In Ancient Rome, for example, a prisoner on his way to execution would be pardoned if he encountered one of the sacred "Vestal Virgins" along the way, but only if this encounter was accidental, a form of good luck that indicated divine favor. Only sacred virgins, who took a thirty-year vow of chastity to the goddess Vesta, could do this, on the theory that their purity could be supernaturally transferred to the criminal, figuratively or spiritually washing away their crimes. This symbolic purity gave the virgins extraordinary authority; in certain situations, they could even intercede to pardon criminals. For example, when the bloodthirsty dictator Sulla ordered that a young Julius Caesar be executed in 82 BC, the virgins' intercession persuaded Sulla to spare him. (Evidently, it paid to be on good terms with these women if one were planning to perpetrate a capital offense.)

... *AND WHY?*
In Ancient Rome, vestal virgins (like Lady Godiva) were thought to have the power to pardon crimes.
How have our understandings of pardons evolved in relation to our social perceptions of purity and redemption?

Vestal Virgins, the Clergy, and Canon Law: AD 476–1575

The power of virgins to symbolically purify criminals continued into the Dark Ages, from about AD 476 to 1000. They could win pardons in some places by offering to marry the accused, and in others by running naked around the precincts multiple times. The famous story of Lady Godiva from eleventh-century England seemed connected to this practice. Godiva's husband, Leofric of Mercia, decided to punish the obstinate people of the city of Coventry with oppressive taxes. When his wife pleaded for their clemency, Leofric refused, only agreeing to grant her request if she rode naked through the city. So Godiva stripped naked, mounted her horse, and rode through the streets. In gratitude, the inhabitants of Coventry stayed indoors and did not watch her—except for one voyeur, from whom we have the origin of the expression "Peeping Tom." In some parts of Europe, touching the king or a local cleric—who were also thought to have a direct connection to God, or whose purity meant they were incapable of sin—was sometimes enough to confer a pardon on the accused, as well.

The magical nature of these ritual pardons arose from their associations with purity, nakedness, physical contact, folk customs, and numerology, and they manifested in various practical forms. Perpetrators could sometimes earn pardons "by ordeal"—that is, if those condemned to death survived up to a certain point in the execution process, they would automatically receive a pardon because it was believed that God demonstrated their innocence by sparing their life. In the ancient city of Basle, in modern-day Switzerland, women sentenced to drowning in the local river would be set free if they reached a certain point downstream alive. More commonly, men sentenced to be hanged would be released if the rope broke.

Religion was responsible for two of the more enduring forms of this kind of pardoning: the right of sanctuary, and the benefit of clergy. The former mandated that criminals who could reach the precincts of a church without apprehension by the authorities could not be punished as long as they did not leave. The practice actually predated Christianity, with pagan Greek and Roman temples sometimes offering protection to fugitives. It only became part of the law of the Roman Empire after the conversion of the emperor Constantine to Christianity in the fourth century AD.

Probably the most famous example comes from fiction. In Victor Hugo's *The Hunchback of Notre Dame* (and its accompanying Disney movie), the hideously deformed hero, Quasimodo, saves his beloved Esmeralda from being sentenced to burning at the stake when he seizes her and carries her into the Notre Dame cathedral, invoking its protection from secular authority and saving her life. The practice endured in places for over a thousand years, bestowing on churches the authority to give safe harbor to perpetrators who had broken secular laws. (Sanctuary was banned in England in 1623 after the Protestant Reformation splintered Roman Catholicism from new Protestant churches.)

A special kind of pardon known as the "benefit of clergy" lasted even longer than Catholic sanctuary. Laws placed clergymen outside the jurisdiction of secular courts and allowed for their trials to occur instead in more lenient ecclesiastical courts under what was known as "canon" law, which frequently resulted in the pardoning of secular, or nonreligious, crimes. In practice, the perpetrator did not have to be an actual clergyman; anyone with some kind of connection to the Catholic Church could access its own independent court system, which applied religious or canon law instead of regular, secular law. Unsurprisingly, the system was rife with abuse, and in 1575, Queen Elizabeth I of England confined its use to a one-time commutation of a sentence of execution.

As a means for dodging a death sentence, this more limited form of a clergy's pardon endured. In eighteenth-century Massachusetts, two of the British soldiers convicted of manslaughter for the Boston Massacre in 1770 avoided execution by invoking the so-called "benefit of clergy." In order to get their sentences commuted, the soldiers merely had to prove they could read Psalm 51 from the Bible, which contains a confession and expression of repentance for sins. The practice was eventually abolished in federal courts in the United States in 1790, and in the United Kingdom, in 1827, though it survived in some American state courts even longer (in South Carolina, until 1855).

These mystical and religious forms of a pardon gradually died out during the Middle Ages because they represented threats to monarchical power. Medieval princes, kings, and emperors wanted to monopolize the authority to punish and pardon crimes, keeping it to themselves, so they seized it from religious and local rivals.

This was not always a smooth process. One of the most notorious flashpoints was the disagreement in 1170 between King Henry II of England and the Archbishop of Canterbury, Thomas Becket, over the "benefit of clergy." Becket resisted Henry's attempts to establish a new system of courts that would submit priests who committed crimes to secular, royal jurisdiction rather than their own, more lenient ecclesiastical courts. When Henry's knights murdered Becket, they sparked outrage among the common people, which forced the king to back down in favor of the religious court system. This victory was temporary, however, as the religious power to pardon gradually became subsumed into the king's centralized, royal, secular authority. This was also true in Ancient Rome, as the variety of groups that could issue forms of pardons—consuls, the Senate, religious leaders—was slowly superseded by the sole person of the emperor. Over the course of history, raw political power in the form of a single monarch usually triumphed over religion, magic, or tradition.

But some governments offered alternative models. The Athenians placed the power to pardon squarely in the hands of the citizenry in the form of the *adeia*, a bill requiring six thousand signatures of eligible citizens in order for a pardon to be issued. In a city with a small population, this meant that pardons were exceedingly rare. Coincidentally or not, although its literature and religion are full of examples of bloody vengeance and penance for crimes, Ancient Greek does not have a specific word for "pardon."

... AND WHY?

Not just kings had the power to pardon in ancient Europe. The clergy could pardon, too. Do the religious underpinnings of the pardon power matter for the modern presidency?

Further north, early German tribes (approximately AD 300–700) bestowed the pardon power not on an individual chieftain or priest, but upon the entire community, which would assemble to discuss and decide whether to grant a pardon. Traces of this tradition carried on long into the Holy Roman Empire (which lasted from around AD 900 through the early nineteenth century) through the use of pardons by "intercession," whereby the whole community was entitled to seek a pardon from the local prince on the defendant's behalf. However, these more community-based forms of pardoning were the exception rather than the rule.

Ascent of the Royal Pardon Power and the Rise of Parliament: AD 668–1600s

The more typical progression of the pardon appeared in medieval England, where the Anglo-Saxon kings gradually wrested the pardon power away from clerics, local barons, communities, and religious or magical folk practices in an effort to secure it for themselves. The earliest explicit example of this assumption of power is that of King Ine of Wessex (AD 668–725), who imposed a law stating that "if anyone fight in the king's house, let him be liable in all his property, and be it in the king's doom whether he shall or shall not have life."

King Edmund, who ruled the English from 939 to 946, acted more explicitly to forestall vendettas by ordaining that anyone who took revenge on a member of the perpetrator's family would answer to the king—specifically, that "anyone who commits [a crime] is to forfeit all that he owns, and it is to be for the king to decide whether he may preserve his life." As historian Naomi Hurnard points out, this proclamation is important for having clearly reserved to the king the authority to commute a capital sentence at his own discretion. Such unchecked authority illustrates the long-standing capricious face of the pardon power. The king could use it to temper harsh criminal laws with the possibility of mercy and forgiveness, but he could also use it to pardon his own supporters, perhaps for murdering or stealing the property of the king's rivals, essentially giving free rein to tyrannical abuses committed in his name. This ugly underbelly of the pardon power—started by King Edmund in the tenth century—continues today.

Following Edmund, William the Conqueror stands out as the next Anglo-Saxon king to seize the pardon power after the Norman conquest of England in 1066. The law codes created by William's son, Henry I, which were known as the *Leges Henrici Primi*, revealed the frequency of and the breadth of offenses that triggered pardons. They also showed the double-faced nature of the monarch's pardon— part divine, part practical. On one hand, as Naomi Hurnard again describes, the codes emphasized the godlike quality of bestowing a pardon, even using explicit theological concepts to characterize the king's mercy. On the other hand, pardons functioned as pragmatic safety valves in a rudimentary criminal justice system whose laws were strict and inflexible. In 1249, for example, a four-year-old child named Katherine Passeavant was charged with homicide for accidentally opening a door and fatally pushing a younger child into a vessel of boiling water. Only by bringing the matter to the king for a pardon was her father able to prevent her from being punished as a murderer.

Cases like this led William Blackstone, the great eighteenth-century expositor of English common law, to declare the pardon power one of the most important benefits of a monarchy. While it allowed for maximal flexibility in the achievement of justice, it also provided the regime with stability. He wrote:

> Indeed one of the great advantages of monarchy in general, above any other form of government; that there is a magistrate, who has it in his power to extend mercy, wherever he thinks it is deserved: holding a court of equity in his own breast, to soften the rigour of the general law, in such criminal cases as merit an exemption from punishment.... To him therefore the people look up as the fountain of nothing but bounty and grace; and these repeated acts of goodness, coming immediately from his own hand, endear the sovereign to his subjects, and contribute more than any thing to root in their hearts that filial affection, and personal loyalty, which are the sure establishment of a prince.

Scholars such as Judith Ferster have also emphasized how the "mirrors of princes" of the fourteenth century—textbooks written for kings and princes instructing them on how best to govern their subjects—showed the extent to which mercy and pardoning were considered essential attributes of good kingship. Like Blackstone, these books' authors regarded the monarch's generous use of pardons as both ethically desirable and practically useful.[177]

Yet in one of the first places to mention how monarchs could receive financial compensation in exchange for a pardon, the *Leges Henrici*—which was a legal treatise written around 1115 that recorded the legal customs of medieval England under King Henry I—spoke of the pardon power's equivalent potential for abuse. Although the practice probably went on for some time on a more informal basis, Henry's official recognition of pay-to-play pardons morphed into pervasive abuses. Henry III (1216–1272) used pardons to appease opposing factions of his courtiers. Edward I (1272–1307) used them as a method of conscription, offering pardons to convicts in exchange for serving in his armies against the Scots. And Richard II (1377–1399) used them as a means of extortion, frequently backing out on them later. As English historian and Anglican bishop William Stubbs later described in his nineteenth-century writings, "this evil was not merely an abuse of the royal attribute of mercy, or a defeat of the ordinary processes of justice, but a regularly systematized perversion of prerogative."

Perhaps the most outrageous example of the pardon power's abuse during this time period involved the Peasants' Revolt of 1381, a mass uprising in England against Richard II's oppressive taxation. Thousands of aggrieved serfs marched to London demanding that the king lift the taxes. The king agreed, granting them all pardons as reassurance against any payback for their rebellion. The crowds dispersed, at which point Richard swiftly rescinded the pardons, had the rebel leaders tracked down, and executed them.

For many historians, therefore, the medieval pardon was not a godlike bestowing of the king's grace, or a flexible tool for the administration of justice; rather, it was an exploitation of the law by ruthless, power-hungry tyrants to serve their military and financial needs. Naomi Hurnard also argues that rather than "softening" the general law, as Blackstone thought of it approvingly, the pardon power served to slow and subvert the growth of English common law by substituting "administrative discretion for judicial decision, uncertainty for the predictability of punishment." What Hurnard's theory, by extension, suggests is that judges lacked the incentive to develop flexible, creative new laws to promote societal health because they knew that the king could unilaterally make these laws irrelevant through prolific use of the pardon power for those he favored. Such abuses arguably reduced the pardon power to a simple exercise of raw power for purely mercenary motives.

... AND WHY?
**Kings abused pardons by extracting payment
in exchange for "mercy."
Does that history justify corrupt
presidential pardons today?**

So, who was correct—Bishop Stubbs, the skeptic of the benefits of a king's blanket power to pardon? Or Blackstone, who believed in its merciful virtues?

The English Parliament evidently found itself in the former camp, having eventually emerged over the years as the legislative body of the English government—and thus, as a potential rival for the king's power. When Parliament first convened at the signing of the Magna Carta in 1215, its members were nobles, bishops, and representatives from each of the counties and major towns of England. As the first writing to acknowledge that the king was not above the law, the Magna

Carta placed limits on royal power by establishing law as a constraint on the monarch's ability to exploit his authority. Parliament could submit petitions to the king, while the king needed Parliament's consent and cooperation in order to govern. If he refused to listen to Parliament, its members, mostly powerful landowners, could withhold taxes and armies that the king needed to secure his position.

The beginning of the fourteenth century saw a succession of attempts by Parliament to rein in the king's pardon powers, although they were largely unsuccessful. In 1309, Parliament issued a petition known as the Stamford Articles to Edward II, complaining about his interference in criminal proceedings. Parliament was particularly incensed about a royal pardon given to Piers Gaveston, King Edward's homosexual lover. Gaveston wasn't from a baronial family, and was thus considered "low-born" under the standards of the day. Still, Edward showered Gaveston and his associates with land, money, and titles. When Parliament exiled Gaveston for abusing his position, Edward pardoned him and welcomed him back to England—although he was eventually murdered. In response to Edward's embrace of Gaveston, furious Parliamentarians tried to force the king to adopt ordinances stripping the king of his pardon power:

> We do ordain, that no Felon or Fugitive be from henceforth protected or defended from any manner of Felony, by the King's Charter of his Peace granted to him, unless in a case where the King can give grace according to his Oath, and that by Process of Law and the Custom of the Realm, and if any Charter be from henceforth granted and made in any other manner to any one, it shall avail nothing, and be holden for none.

86

. . . AND WHY?

As far back as the 1300s, the English Parliament—England's equivalent of the US Congress—tried to constrain the king's power to pardon. What about the pardon power allowed it to evade limitations for centuries?

After the king disregarded these laws, Parliament tried to limit the king's pardon power again—in 1328, 1336, 1340, 1347, 1351, and 1389. In the sixteenth century, the House of Tudor monarchs (1486–1603) ultimately began to curb the power of the baronial class that made up much of Parliament and focused power back into the hands of the king or queen. Henry VII (1485–1509) created the notorious Star Chamber, a special royal court that he could use to mete out arbitrary punishment to nobles who opposed him. He also drove into exile many of the Parliamentary barons who had sided with his rival, Richard III, and then forced a weakened Parliament to pass so-called "bills of attainder" allowing him to execute others without trial. (Article I of the US Constitution bans bills of attainder, precluding the US Congress—versus judges and juries—from deciding if an individual violated a law and should be punished.)

With Parliament no longer able to resist the monarchy's pushback, its string of failures to curb the pardon power culminated in a craven Act of Parliament in 1535, which unequivocally restored all pardon power to the king:

> Be it enacted by authority of this Parliament that no person or persons of what estates or degrees soever they be of . . . shall have any power or authority to pardon or remit any treasons, murders, manslaughters or any kinds of felonies . . . but that the King's Highness, his heirs and successor Kings of this realm, shall have the whole and sole power and authority

thereof united and knit to the Imperial Crown of this Realm, as of good right and equity it appertaineth, any grants, usages, prescriptions, act or acts of Parliament, or other things to the contrary thereof notwithstanding.

A similar process occurred in France, where House of Bourbon kings seized virtually unchecked power to pardon from the nobility and clergy by the end of the seventeenth century. France had been wracked with centuries of sectarian wars, in which some nobles—with their huge estates and private armies—could command more power even than the king himself. Louis XIV (1643–1715), the famous Sun King of Versailles, aggrandized supreme power to himself within France in a similar fashion as the kings in England. Across Europe, this process was called "absolutism," by which monarchs became absolute rulers and lawmakers of their respective nation-states rather than remain dependent on the consent of the nobility or some representative or legislative body. It also occurred in Spain, Austria, and Prussia, modern Germany's predecessor.

Europeans Settle in America:
Early 1600s

In the seventeenth century, Europeans also began to settle in North America. Sometimes they fled to escape political or religious persecution; sometimes they came for profit and glory. But either way, they brought their absolutist political models with them, which meant a strong central executive authority figure in each colony who served as a representative of the monarch back in Europe, and thus acted in the king's name in the colonies. As a consequence, the European, absolutist version of the pardon power as unchecked and exclusive to the sovereign was simply transposed onto the executive authority in each colony. For example, Baron Baltimore in Maryland, William Penn in Pennsylvania, and Sir Ferdinando Gorges in Maine all had full and absolute power to pardon. The philosopher John Locke's Fundamental Constitution of the Carolinas—the governing document for North and South Carolina—gave a similar power to the executive of those states. By the dawn of the seventeenth century, therefore, the exclusive authority of kings to pardon, for better or worse, was at its absolute zenith and spreading across the globe.

The Age of Enlightenment, however, was just around the corner.

Decline of the Pardon Power: 1600s–1791

By the end of the seventeenth century, the English Parliament felt ready for another go at reining in the king's power to pardon. What had changed? Well, most dramatically, the English Civil War had happened. This conflict, waged between supporters of Parliament and supporters of King Charles I (1625–1649), engulfed the entire British Isles in a decade of savage, mutually destructive violence.

Charles believed that as monarch he had a divine right to rule the British Isles with complete personal control over all issues of governance and religion. For years, he tried to rule without Parliament (a period alternately known as the "Personal Rule" or the "Eleven Years' Tyranny," depending on which side you supported), but he needed Parliament's approval to raise taxes.[178] When he became ensnared in a religious war with the Scots, who were deeply suspicious of Charles's attempts to impose a uniform book of prayer upon them, he found himself forced to reconvene Parliament and ask for money to support the war effort. The emboldened Parliamentarians—knowing they finally had the king over a barrel—made a number of demands to limit the power available to the monarch (including the abolition of Henry VII's hated Star Chamber). The King refused, and England collapsed into civil war.

Monarchists who supported King Charles I, who were known as "Cavaliers," based their support on the belief that the king was the source of all law. Parliamentarians, known as "Roundheads," justified their cause with ideas that sound modern and radical—most importantly, that Parliament should be sovereign because it represented the people. Roundheads likewise believed that Parliament should be the final arbiter of crime and punishment—not the king.[179] Such ideas were, of course, abhorrent to Charles, who thought he had the divine right to punish and pardon as he saw fit. This stark difference of opinion made reconciliation impossible.

In 1645, the Roundheads won a crushing victory over the king's forces at the Battle of Naseby following a cavalry charge led by a Parliamentarian officer named Oliver Cromwell.[180] Charles was taken prisoner, and the Parliamentarians attempted to negotiate some kind of settlement in which the king could continue to reign, but with limited powers. Charles persisted in his defiance, however, and temporarily escaped in 1647 to raise new armies against his captors. He was ultimately recaptured. Led by Cromwell, the Parliamentarians decided to try, convict, and execute Charles for high treason in 1649. That same year, the monarchy was abolished, and an English republic, with Cromwell and Parliament at its head, emerged.

By the time the monarchy was restored in 1660—shortly after Cromwell's death—its power was irrevocably weakened. This new, weakened monarchy set the stage for the Glorious Revolution of 1688. By that point, Parliament had finally wrested power from hereditary monarchs like Charles and ushered in the democratic constitutional monarchy that Great Britain follows to this day. Under the modern British political system, the monarch is technically the head of state, but actual power is lodged in Parliament as the representatives of the people. These representatives—not the monarch—make the laws. The period after the English Civil War was accordingly characterized by a newly powerful Parliament flexing its muscles, with monarchy on the defensive. The question of the king's power to pardon finally came to a head because of what historians call the "Danby Scandal."

Thomas Osborne, who was also known as Lord Danby, was a close advisor to King Charles II and one of the most powerful figures in England at the time—even though he was personally unpopular due to his arrogance and corruption. (Scottish philosopher and historian Gilbert Burnet said he was "the most hated minister that had ever been about the king.") Tensions between the king and Parliament were still high, especially around the subject of foreign policy. On the European continent, the Catholic monarchy of France and the Protestant Dutch republic were at loggerheads over religion. England had to decide which side to back. Parliament naturally leaned toward the Dutch because they were Protestants; King Charles, naturally, favored his fellow hereditary monarch, the Catholic Louis XIV in France.

Although personally anti-French, Danby was first and foremost a suck-up, and blindly followed Charles's orders to favor the French. In 1678, Danby's enemies in the government leaked a secret letter from him to Lord Montague, the British ambassador to France. In the letter, Danby promised the French that the British would remain neutral in any conflict between them and the Dutch, in exchange for a bribe of 600,000 livres (the French currency from 781 to 1794). Although it was obvious that Danby had only been acting on Charles's orders, Parliament decided it could clip the king's wings by focusing on the easier target, Danby. It impeached him. (Impeachment in this context meant not only removal from office, but also included criminal consequences.) Charles defiantly announced a full royal pardon for Danby.

Cue constitutional crisis.

Although ostensibly concerned with foreign policy, the clash implicated everything that the Parliamentary party had fought for over the previous decades. Parliament—the representatives of the people—thought it was in the country's best interests to support the Dutch. The king had deliberately tried to subvert its position through personal greed, and now sought to escape the consequences of his actions by pardoning the instrument of his subterfuge, Danby. After all the bloodshed of the Civil War, did the king still really have the unlimited power to subvert the will of the people and rescue his cronies as he did in the Middle Ages? Sir Francis Winnington, member of Parliament, dramatically declared that "there's an end of all Justice among men if such Pardons are allowed." (Attentive readers will note the parallels with debates today; similar concerns were also raised at the Constitutional Convention in Philadelphia, as we shall see.)

Despite the king's pleas and opposition from several prominent lords, Parliament refused to back down. Too much was at stake. It pronounced that a royal pardon was no defense to impeachment by Parliament.

Danby was sent to the Tower of London, where he would remain imprisoned for five years. There was nothing the king could do. Danby was so unpopular at this point that even powerful members of Parliament who might have been inclined to support the king's position sided against him because they were so determined to bring Danby down. Parliament's position was officially written into the law of the land in the Act of Settlement of 1700, which barred the Crown from pardoning impeachments. For the first time since the Dark Ages, the monarch's power to pardon had been restricted in some way. Never again would the king of England have the absolute power to pardon. Parliament—i.e., the people—was now sovereign. Oddly, this is in stark contrast to how broadly the president's pardon power is perceived under the US Constitution. And the president is not even a king.

The Act of Settlement turned out to be just the first blow in a century of actions that narrowed the king's pardon power. After the conflict in England came the Age of Enlightenment, an intellectual, scientific, and political movement that dominated Europe in the seventeenth and eighteenth centuries. The Enlightenment focused on reason and individualism, putting the pardon power under ferocious attack from some of the most important thinkers of the age. These attacks went beyond accusations that the pardon power led to abuse and financial exploitation. They involved foundational disputes over the best way to structure government, with the emerging philosophies of liberalism and republicanism driving the shift away from unlimited power of monarchs. Many of these philosophers thought that governmental power should be vested in the people, who alone should have the authority to pass criminal laws through elected legislatures. To the extent the pardon power allowed monarchs to subvert the popular will by unilaterally pardoning violators—including his lackeys, like the Earl of Danby—it impermissibly encroached on the power of the people.

Enlightenment Period Debates:
1650–1800

One of the most impassioned critiques in this regard came from arguably the greatest philosopher of the eighteenth century, German writer Immanuel Kant. In his book, *The Metaphysical Elements of Justice*, Kant disputed the fundamental idea that crimes were offenses perpetrated against the monarch. Unless the offender actually hurt the king individually, he argued, his crimes were instead offenses against the community, because they are the ones actually injured by crime and violence. Thus, only the community has the right to punish. To give the pardon power exclusively to the ruler allowed him to usurp the rights of the people. Kant also found the pardon power itself troubling—regardless of whether a king or Parliament wielded it—because it had no limits. The "right to grant clemency to a criminal," he wrote, "is the slipperiest one for [the sovereign] to exercise," and risks becoming an instrument of tyranny.[181]

In England, the philosopher Henry Fielding likewise argued that having a pardon power actually encouraged *more* unjust laws because it allowed lawmakers and judges to operate with a false belief that the pardon power worked as a safety valve in the event of mistakes. "This I am confident may be asserted," he wrote, "that pardons brought many more men to the gallows than they have saved from it." Furthermore, Fielding asserted, if criminals had enough money, they always had a chance of securing a pardon from the sovereign, which undermined the rule of law enacted by the people's representatives in the legislature.

Analyzing the power from a strictly cost–benefit standpoint, English philosopher Jeremy Bentham agreed, arguing that the pardon power triggered a slippery slope of problems that could ultimately lead to societal ruin: "From pardon power unrestricted, comes impunity to delinquency in all shapes: from impunity to maleficence in all shapes . . . dissolution of government: from dissolution of government,

95

dissolution of political society."[182] The pardon power meant that the threat of punishment didn't deter criminals from committing crimes as effectively as it would without such a (literal) get-out-of-jail-free card. This, in turn, meant more crime than there should be under the existing laws.

Additionally, Fielding pointed out, it paradoxically meant *more* punishment than without the pardon power—and therefore, more overall societal misery—because many of the criminals who might have been deterred by the absence of a pardon power do not in fact get pardoned. They instead end up being imprisoned or executed for crimes they may not have otherwise committed. A primary justification for the pardon power—mercy—falls apart under Bentham's analysis.

The Italian jurist Cesare Beccaria—whose treatise, *On Crimes and Punishments*, would have a huge influence on the Founding Fathers—mounted a similar attack. For Beccaria, a perfect legal system had no need for a pardon power because crimes would exactly match punishments. The pardon power rescues from punishment only a small number of criminals who violated laws that applied to everyone. But because it exists, people are less deterred from committing crimes because there's always the possibility of that stopgap. As a result, the pardon power actually encouraged legislators and judges to impose *harsher* punishments on the people who don't get pardons in order to make up for the deterrence deficit. Ordinary people who might not have the money or influence to obtain a pardon end up getting punished more harshly than their crimes actually merited. A pardon power, therefore, actually impeded the development of more appropriate (in his view, milder) punishments.

The French Baron de Montesquieu—another huge influence on the Framers of the US Constitution—agreed. (His book, *The Spirit of the Laws*, was the first major work to advocate for the separation of governmental powers into legislative, executive, and judiciary, which became the structural basis of the federal government under the Constitution.) While the pardon power might be appropriate in a monarchy where the king is sovereign, he wrote, "it is less needed in a republic where virtue reigns." Worse, the pardon power actually *violates* separation-of-powers principles by allowing the president to essentially override the will of *both* the legislature and the judiciary when it comes to criminal laws and punishment. Even Blackstone, who approved of the pardon power under a monarchy, thought that "in democracies, . . . this power of pardon can never subsist; for there nothing higher is acknowledged than the magistrate who administers the laws: and it would be impolitic for the power of judging and of pardoning to center in one and the same person."

In order to be considered "enlightened" in the eighteenth century, therefore, opposition to the pardon power was typical. The pro-republic approach of the Enlightenment—in which the power of government lies in a body of citizens who vote for officers and representatives responsible to them—fueled the French Revolution, which began in 1789, shortly after the US Constitution was ratified. Much of the fury the French revolutionaries felt was directed at the absolutist monarchy established by Louis XIV. So when the monarchy was abolished, the new republican National Assembly (a predecessor to the modern French Parliament) did away with the pardon power in 1791. From the height of its strength in both England and France a hundred years previously, it seemed as though the unlimited power to pardon was irrevocably broken.

The American Revolution: 1765–1783

By the time of the American Revolution, the pardon power in England was already divided between the monarch, Parliament, and the church. It did not, in other words, belong entirely to the king. Because criminal laws were harsh in England, the pardon power still played an important role in ensuring justice. By 1819, for example, 220 felony offenses in England were punishable by death. But due to pardons, only 97 of the 1,254 criminal defendants sentenced to death the prior year were finally executed.[183] The king pardoned the others, often at the recommendation of a court.

The pardon power also produced variations in modern-day criminal law, such as differences between manslaughter and murder; crimes of passion or mistake versus intentional crimes; excuses like insanity; and justifications like self-defense. Today, these concepts are already baked into the criminal laws; when properly applied, they produce acquittals and lesser sentences. Remnants of the English pardon power—i.e., some of the reasons why kings issued pardons—now appear in the criminal laws themselves, calling into question whether an unconstrained pardon power for presidents and governors makes sense at all anymore. If the criminal laws take care of the factual nuances that distinguish between indicting or not indicting, convicting or acquitting, and imposing lesser or greater sentences, what's the point of keeping the pardon power as a last-ditch lever of mercy?

In England, pardons were also bought and sold by both the Crown and the Church, thus becoming an important source of income for those in power. In one case, King James II (1633–1701) exchanged a pardon for 16,000 pounds sterling, of which he received "one half and the other half was divided among the two ladies then most in favor." By the seventeenth century, many defendants convicted of capital offenses and sentenced to death were offered pardons if they voyaged to the

New World, either working as ship hands or on plantations to satisfy the government's labor shortages. Anywhere from 15,000 to 100,000 convicted felons were sent from England to America. By 1663, officials in Virginia feared there were so many that they might rebel.

In 1776, the thirteen American colonies did in fact revolt against British rule and declared independence.[184] The founding document in which they declared their intentions was explicitly based on many of the ideas of the English Civil War and the Enlightenment—particularly the idea that sovereignty should be lodged not in hereditary monarchs, but in the people. Indeed, most of the content of the Declaration of Independence deals with specific complaints against King George III for abusing his powers as a monarch. The pardon power is not explicitly mentioned, but as one of the key prerogatives of the sovereign, the Framers of the Constitution would have been well aware of its history as a tool of potential abuse and tyranny. After a disastrous defeat in the Revolutionary War, the British recognized American independence at the Treaty of Paris in 1783 and the last British troops left New York in November of that year.

But this was not the end of the story. Amid interstate squabbling and violent local rebellions, the infant republic was on the verge of collapse. In 1787, delegates from each of the states descended on Philadelphia to come up with a system that might enable the former colonies to thrive while also preserving the freedoms they had fought so hard to secure. As a central facet of the king's power which the colonies had just spectacularly rebuked, the pardon power was something the delegates had to address. In its rebuke of a monarchy, would the new republic incorporate the king's power to pardon or reject it as it had done with so many other facets of British rule? And if it included the pardon power, would it be unlimited—as in medieval times—or shared with the legislature, as was the convention in England at the time?

The Constitutional Convention: 1787

Perhaps the most fundamental distinction between modern American government and the authority of English monarchs is that power under the US Constitution comes from the people. The authority of English kings, by contrast, was believed to come from God. The Constitution is a sort of social contract whereby the public agrees on the terms of self-governance and chooses elected officials whom they believe will exercise that power on their behalf. If elected representatives act criminally, corruptly, or out of self-interest, the structure guarantees that one or more mechanisms of oversight exist to hold public officials accountable to the people. Not so for absolute monarchs. Accountability thus underlies the entirety of American government in some way or another.

As first envisioned by Montesquieu, the US Constitution accordingly breaks up the national government into three bodies—judicial, legislative, and executive—and gives each a discrete role. Judges and juries decide whether a law has been violated and, if so, what punishment is warranted. The legislature enacts the laws and is accountable to the citizenry through voting. The executive branch primarily acts as law enforcement officer and prosecutor, identifying people who may have violated laws and representing the government in arguing that courts should hold them accountable. Presidents, like Congress, are elected. Federal judges are not, but it's their appointment without election that is precisely why they are best suited to manage trials, convictions, and sentences: They don't need to worry about political retribution. Given these three distinct roles, the pardon power seems out of place as a potential infringement on the role of judges, juries, and legislatures—and one that's susceptible to abuse in light of presidents' vulnerability to political influence.

100

By contrast, the English monarch's power to rule and punish theoretically came from God, and crimes committed against the Crown were therefore considered crimes against God. St. Paul himself—one of the most important Christian apostles who spread the teachings of Jesus in the first century BC—wrote in a letter to the Romans:

> Since all government comes from God, the civil authorities were appointed by God, and so anyone who resists authority is rebelling against God's decision, and such an act is bound to be punished. . . . The authorities are there to serve God; they carry out God's revenge by punishing wrongdoers.

By the same token, just as the Bible brims with instances of God showing forgiveness, the monarch can show God's mercy by forgiving wrongdoing in the form of a king's pardon. As we've seen, both the Crown and the Church used the pardon power to raise money and secure powerful allies—a corruption that ultimately led Martin Luther to break from the Catholic Church and found the Protestant religion in the sixteenth century.

Because many of the eighteenth-century philosophers significantly influenced the Framers, a revolution founded on Enlightenment principles looked as if it might sweep the pardon power away—along with all the other powers King George III held over the American colonies. This is certainly what happened in the immediate wake of that other great eighteenth-century revolution, which occurred in France. Individual colonies took the same approach: The constitutions of Georgia, Delaware, North Carolina, and New Hampshire explicitly forbade executive pardons.

Moreover, a number of the Framers of the Constitution were highly suspicious of the pardon power. Thomas Jefferson was a close reader of Cesare Beccaria, the eighteenth-century Italian philosopher, and Montesquieu. A contemporary edition of Jefferson's *Legal*

Commonplace Book included passages from Beccaria's *On Crimes and Punishments*, in which he argued that clemency would no longer be needed under a milder, more democratic criminal justice system. In his 1776 draft constitution for Virginia, Jefferson explicitly denied to the governor, other state executive officials, and the legislature the "prerogative . . . of pardoning crimes, or remitting fines and punishments."[185]

Other powerful delegates in Philadelphia were known skeptics of an unlimited pardon power for future presidents. Roger Sherman of Connecticut proposed a Senate check on presidents' ability to pardon, which would have empowered the president "to grant reprieves until the ensuing session of the Senate, and pardons with consent of the Senate." Virginia's James Madison liked the idea of involving the Senate "as a Council of advice, with the President," as "the pardon of treasons was so peculiarly improper for the President." However, Edmund Randolph, also from Virginia, "could not admit the Senate into a share of the Power" as "the great danger to liberty lay in a combination between the President & that body." Virginia's George Mason thought so, as well: "The Senate has already too much power." The idea of adding Senate approval to presidential pardons accordingly died.

The Framers also specifically debated the question of excluding pardons for treason—and rejected the idea. (Treason did make it into Article III, Section 3, Clause 1 of the Constitution, which states: "Treason against the United States, shall consist only in levying War against them, or in adhering to their Enemies, giving them Aid and Comfort. No person shall be convicted of Treason unless on the testimony of two Witnesses to the same overt Act, or on Confession in open Court."[186]) Randolph and Mason—again, both delegates from Virginia—argued that presidents should not have the power to pardon the crime of treason. Randolph made a motion to add to the Constitution's text the words, "except cases of treason," arguing that otherwise it's too tempting for a president to engage

102

in self-dealing—precisely what the English king did for the Earl of Danby and his co-conspirators. If a president had the power to pardon acts of treason, he could pardon his own supporters who tried to subvert the legislature. Perhaps he could even pardon *himself* if he were found guilty of trying to overthrow the republic and set himself up as a dictator. According to Mason:

> [The President] ought not to have the power of pardoning, because he may frequently pardon crimes which were advised by himself. It may happen, at some future day, that he will establish a monarchy, and destroy the republic. If he has the power of granting pardons before indictment, or conviction, may he not stop inquiry and prevent detection? The case of treason ought, at least, to be excepted. This is a weighty objection with me.

Added Randolph: "The prerogative of pardon in these cases was too great a trust. The President may himself be guilty. The Traytors may be his own instruments."

James Wilson, who represented Pennsylvania at the convention along with Benjamin Franklin and later served on the US Supreme Court, disagreed, responding that "Pardon is necessary for cases of treason, and is best placed in the hands of the Executive. If he be himself a party to the guilt he can be impeached and prosecuted." Wilson was more concerned that the US Congress would be given the pardon power instead of presidents. He believed that a "Legislative body is utterly unfit for the purpose. They are governed too much by the passions of the moment. In Massachusetts, one assembly would have hung all the insurgents in that State: the next was equally disposed to pardon them all." Randolph's bid to exclude treason from the pardon power failed.

In sum, Mason, Randolph, and Sherman all appeared to favor a highly limited form of the pardon power—if not its complete elimination. This was unsurprising. The American experiment was a live manifestation of Kant's Enlightenment vision. How could the executive branch have a pardon power when that was a prerogative of the despised sovereign in England, the king? In America, the people would be the sovereign, not the head of the executive branch. With the trend of history and philosophy seemingly moving in only one direction, an observer might have confidently speculated that there would be no pardon power in whatever constitutional document that came out of the Convention.

But that did not happen. The skeptics came up against a unified and disciplined group of delegates who wanted a strong central government with an executive powerful enough to enforce his will on the states. Among them were James Madison and the powerful South Carolina delegates, Charles Pinckney and John Rutledge. Madison pointed out that impeachment already existed as a constitutional remedy against a president who might use his pardon powers corruptly (presumably not envisioning a scenario in which a president commits treason, but the Senate refuses to convict him). Yet their most eloquent proponent was Alexander Hamilton of New York. In the *Federalist Papers*, Hamilton would later explain his support for giving the power exclusively to the executive branch, in words that echo Blackstone's:

> Humanity and good policy conspire to dictate, that the benign prerogative of pardoning should be as little as possible fettered or embarrassed. . . . As the sense of responsibility is always strongest, in proportion as it is undivided, it may be inferred that a single man would be most ready to attend to the force of those motives which might plead for a mitigation of the rigor of the

law, and least apt to yield to considerations which
were calculated to shelter a fit object of its vengeance.
The reflection that the fate of a fellow-creature
depended on his sole fiat, would naturally inspire
scrupulousness and caution.... On these accounts,
one man appears to be a more eligible dispenser of
the mercy of government, than a body of men.[187]

As far as we know, that was basically that. No more debate, no
more resistance. When we next encounter the federal pardon power,
it's in Article II.

...AND WHY?

**The Framers debated the scope of the pardon power and
ultimately rejected adding constraints like Senate approval.
How might the federal criminal justice system be different
today if they had imposed such limitations?**

The lack of resistance is remarkable. Although New York's George
Clinton warned that the pardon power would result in a "vile and
arbitrary aristocracy or monarchy," Mason was the only Anti-Federalist who refused to sign the finished document. (Clinton was also
an Anti-Federalist who unsuccessfully advocated for a Bill of Rights.)
Possibly fearing a radical democracy, the Federalists—including
Hamilton—evidently wanted a system that retained elements of
the British authoritarian monarchy. The pardon power operated as
a check on the legislature and the judiciary—and by implication, a
check on the power of the people themselves. As North Carolina's
James Iredell, also a Federalist, later admitted:

Nobody can contend upon any rational principles, that a power of pardoning should not exist some-where in every government, because . . . it could scarcely be avoided, that when arms were first taken up in the cause of liberty, to save us from the immedi-ate crush of arbitrary power, we should lean too much rather to the extreme of weakening than of strength-ening the Executive power in our own government.

Iredell was not alone in his belief that the legislature was the most powerful branch and it needed to be checked. The pardon power, at least in theory, gave the president the ability to prevent Congress from arbitrarily punishing citizens by passing unfair laws. If Congress wanted to target or proscribe certain groups—say, by passing a law making it a crime to have red hair—the president could prevent this abuse of power by simply pardoning all the members of that group for violating the law. (Recall that the Bill of Rights, as well as the post–Civil War Fourteenth Amendment, with its particular promise of equal protection under the law, both came later.)

In the end, the Framers perceived the two primary reasons for pardons—mercy and amnesty—as more central to the aims of the Constitution than preventing presidents from pardoning treason, even if it benefits themselves. Moreover, in the early days of the republic, judges did not have much discretion to set aside jury verdicts or order new trials, making appeals for mercy to the president an important safety valve for the criminal justice system. In 1790, Congress intro-duced discretionary sentencing with the Crimes Act, but mandatory death sentences still applied to certain offenses. The law applicable to the District of Columbia was divided between Virginia and Mary-land, producing disparate sentences for the same offense—the death penalty on one side of DC and a whipping on the other side—and as a result, numerous pardon applications. A single criminal code was not enacted for Washington, DC, until 1831.

Whatever the rationale for including the pardon power in the Constitution, the end result was that Americans had thrown off the yoke of a monarch only to give the head of their new executive branch similar power over them—more power, in fact, than King George III had had at the time of the American Revolution. In the pages that follow, we will see the consequences of their decision.

2

From Kings to Presidents

Any discussion of the US pardon power must start with the Constitution's text. Article II, Section 2, clause 1 of the United States Constitution gives the president the power "to grant reprieves and pardons for offenses against the United States."[188] Many people construe this power as unlimited and absolute, believing that the president can pardon whom she wants, when she wants, for whatever reason she wants (so long as it's a federal—versus a state or local—crime). The Constitution bans pardons only for "impeachments." Otherwise, this constitutional language contains no caveats, limitations, definitions, or exceptions.

The language does not include the word "absolute" when referring to the president's power to grant a pardon, however. It does not say presidents can grant "any" pardons for "all" offenses. It seems perfectly reasonable to read the language, then, as allowing the president to grant "some" pardons, leaving it to the other branches of government—either Congress, through legislation, or the courts, through judicial review—to decide which ones are okay and which are not. And if Congress were to pass a law outlining a dubious set of standards presidents must apply to pardon applications, that law could be challenged in court. If it were to enact statutory limits on the pardon power, according to the Supreme Court's own ruling in the 1803 case, *Marbury v. Madison*, the Court would decide what the pardon power language in the Constitution means with more specificity, including whether it's unlimited or susceptible to reasonable constraints.[189]

... AND WHY?

The Constitution cites the president's power "to grant reprieves and pardons for offenses against the United States ... except in Cases of Impeachment." Are corrupt pardons so obviously allowed? Do they foster mercy? Amnesty?

But the exercise of judging is not a linear, black-and-white, or ideological process. It's methodical, multilayered, and demanding of the exercise of, well, judgment—reason, deliberation, and discernment. Judges start with the text of the Constitution. If there's no answer to a question in the plain text, they look to a host of other clues to decide its meaning, such as modern or contemporary definitions of a term, writings by the text's drafters, prior precedent by the Supreme Court, the purpose of a provision, and even other cases interpreting similar language in other parts of the Constitution. Against that backdrop, the pardon clause is relatively unique to the extent that the scholarly and popular consensus appears to be that the power is unlimited—like that of a king or queen prior to the emergence of the British Parliament—rather than subject to interpretation under the circumstances of a particular case. Imagine a president who pardons a group of aides that siphoned off millions of tax dollars to an offshore account in the president's name while he was in office. If that corrupt act of self-enrichment were put through the traditional scrutiny of a court applying basic tools of constitutional analysis, he would presumably be denied the benefit of the pardons. The assumption that such an act is somehow above the law in America makes no logical sense.

Although the Supreme Court has had several occasions to interpret the pardon power language, there undoubtedly remains room for the modern Court to tailor it for purposes of addressing some of the concerns set forth in this book. The Court does this kind of thing all the time. It has read many tests into the words "due process" and "equal protection" in the Fourteenth Amendment, for example—not to mention the legions of cases interpreting the freedom of speech and religion articulated in the relatively scant words of the First Amendment. Although the First Amendment *protects* "freedom of speech," *restrictions* on speech exist. It's a federal felony to knowingly and willfully make any threat to "inflict great bodily harm upon the president of the United States," for example—even if done in protest over how the president is wielding power. The point is not to say that those who read the pardon language as absolute are definitely wrong—just that the pardon power language, like most of the Constitution, does not come with an instruction guide along with it. That's what the Supreme Court is for, according to *Marbury v. Madison*.

Nonetheless, the Supreme Court has, for the most part, construed the pardon power as extremely broad. For presidential pardons and commutations, obtaining judicial review of a decision is nearly impossible. Although the Court has never ruled that pardon decisions are "political questions"—a doctrine that it uses to essentially beg off deciding certain cases because they are political hot potatoes better left to Congress and the president to resolve—there is certainly no routine opportunity for an individual charged or convicted of a federal crime to argue to a federal judge that the president was wrong to turn down a pardon application because they were especially worthy. Weighing the pros and cons of the facts bearing on an individual pardon or commutation decision remains wholly within the discretion of the president.

But a close reading of the Court's case law interpreting the pardon power reveals that the presidential pardon power *does* have legal limitations.

Express Constitutional Limits
on the Pardon Power

Consider the text of the Constitution itself, which provides two limits on the president's pardon power. First, pardons may only be granted for "offenses against the United States." This means that state criminal offenses and federal or state civil claims are not covered. (A civil offense is one that produces money damages or injunctions, but not jail time. New York Attorney General Letitia James's 2023 fraud trial against Donald Trump is a civil case, for example.) The Court affirmed this limitation in the 1925 case *Ex parte Grossman* when it noted that the Constitution draws a line between offenses against the United States and other offenses. Second, the authority cannot be used "in Cases of impeachment."[190] If a federal judge, a member of the president's cabinet, a vice president, or a president are impeached, a president can't erase that impeachment with a pardon.

Keep in mind, however, that there is a legal difference between an impeachment and a conviction after an impeachment trial. As seen most recently in the two impeachments against former president Donald Trump, an impeachment is just a charging document—somewhat like an indictment in a criminal case or, more aptly, a complaint in a civil case. It's more like a complaint in a civil case because a conviction on an impeachment charge can't land a person in jail; it basically means they're fired. Most of us don't get a full trial before the US Senate before losing a job![191] The Constitution does not clarify whether or not a president can pardon a *conviction* for impeachment, or just the impeachment. Presumably, neither is allowed. Hamilton explained in *Federalist* No. 69 that impeachment exists in the Constitution to hold presidents accountable for wrongdoing, so presidents cannot pardon impeachments: "A President of the Union, . . . though he may even pardon treason, when prosecuted in the ordinary course of law, could shelter no offender, in any degree, from the effects of impeachment [and] conviction."[192] Hamilton believed that the threat of impeachment was what distinguished presidents from governors, and that it also explained why presidents can pardon for treason but many governors cannot.

"Strict" readers of the Constitution—the folks on the Supreme Court who claim to apply the plain language of the text and that's that—might argue that, because the text precisely mentions two exceptions to the pardon power, that list must be exclusive; no other exceptions are allowed. The Framers did not include an exception for treason or require consent of the Senate, and if they wanted additional constraints, they would have added them. Luther Martin, a delegate from Maryland, had also proposed adding the words "after conviction" to the pardon language, but was persuaded that pre-conviction pardons might be warranted in some circumstances. Even today, if the Supreme Court were faced with a case challenging a presidential pardon that the public considered extremely offensive or even illegal, its conservative majority might seize on the historical fact that the Framers specifically rejected language limiting the pardon power as proof that the president's pardon power is very broad. In other words, they put on the table the possibility of narrowing the power further, but did not, and it's not the role of the Supreme Court or Congress to do that now. Only a constitutional amendment will do the trick.

In practical terms, however, the Supreme Court generally strives to read the Constitution as a whole—or in such a way as to give meaning to all of it. If two provisions conflict, courts should find a way to apply them both. If a president were to announce that only people of Caucasian descent qualify for pardons, for example, that decision would bump against the Fourteenth Amendment's Equal Protection Clause, which the Court has held applies to the federal government and bans discrimination on the basis of race. A court could nonetheless read the pardon power as allowing that sort of thing on the rationale that pardons are supreme and absolute.

But a court could also decide that handing out pardons to favor one race over another doesn't serve the purpose of pardons in the first place, so honoring both the pardon power and the Fourteenth Amendment is the way to go. Of course, it's unlikely that a president would make such discriminatory intent public, and Black individuals denied a pardon would undoubtedly have a very hard time proving that a president made the decision for racist reasons and not because of the factual particularities of each specific case that have nothing to do with race. But the broader point remains: To say that the pardon power has no constraints whatsoever isn't logically sound.

Other Constraints on the Pardon Power
(Yes, They Exist!)

The assumption that presidents' power to pardon has no limits doesn't hold up under the case law, either. Limits *do* exist under Supreme Court precedent. The fact that the Supreme Court has already recognized some limits on the pardon power—without the Constitution expressly stating them—means that the widespread reading of the president's pardon power as totally absolute except for impeachment is already wrong. It also means that if a corrupt pardon were ever to make its way to the Supreme Court, it should take the case and hold that the pardon power can't be used that way.

Here are some of the recognized or potential limitations on the pardon power that are already in play:

1. **Can a presidential pardon trigger the government's reimbursement of money paid by a criminal defendant as part of their sentence?** Answer: No—not unless Congress says so. This is a clear limit on the pardon power, which most folks overlook.

2. **Does a presidential pardon wipe out all repercussions flowing from a criminal conviction, such as poor job prospects?** Answer: No. The Supreme Court has stated that a pardon implies the acceptance of guilt for a crime, and lower courts have upheld restrictions on job prospects caused by a criminal conviction, despite a pardon.

3. **Can a president secretly pardon someone, tell no one, and it takes effect?** Answer: No. A pardon is effective only once it's accepted. And if you want your pardon to count in court, you have to actually show it to the judge.

4. **Can a president issue a pardon to force someone to testify when they invoked their Fifth Amendment privilege against**

self-incrimination? Answer: No. The Fifth Amendment trumps a presidential pardon.

5. **Can a recipient refuse to accept a pardon?** Answer: Yes. People can refuse pardons, especially if they come with conditions they don't like; what's unclear is how far a president can go in imposing conditions that cause other problems.

6. **Do other parts of the Constitution—like the Due Process Clause's protections against procedural unfairness—bind presidents when they pardon?** Answer: The Supreme Court hasn't ruled it out, but frankly it's hard to imagine a successful case raising a due process challenge to a decision to deny a pardon.

7. **Can a president pardon hypothetical, future crimes that have not been committed yet?** No.

8. **Can a president issue a blanket pardon for any conceivable crime committed during a past time period?** Answer: Probably not.

Given that this list includes established (albeit, relatively minor) limits on the pardon power, common sense may pose the question of why it is universally accepted that presidents can pretty much do whatever they want when it comes to pardons. The answer may lie in a few lines of rhetoric from some old Supreme Court opinions.

The Civil War Pardon Cases

The 1867 case, *Ex parte Garland*, is important here because the Court referred to the president's authority to pardon as "unlimited," apart from cases of impeachment, for the very first time.[193] Approximately a century later, the Court stated in *Schick v. Reed* that the Constitution gives the president "plenary authority to forgive [a] convicted person in part or entirely, to reduce a penalty in terms of a specific number of years, or to alter it." The word "plenary" means complete in all respects—unlimited, full, entire—so it's long been widely assumed that the pardon power cannot be questioned under any circumstances. Considered in context, however, these cases are probably distinguishable—meaning, they can be explained away based on their specific facts and circumstances without creating an impenetrable rule for all presidents for all time, particularly when compared to modern-day pardons involving unfairness, self-dealing, and even possible corruption.

The *Garland* case arose shortly after the Civil War. On February 8, 1861, seven states in the Deep South whose economy relied heavily on agriculture and enslaved human labor—South Carolina, Mississippi, Florida, Alabama, Georgia, Louisiana, and Texas—seceded from the Union, forming a provisional Confederate government. In April, the war broke out. More states (including Arkansas, which matters in *Garland*) joined the Confederacy, whose government included full delegations of "representatives" and "senators" in a separate "Confederate" Congress.

On January 24, 1865, the US Congress passed a law banning Confederates from practicing law unless they took a loyalty oath affirming that they never voluntarily supported any "pretended government" in a hostility against the United States. The oath went as follows:

> I . . . do solemnly swear (or affirm) that I have never voluntarily borne arms against the United States since I have been a citizen thereof; *that I have voluntarily given no aid, countenance, counsel, or encouragement to persons engaged in armed hostility thereto*; that I have neither sought nor accepted, nor attempted to exercise the functions of *any office whatever, under any authority or pretended authority in hostility to the United States*; that I have not yielded a voluntary

support to any pretended government, authority, power, or constitution with the United States, hostile or inimical thereto. . . . [S]o help me God.

Augustus Hill Garland was admitted to the Arkansas bar in 1860 and served "in the Congress of the so-called Confederate States" after Arkansas seceded in 1861. When the war ended and Arkansas rejoined the Union, President Andrew Johnson—who assumed the presidency following Abraham Lincoln's assassination, just days after the Union victory—gave Garland a full pardon "for all offences committed by his participation, direct or implied, in the Rebellion."[194] Johnson had attached a different oath to the pardon than the one Congress enacted and Garland took Johnson's oath, knowing that taking the congressionally mandated oath would have disqualified him from law practice given his participation in the rebellion. He petitioned the Supreme Court for permission to continue as an attorney in light of his pardon, but without having taken the oath required by Congress.[195]

As framed by the Court, the legal question before it was "whether the bar admission law passed by Congress infringed on the president's pardon power"—that is, did the law banning Confederates from practicing law unconstitutionally constrain the president? The Court answered yes—the law did unconstitutionally undermine the pardon power. As a consequence, Johnson's pardon of Garland for all offenses related to his allegiance to the Confederacy relieved him of all "penalties and disabilities attached to the offence of treason," placing him "beyond the reach of punishment of any kind," including disbarment from the Arkansas bar.[196] The Supreme Court's decision in the *Garland* case has been understood to mean that Congress can't pass *any* laws narrowing the presidential pardon power. It turns out that this is wrong.

... AND WHY?

**The oldest US pardon cases date from the Civil War.
The Supreme Court held that pardons overrode
laws passed to punish former Confederates.
Mercy? Amnesty? Or both?**

Four years later, in 1871, the Court had before it another case involving Confederate pardons. Following the bitter war, President Lincoln wanted to heal the country quickly and directed his generals to offer terms to Confederate officers, enabling a majority of soldiers who surrendered to return home without legal consequences for their rebellion against the United States. On December 8, 1863, in his annual message to Congress outlining his plans for Southern Reconstruction, Lincoln issued a proclamation offering a full pardon to anyone who supported the Confederate Army. The pardon would restore all rights to Confederate property (except ownership of formerly enslaved people) confiscated during the war, so long as recipients took an oath of allegiance to the Constitution of the United States. Lincoln also envisioned that his pardons would exclude officials in the defunct Confederate government, as well as anyone who mistreated prisoners.

Congress initially reacted negatively to Lincoln's pardons. Thinking that Lincoln was being too lenient on former Confederate loyalists, it passed the Wade-Davis Bill that would have required half of all former Confederate states' voters to swear allegiance to the United States and promise they had not supported the Confederacy in order to rejoin the Union. Lincoln vetoed the bill.

Around the same time, Congress passed a series of laws providing that Confederate property used in the war could be seized and forfeited, and outlining punishment for treason, among other things. On July 12, 1862, it passed a law stating that anyone who engaged in the rebellion and did *not* "return his allegiance" to the United States within sixty days of Lincoln's proclamation shall forfeit all their property. Then, on March 12, 1863, Congress pulled back a bit, passing another statute that permitted owners of property confiscated during the war to receive the *proceeds* from the sale of their property if they *didn't* participate in the rebellion.

V. F. Wilson had voluntarily participated in the rebel confederacy, but took Lincoln's oath of allegiance, so in theory he was entitled to his property under Lincoln's proclamation, but not under the statute passed by Congress. After his death, John A. Klein, administrator of Wilson's estate, applied to a court to recover the proceeds of the sale of cotton seized from Wilson during the war under the 1862 statute, reasoning that because Wilson took Lincoln's oath, he was effectively pardoned, and his property would not be forfeited.[197]

The 1862 law memorializing Lincoln's proclamation was repealed in 1867. Then, in 1870, Congress passed a new law as part of an appropriations bill that not only prohibited the use of President Lincoln's pardon, but also established that accepting the pardon was proof that the recipient had *supported* the rebellion during the War and was therefore unable to get proceeds from the sale of their seized property.

Klein's case made its way to the Supreme Court, which held that the 1870 law turning the tables on Lincoln's pardon—i.e., treating its acceptance as proof of rebellion and thus disqualifying recipients from getting seized property back—was unconstitutional because it "is clear that the legislature cannot change the effect of such a pardon any more than the executive can change a law." Through its decision in *Klein*, the Supreme Court reaffirmed that a pardon is more controlling than a conflicting law passed by Congress. (Although as we'll see below, some things Congress does *can* override a pardon.)

Meanwhile, Andrew Johnson assumed the presidency on March 4, 1865, a month before the Civil War officially ended on April 9,

1865. On May 29, he extended amnesty to former Confederate troops but included over a dozen exceptions—more than double the exemptions under Lincoln's amnesty grant—including for people who participated in the rebellion but owned property worth over $20,000. He also required that recipients swore a loyalty oath to the United States and that they would free any persons they had enslaved. The final surrender of Confederate troops occurred on June 2, 1865. Those who did not qualify for his amnesty grant could apply for a special pardon from Johnson.

By June 5, 1866, Johnson had issued 12,652 pardons, including for members of Congress. On December 25, 1868, he gave a final mass pardon to all Confederate soldiers "unconditionally, and without reservation," explaining that his action would "renew and fully restore confidence and fraternal feeling among the whole, and their respect for the attachment to the national government, designed by its patriotic founders for the general good." Soldiers seeking return of their confiscated property were thus finally relieved of having to establish their loyalty first.

Garland and *Klein* are among a series of cases involving presidential pardons around the Civil War, and are often cited to support a sweeping reading of the presidential pardon power today. But the circumstances of these cases were unique. Both Lincoln and Johnson needed to unite the country after a bloody civil war. They used the pardon power for amnesty—extending it to a group of people for political offenses rather than exercising it as a show of mercy on particular individuals with exceptionally harsh sentences. So it's not altogether obvious that the Court's broad rhetoric in these early cases justifies unlimited presidential authority and discretion to pardon specific individuals in modern times.

Constraint Number 1:
A Pardon Recipient Is Still Stuck with the Bill

In another Civil War–related case, *Knote v. United States*, the Supreme Court in 1877 quietly recognized a limit on the pardon power.[198] The claimant's West Virginia land was seized during the war because he had assisted in the rebellion. He filed a lawsuit to get the property back, again under President Johnson's pardon in 1868. Citing *Garland*, *Klein*, and other Civil War cases, the Supreme Court offered this explanation of the scope and effect of a presidential pardon:

> A pardon is an act of grace by which an offender is released from the consequences of his offence, so far as such release is practicable and within control of the pardoning power, or of officers under its direction. It releases the offender from all disabilities imposed by the offence, and restores to him all his civil rights. In contemplation of law, it so far blots out the offence, that afterwards it cannot be imputed to him to prevent the assertion of his legal rights. It gives to him a new credit and capacity, and rehabilitates him to that extent in his former position.

After *Garland* and *Knote*, which said that a pardon "blots out" an offense, it became generally understood that a full pardon restores basic civil rights, such as the right to vote, serve on juries, and the right to work in certain professions.

Yet at the same time, the *Knote* Court made clear that a pardon "does not make amends for the past" or otherwise operate to return the offender to the status quo that existed before his prosecution. The language, once again, bears repeating at some length because it offers the best clues as to how the Supreme Court has understood the purposes and functions of the pardon power:

It affords no relief for what has been suffered by the offender in his person by imprisonment, forced labor, or otherwise; it does not give compensation for what has been done or suffered, nor does it impose upon the government any obligation to give it.

In other words, a pardon does *not* give a recipient the right to obtain *financial compensation* from the government for the harms suffered by the prosecution or imprisonment. Anything that happened in the past as a result of "judicial proceedings, that which has been done or suffered while they were in force, is presumed to have been rightfully done and justly suffered."

...AND WHY?

In 1877, the Supreme Court called the pardon an "act of grace" that "blots out the offense," but not the punishment already suffered. Is this nod to mercy justified today?

So what does this all mean?

Practically speaking, *Knote* held that a president's pardon cannot extend to a payment of money from the government to the pardoned individual. Money "can only be secured to the former owner of the property through an act of Congress" under the Constitution, which states in Article I, Section IX, Clause 7 that "No money shall be drawn from the Treasury, but in Consequence of Appropriations made by Law." Congress's power of the purse controls the pardon power—not the other way around.[199] Bear in mind that Article II of the Constitution, which contains the pardon power, has no such limit. The Supreme Court got there by reading it in tandem with the appropriations language of Article I. It didn't have to.

In more recent cases, courts have backed away from the "blot-out" language of *Knote*, reading that case as only limiting the president's power to trigger money awards as part of a pardon—not to wipe clean the entire criminal conviction and its implications. In 1986, for example, Independent Counsel Lawrence E. Walsh was appointed "to investigate . . . alleged violations of federal criminal laws . . . in connection with the sale or shipment of military arms to Iran" under the administration of President George H. W. Bush. The CIA's deputy director for operations, Clair E. George, was indicted on ten counts of false statements, perjury, and obstruction of justice after testifying multiple times before Congress, the Office of Independent Counsel, and a grand jury. Following a mistrial, George was ultimately convicted on two counts—one for making a false statement and the other for perjury.

On December 24, 1992, after the jury verdict but before the judgment of conviction was officially entered on the court's docket, Bush gave George a "full, complete, and unconditional pardon." George later sued the government for reimbursement of $1,297,950.18 in attorneys' fees incurred as a result of the prosecution. Under a federal statute, courts could award subjects of the independent counsel's investigation attorneys' fees "if no indictment is brought against this individual." Clair argued that the pardon blotted out all repercussions, including the financial costs of defending himself. The US Court of Appeals for the DC Circuit (a court that's only one step removed from the Supreme Court when it comes to important cases implicating the federal government) rejected his claim, citing *Knote* and the Appropriations Clause, which gives Congress the exclusive power to allocate the spending of federal dollars. It wrote: "The question then arises: Can the pardon annul, expunge, or otherwise nullify George's indictment so he can receive the fees pursuant to the statute? The answer is no; the pardon does not remove his disability."

Constraint Number 2:
Congress Can Limit a Pardon Recipient's Job Prospects

The US Court of Appeals for the Seventh Circuit went even further to limit the pardon power, holding that the Commodity Futures Trading Commission (CFTC) could deny an individual's application to register as a floor broker despite a presidential pardon. In 1985, Judd Hirschberg became a registered floor broker with the CFTC—essentially a fiduciary who conducts transactions for clients on an exchange floor. He was later convicted in federal court on four felony counts of mail fraud after he collected $43,300 from his insurance company after falsely claiming that his car had been stolen. The CFTC revoked his registration in 1994. In 2000, President Bill Clinton pardoned him. Hirschberg applied again for registration as a floor broker. When he was denied, he sued.

The question before the appellate court was whether the statute allowing the CFTC to revoke or deny registrations was nullified by the pardon. It concluded no—even though the CFTC considered the conduct underlying the conviction in banning him from re-registering as floor broker. Hirschberg argued that the pardon erased the entire conviction, so it was unconstitutional for the CFTC to punish him based on the same facts. The court disagreed, holding that the CFTC's denial did not unconstitutionally undermine the president's power to pardon because "[t]he effect of a pardon is not to prohibit all *consequences* of a pardoned conviction, but rather to preclude future *punishment* for the conviction." Being denied registration as a broker was not punishment as a result of the underlying conviction; rather, it bore on his "honesty and integrity," which were "legitimate qualifications for the job." Hirschberg was "unfit to be floor broker," whether or not his conviction for actual fraud was pardoned.

Moreover, in 1914, the Supreme Court in *Carlesi v. New York* had already determined that although a pardon may erase a punishment for a crime, it doesn't erase the underlying facts associated with the conviction.[200] That case involved a crime of "forgery in the second degree as a second offense" under New York State law. The defendant had already received a presidential pardon for a related federal crime, and argued that it "operates to restrict and limit the power of the State of New York" to consider the prior offense "as adding an increased element of aggravation" for the second forgery charge. The Court said no, concluding that by merely considering the pardoned crime as an element of the new offense, the New York law was not "repugnant to the Constitution."

Borrowing from the history of monarchical pardons under English common law, the Supreme Court has placed a number of additional conditions on presidential pardons.

Constraint Number 3:
Unknown Pardons Don't Count

The Supreme Court has also indicated that a pardon has to be communicated to a recipient and made known to a court for it to take effect. Secret or unknown pardons don't count.

In the 1833 decision in *United States v. Wilson*, the defendant was indicted twice: once for stealing US mail and endangering the life of the mail carrier, which triggered the death penalty; and the other for stealing US mail without putting a life in jeopardy (a lesser offense), which carried a fine and imprisonment.[201] The defendant pleaded guilty to robbing the mail, but later withdrew his plea. President Andrew Jackson had previously pardoned him for the capital offense, saving his life. When the court asked whether the pardon impacted the lesser offense, the defendant's lawyer didn't invoke the pardon, stating that it only applied to the death sentence.

On appeal, the defendant argued that the pardon automatically covered both offenses despite what his lawyer told the judge. The Supreme Court disagreed, holding that courts cannot give effect to a pardon that the defendant declined to raise in court: "A private deed, not communicated to him, whatever may be its character, whether a pardon or release, is totally unknown and cannot be acted on." The Court further explained:

> A pardon is a deed, to the validity of which delivery is essential, and delivery is not complete without acceptance. It may then be rejected by the person to whom it is tendered, and if it be rejected, we have discovered no power in a court to force it on him. . . . These circumstances combine to show that this, like any other deed, ought to be brought judicially before the court by plea, motion, or otherwise.

The Court thus upheld the defendant's conviction for robbing the mail despite a presidential pardon from an earlier capital conviction for the same conduct.

Presumably, then, under *Wilson* a secret pardon that sits in a drawer would have no effect unless and until it's actually accepted by the pardoned individual and ultimately produced to a court. If President Trump executed "secret" pardons for his children and hid them away, as some people have speculated, those pardons might not be legally effective if they were not accepted while he was still president. And even then, the pardon must be produced to a court if a recipient expects to have a pardon actually impact a prosecution, conviction, or sentence. Just saying that you have a pardon is not enough. For a pardon issued by Trump for himself, it's a bit trickier: A self-pardon would technically be communicated to himself when he made it for himself. We'll deal with the self-pardon conundrum, which poses a host of other theoretical and pragmatic problems, later in the book.

Constraint Number 4:
Pardons Are Worthless If Recipients Reject Them

In 1915, the Supreme Court underscored that a pardon must be accepted to have any legal effect. *Burdick v. United States* involved a newspaper editor, George Burdick, whose paper, the *New York Tribune*, had reported that someone was illegally smuggling jewels into the United States.[202] A federal grand jury subpoenaed Burdick, who refused to testify about his source of the information, invoking the Fifth Amendment privilege against self-incrimination. In 1914, President Woodrow Wilson pardoned Burdick in an attempt to force him to testify; without the threat of criminal indictment, there would be no need to plead the Fifth. The Wilson administration suspected that the information Burdick leaked came from the Customs Service, and potentially involved a bribe. Burdick refused to accept the pardon and was fined and jailed until he complied with the subpoena. As in the *Wilson* case, the Supreme Court held that Burdick was entitled to reject the pardon and continue his refusal to testify, observing that a pardon carries "an imputation of guilt and acceptance of a confession of it." The Court conceptualized a pardon as a sort of contract—"a private deed" mercifully bestowed on a particular individual. Like any contract, it can be rejected."[203] It also made clear that presidents cannot force people to forego the constitutional right against self-incrimination by bestowing the benefits of a pardon.

Here again, then, as with the Appropriations Clause, the Court read Article II's pardon power language in tandem with another part of the Constitution—the Fifth Amendment—rather than relying on the bald assumption that all pardons are absolute and the president can do whatever he wants with pardons.

... *AND WHY?*

**So what's the hot take, so far, on the scope of the pardon power?
Given the limits the Supreme Court has already recognized,
does it make sense to assume that presidents have an absolute
and unconstrained right to issue pardons as they see fit?**

* * *

Constraint Number 5:
Pardons with Conditions Are Okay

A person's right to reject a pardon also bears on the subject of conditional pardons. A conditional pardon is one that requires a recipient to satisfy some sort of prerequisite before the pardon can take effect, or to do something specific in order to prevent a pardon from becoming void.[204] The Supreme Court has for a long time accepted the constitutionality of conditional pardons, which our legal system borrowed from English common law history along with the pardon power itself. Presidents Lincoln and Johnson issued conditional pardons for former Confederate soldiers in exchange for loyalty. Other presidents have conditioned pardons on recipients' providing restitution—or payback—to their victims, dropping their legal claims against the government, and agreeing to deportation from the United States. In 2001, President Clinton issued pardons that required periodic drug tests.

Conditional pardons stretch as far back as 1855, when the Supreme Court issued a decision in *Ex parte Wells*, which involved a conviction for murder.[205] After the defendant William Wells was sentenced to hang, President Millard Fillmore granted him a pardon "upon condition that he be imprisoned during his natural life; that is, the sentence of death is hereby commuted to imprisonment for life in the penitentiary of Washington." Wells later argued that the conditional pardon was unconstitutional because it effectively changed the law, "legislat[ing] a new punishment into existence." The Court disagreed. An individual who accepts a pardon on certain conditions "cannot complain if the law executes the choice he has made."

The 1974 decision in *Schick v. Reed* involved a conditional pardon issued by President Dwight D. Eisenhower who commuted the sentence of Maurice Schick from death to life imprisonment on the condition that he would never be eligible for parole.[206] Eisenhower specifically stated: "This commutation of sentence is expressly made on the condition that the said Maurice L. Schick shall never have any rights, privileges, claims, or benefits arising under the parole and suspension or remission of sentence laws of the United States."

Schick had been court-martialed—or put to trial before a military court—and sentenced to death for the brutal murder of an eight-year-old girl while he was a master sergeant in the US Army stationed in Japan. He admitted to the killing, but claimed that he was insane at the time. After serving twenty years, he filed a lawsuit seeking to require the US Parole Board to consider him for parole, arguing that he made a "bad bargain" by accepting a no-parole condition in place of a death sentence. He reckoned that he would have been better off appealing his death sentence because the Supreme Court had handed down *Furman v. Georgia* in the interim, which declared certain manifestations of the death penalty unconstitutionally cruel and unusual punishment in violation of the Eighth Amendment.[207] The Supreme Court rejected his claim, calling it elementary that under English common law, "the king may extend his mercy on what terms he pleases, and consequently may annex to his pardon any condition that he thinks fit."

In *Hoffa v. Saxbe*, decided that same year, a lower federal court rejected a bid by James R. Hoffa, former president of the International Brotherhood of Teamsters, to undo conditions attached to his sentence commutation.[208] Hoffa was convicted of various federal crimes and sentenced to thirteen years in prison. President Richard Nixon commuted his sentence to six and a half years on the condition that Hoffa refrain from union management. Hoffa accepted the condition and supported Nixon's 1972 reelection bid, but later argued that the condition "unlawfully infringes on his First Amendment rights of speech and association, amounts to additional punishment and a bill of attainder as well as contravening the double jeopardy clause, all in violation of the Fifth Amendment." He also claimed "that the condition was imposed outside the normal pardon application procedures, without due process of law, and in spite of the fact that Mr. Hoffa never 'accepted' the condition."

A federal trial court in Washington, DC, rejected all of Hoffa's arguments, concluding "that the President may exercise his discretion under the Reprieves and Pardons Clause for whatever reason he deems appropriate and it is not for the courts to inquire into the rationale of his decision." Hoffa had also alleged "that the condition was formulated and imposed as the result of a conspiracy involving the President." The court—whose decision was not binding like one from the Supreme Court—suggested that political self-interest is no reason to invalidate a pardon:

> If . . . the President participated in the alleged conspiracy, it necessarily follows that the President was also fully aware of the considerations motivating the final decision to commute Hoffa's sentence. There is no claim that the President was in any way deceived or misled into acting upon Hoffa's application for clemency. Plaintiff essentially charges that the President acted, at least in part, with a view toward gaining political advantage. But this fact alone, even if proven, would never be enough to vitiate an otherwise proper exercise of Constitutional power for the same reason that one cannot attack the validity of an Act of Congress on the grounds that the Congressmen who voted in favor of it did so for improper motives.

Hoffa disappeared on July 30, 1975, while waiting to meet with business associates who were well-known Mafia figures. Some believe he was attempting to reassert himself into the Teamsters, defying the terms of Nixon's commutation. In 1982, a Michigan probate court declared him dead.

As a matter of sheer logic and common sense, the *Hoffa* court probably overstated the scope of a president's power to make conditional pardons. As a student author put it for the *Harvard Law Review*, if that were true, the president "could pardon, and thereby re-enfranchise, thousands of convicted felons in key swing states upon the condition that they vote for his or her party in the upcoming election. Pardon recipients who failed to fulfill the condition would be thrown back in jail."[209] Or the president could "pardon a healthy prisoner upon the condition that the prisoner donate her kidney to the President's ailing cousin, or commute a death sentence upon the condition that the prisoner be strung up by his ankles and tortured in the Rose Garden for the First Family's entertainment."

These hypotheticals seem far-fetched, but so is the assumption that the president is actually more like a king than an accountable, elected representative of the voting public when exercising the power of the pardon. Presumably, pardons conditioned on waiving constitutional rights—like the right speak freely under the First Amendment—would be unconstitutional. We've already seen that the pardon power cannot override the Appropriations Clause or the Fifth Amendment's protection against self-incrimination. But what about the Due Process Clause?

Constraint Number 6:
Possible Due Process Protections around Pardons

In a series of cases culminating in *Ohio Adult Parole Authority v. Woodard* in 1998, the Supreme Court indicated that there might be a scenario in which due process protections might apply to pardon decisions.[210] The Court just hasn't seen that case yet.

First, a brief explainer on due process. There are two Due Process Clauses in the Constitution. The first, found in the Fifth Amendment, applies to the federal government (and thus to the president, in theory, when pardoning). The Fourteenth Amendment's Due Process Clause applies to the states (and thus to governors when pardoning—more on how state clemency works later in the book). Due process has its roots in England's Magna Carta. In 1215, King John agreed to a list affording his subjects certain rights in order to make peace with a group of rebel barons who were fed up with the unlimited powers of the monarchy. The list included a provision prohibiting the king from taking someone's life, liberty, or property without some measure of process, including *notice* that a law may have been violated and an *opportunity to be heard* before the king took away life, liberty, or property.[211] Even today, a classic form of notice is a criminal indictment setting forth the charges against an individual and citations to the relevant law, and an opportunity to be heard is a full-blown jury trial on those charges.

When it comes time to make a request for a pardon, most petitioners presumably have already received some due process—that is, the government issued an official charging document against them, such as an indictment, and they had an opportunity to be tried before a jury of their peers. If a defendant decided instead to strike a plea deal, that's considered a waiver of the constitutional right to a criminal trial.

As we shall see, incarcerated individuals have argued in a number of Supreme Court cases that the Due Process Clause of the Fourteenth Amendment applies to clemency decisions in addition to the process that led to their underlying conviction. They claimed, in essence, that before a state can continue to imprison someone after they made a pardon request, the governor's office or other government entity charged with making a pardon decision has to afford the requester a meaningful opportunity to be heard on the clemency request, too. After all, *ongoing* incarceration is a deprivation of liberty. Keep in mind that the Due Process Clause doesn't always guarantee a full-blown jury trial. Under certain circumstances, the most "process" you are owed could be an oral hearing before a judge, or even the right to submit a written brief or letter setting forth arguments in your favor. So in arguing for due process with respect to a clemency petition, they weren't arguing for a second trial—just a guarantee of some sort of fair process around their pardon applications.

Due process analysis gets nuanced and complicated from there. The gist of it for purposes of clemency proceedings is this: The Supreme Court has never ruled that any particular procedure must be followed before governors grant or deny clemency requests under the Due Process Clause. But it hasn't ruled out the notion, either. The question of whether due process applies to pardon decisions has arisen exclusively with convictions under state law—which implicates governors' pardon powers—rather than under federal law, which would implicate presidents' powers. Nonetheless, the Supreme Court's case law under the Fourteenth Amendment's Due Process Clause (for states) would likely inform how it would handle a due process claim under the Fifth Amendment (for the federal government).

The most recent case on this subject is *Ohio Adult Parole Authority v. Woodard*, from 1998. Eugene Woodard, while on death row for aggravated murder during a carjacking, sued the Ohio Adult Parole Authority, arguing that its clemency procedures violated due process because the parole authority only gave him seven days to plead his case for clemency. The Supreme Court rejected his claim, reasoning that there is no special liberty interest in clemency once the state validly secured a conviction and the defendant was properly sentenced. In other words, once Woodard was incarcerated, no *new* right to due process attached—his rights were satisfied when he was arrested, charged, and convicted through a trial, appeal, and other post-conviction procedures.

The Court noted that a new liberty interest might arise in clemency if the government took *new actions* to change the prisoner's situation—like transferring him from one prison to another, to a more severe one, or from a prison to a psychiatric hospital. In that instance, the prisoner would have an interest in protecting his "liberty" from a particular prison condition. But with just a clemency question, any changes in how a governor decides whether to grant or deny a clemency petition did not alter an inmate's conditions of confinement. They merely alter the defendant's *expectations* that he might be able to receive a pardon or a commutation of a sentence, or so the Court reasoned. The Court went on to suggest that if there were clemency procedures in place that made it *mandatory* that someone receive a pardon if certain criteria are satisfied, then a prisoner could argue that keeping him incarcerated triggers a new liberty interest. But clemency, virtually by definition, is discretionary. Presidents and governors hold the power to pick and choose winners and losers, and those choices are not reviewable by any court.

As the *Woodard* Court observed, due process protections actually create a perverse incentive. If a governor or the White House were to establish definitive criteria for pardons, the inmate population—and the public—would have a clear idea of who is eligible and who is not. The downside, however, is that definitive criteria would mean that people who don't get pardons could sue the governor or the president in court under the Due Process Clause. The criteria themselves would create an expectation of a certain process which, if not adhered to, would be a constitutional violation. With no set process, there's no expectation of process. As the Supreme Court explained, this approach "creates disincentives for States to codify" standards.[212] It would also put courts in the position of conducting day-to-day oversight of pardon decisions for compliance with the Due Process Clause. Courts don't want that.

... AND WHY?

Why not just have clear procedures and standards for pardons and make them apply equally and fairly? It might hamper a president's discretion, for one thing. It would also give claimants a constitutional right to sue under the Due Process Clause (and the government doesn't want that).

Even if the government doesn't come up with a list of factors promising pardons under certain circumstances, the lower appeals court in *Woodard* recognized that in the future, a bare-bones case of a pardon may warrant due process scrutiny. Due process, at its essence, aims to prevent arbitrary decision-making.

> The Court offered some hypotheticals of what could cross the line: For example, a procedure in which a governor or parole board merely pulled names out of a lottery bin or flipped coins to make clemency decisions would undoubtedly constitute a "meaningless ritual." Similarly, a death-penalty "clemency hearing" occurring immediately after conviction but before commencement of a defendant's sentencing proceeding would be almost equally without meaning.

Justice Sandra Day O'Connor, in her concurring opinion in the Supreme Court's decision in *Woodard*, similarly suggested that the president could not grant pardons that imposed conditions that would violate the Eighth Amendment's ban on cruel and unusual punishment, such as castration of a sex offender. But just as governors or presidents are unlikely to bind their own hands by producing very precise criteria for pardons and commutations, they are just as unlikely to be arbitrary about the decisions so as to be devoid of any common sense.

Of course, there are many "harder" and more realistic scenarios than flipping a coin. A pardon board could include a decision-maker who is racist or believes that criminal laws are too lax, refusing as a matter of "principle" to pardon people of color or anyone convicted of crimes involving a firearm. Or maybe the decision-maker personally knows the family of the victim and is biased against the petitioner by hearsay rumors that were too unreliable to make it into evidence at trial or at sentencing. If a petitioner is in prison for life, he would have no opportunity to challenge those false facts—a central component of due process—even though those facts prevent him from having a shot at liberty before he dies, while the guy in the cell next to him, who committed an even more heinous crime, gets pardoned.

Consider the story of Isaac B. Desha, son of then-governor Joseph Desha of Kentucky, who was charged with the brutal murder of Francis Baker in 1824.[213] Isaac was convicted by a jury and sentenced to death. On July 13, 1826, the day before his scheduled execution, Isaac attempted suicide, unsuccessfully. Governor Desha immediately issued a pardon for his son, possibly saving his life. Desha's pardon of a close family member isn't an isolated incident. In 2001, on his final day in office, President Clinton pardoned his half-brother Roger Clinton in connection with a 1985 conviction for cocaine distribution.[214] Similarly, Arkansas governor Mike Beebe pardoned his son Kyle for a 2003 conviction related to possession of marijuana (Bill Clinton also served as the governor of Arkansas from 1983 through 1992).[215]

The trouble is, society tolerates exactly this kind of arbitrary decision-making when it comes to pardons. Like the process for deciding on pardons, the configuration of pardon boards gets no review by a court, including under the Due Process Clause.

In *Young v. Hayes,* the US Court of Appeals for the Eighth Circuit did find that the due process line was crossed in 2000 when a city attorney threatened to fire a junior lawyer who had information helpful to a death row inmate's clemency petition.[216] The court wrote: "The

Constitution of the United States does not require that a state have a clemency procedure, but, in our view, it does require that, if such a procedure is created, the state's own officials refrain from frustrating it by threatening the job of a witness." *Young* thus made clear that a viable due process challenge to pardons is *not* legally impossible. Moreover, the fact that some constitutional line in the sand exists dispels the notion that the pardon power is absolutely absolute.

Constraint Number 7:
No Pardons for Future Crimes

Given the two federal indictments against Donald Trump relating to his conduct in office (the January 6, 2021, insurrection at the Capitol and his packing classified information in the White House and unlawfully transferring it to his estate in Mar-a-Lago), the last two constraints on the pardon power could be especially timely.

The first is the ban on pardons for future crimes. In *Ex parte Garland*, the Supreme Court wrote that pardons extend "to every offence known to the law, and may be exercised at any time after its commission." Given the Court's use of the word "after" in this sentence, *Garland* has been universally construed to mean that presidents cannot pardon people for crimes that have yet to be committed.[217] So, for example, if a president were to issue a self-pardon on the first day in office as a form of blanket immunity for any future criminal conduct he might engage in over the next four years, it would be invalid.

Constraint Number 8:
Blanket Retroactive Pardons?

However, an open question remains over whether a president could issue a blanket pardon that applies to all conceivable crimes that may have occurred during a specific time period in the *past*.

President Gerald Ford muddied the waters in pardoning President Richard Nixon of "all offenses against the United States" during his administration, without identifying any specific crimes.[218] Nixon was never charged, and the pardon was never challenged in court, so it does not operate as a legal precedent for broadly worded pardons; its influence is merely historical, although importantly so.

Arguably, a blanket pardon would to be too vague to stick, but the Supreme Court has never recognized a specificity requirement for pardons, either. Recall that in 1915's *Burdick v. United States*, the Court wrote that a pardon "carries an imputation of guilt; acceptance of a confession of it."[219] If that is true—a point that some commentators dispute—then as a matter of logic, a blanket pardon for unspecified crimes could be illegitimate, as the recipient would have no idea what they were admitting to or accepting.

The *Burdick* Court also rejected President Wilson's attempt to force a pardon as a means of circumventing Burdick's ability to claim the Fifth Amendment privilege against self-incrimination (implying that if Burdick were to accept the pardon, it would waive the privilege and he'd have to testify about a leak of government information). This creates its own problem. Consider Trump's pardoning of his first national security advisor, Michael Flynn, for "any and all possible offenses" within the jurisdiction of Special Counsel Robert Mueller's investigation into Russian interference in the 2016 presidential election.[220] Flynn pleaded guilty in 2017 to lying to the FBI about his contacts with a Russian ambassador during the campaign. If Flynn were later called to testify before a grand jury, his lawyers would have a quandary on their hands. If he testified and the grand jury indicted him based on that testimony, he would presumably use the pardon to claim immunity from prosecution. But without a Supreme Court ruling in hand making it clear that nonspecific pardons are valid, he'd be testifying at his own risk.

In addition, blanket pardons could frustrate the government's ability to later investigate and prosecute wrongdoing in office. A president could just pardon his entire staff on the way out the door, possibly greenlighting crime sprees in the Oval Office for future presidents because the government could not dangle the possibility of immunity to motivate witnesses to testify. Normally, prosecutors promise not to charge witnesses with crimes bearing on their testimony as an incentive to get them to cooperate. With immunity, the witnesses no longer need to raise the Fifth Amendment's protection against self-incrimination because they couldn't incriminate themselves, no matter what they say.

A blanket pardon would presumably immunize witnesses and allow them to testify freely, but because it's unclear how precise a pardon must be, prosecutors and witnesses would be flying blind. Witnesses could claim the pardon to avoid prosecution, but still refuse to testify for fear of legal holes in the pardon. This would thrust the government in a bind: hold the witness in contempt, or give them express immunity so prosecutors can get to the evidence—a choice that would essentially be forced by the pardon. Either way, the uncertainties would compromise access to the truth and enforcement of the rule of law. Blanket pardons should be a no-go.

3

From Presidents to Governors

Although clemency can be granted at the state level for state crimes, only three states recognize an unrestricted power in the executive branch to issue a pardon. In 2023, the likelihood of a prisoner receiving clemency remains accordingly low.[221]

Some states exercise clemency powers more frequently than others. A study last updated in October 2022 identified the following states as granting a significant number of pardons, i.e., 30 percent or more of those requested: Alabama, Arkansas, Connecticut, Delaware, Georgia, Idaho, Illinois, Louisiana, Nebraska, Nevada, Oklahoma, Pennsylvania, South Carolina, South Dakota, and Utah.[222] In many states, the number of pardons fluctuates depending on the governor at any given point in time. Twenty states and the District of Columbia have granted virtually no pardons in the last twenty years.

Bear in mind that in 2020, the FBI identified nearly 9 million criminal offenses reported across 9,880 law enforcement agencies, which together cover over 177.5 million people.[223] The vast majority of these represent state-law crimes. Of the 9 million offenses, over 60 percent were for crimes against property, such as burglary, theft, arson, vandalism, and shoplifting. Only 25 percent were crimes against a person, such as assault, battery, and domestic violence. In fiscal year 2020, federal, state, and local governments together spent $275.5 billion on crime and justice, amounting to 2.7 percent of total spending, or $838 per taxpayer—a number that has more than tripled since the 1980s. In 2021, there were 5.4 million people in the US prison system. Meanwhile, the number of violent crimes per 100,000 people has dropped from 600 in 1980 to under 400 in 2020. In light of these figures, the rare use, and even absence, of clemency at the state level raises questions as to whether pardons serve their legitimate purposes—mercy, amnesty, and pragmatism.

... AND WHY?
Most states use pardon boards, which avoid lodging too much unaccountable power in one person. Should the federal system follow suit?

States use a few basic models to administer pardons. Although state constitutions typically conferred pardon power on governors in the nineteenth century, the power has mostly shifted to external pardon boards. In some states, a committee issues pardons with no involvement of the governor, whose only role is to make appointments to the committee. In six states, an independent board processes applications for clemency. In two of these, Alabama and South Carolina, the governor remains responsible for pardons and commutations in capital cases. In Idaho, the governor must approve the board's decision for certain serious crimes.

Twenty-two states' governors share the pardon power with a board. Either the governor sits on the board, it must consult with the board, or the board acts as a gatekeeper. In Rhode Island, a state with a gate-keeping board, the state senate must advise on and consent to every pardon. In Delaware, the governor can only grant a six-month reprieve under that state's pardon power; any other form of pardon requires a written recommendation by the board of pardons, which is established under the Delaware Constitution. In nineteen states, the governor may consult with the board, but retains the ultimate pardon authority. In the remaining five states, there is no statutory advisory process that qualifies the governor's pardon power in any way. In Texas, the governor's uni-lateral authority is limited to a thirty-day reprieve. Only the president can pardon convictions under the local laws of Washington, DC.

... AND WHY?
Unlike for US presidents, the Florida governor's power to grant reprieves is limited to sixty days, and any pardon or commutation of a sentence in Florida requires the consent of two members of the cabinet. Surprising?

States also have varying standards for clemency eligibility and different mechanisms for public transparency and oversight. Unlike the US Constitution, many state constitutions contain an exception for treason, which cannot be pardoned. Forty state constitutions also forbid the use of pardons for impeachments, or limit pardons to actual convictions.

Some states' clemency laws show leniency for death penalty cases, claims of innocence, and first-time convictions—none of which appear in the DOJ's criteria for presidential pardons and commutations, as we shall see. Pennsylvania's constitution requires the unanimous recommendation of the pardon board in death penalty cases, and some anti–death penalty governors have refused to sign death warrants.[224] That state has also produced a relatively high number of inmates on death row. In South Carolina, the governor can only grant reprieves and commute death sentences to life in prison.[225] By law, everything else goes to the probation, parole, and pardon board.[226] And in Louisiana, the constitution automatically pardons first-time offenders—restoring full citizenship rights—so long as they complete their sentences for specific offenses like purse-snatching, aggravated assault and battery, and illegal weapons use.[227]

Because each state has its own constitution, each also has its own set of judicial rulings issued by the state court judges interpreting its constitution's provisions on pardons. Like under the federal Constitution, the language of state constitutions is not uniformly clear, leaving judges with the task of deciding what information to use to resolve ambiguity—such as the constitutional text, the constitutional history, and the rationales or goals behind the inclusion of a pardon power under that state's constitution. Although the language of state constitutions varies across the country, state courts have to a large extent rejected legal challenges to denials of clemency.

An example: During his last days in office, Mississippi governor Haley Barbour, a Republican, granted executive clemency to 215 people in 2012.[228] Democrat Attorney General Jim Hood sued in state court, alleging that the pardons violated Mississippi's constitution, which states that "after conviction no pardon shall be granted until the applicant therefor shall have published for thirty days."[229] Hood argued that Barbour's last-minute pardons failed to satisfy the thirty-day publication mandate, and were invalid. The Supreme Court of Mississippi upheld the pardons as "facially valid"—meaning there were not obvious flaws—even though they were not published.[230] The court recognized that the state's constitution "clearly does" require that pardon applicants publish their petitions, but held that "[t]he controlling issue is whether the judicial branch of government has constitutional authority to void a facially-valid pardon issued by the coequal executive branch." On this question, the court answered "no," effectively rubber-stamping a pardon that did not comply with the Mississippi constitution.

In addition, Pennsylvania voters passed a 1997 amendment to the Pennsylvania constitution that altered the voting procedures used by the board of pardons to make clemency recommendations to the governor.[231] Prior to 1997, the Pennsylvania constitution required a majority of the five-member board to agree on a pardon recommendation. However, in 1994, a prisoner who received a commutation of his life sentence as a result of the board's majority went on to commit a murder in the state of New York. The incident prompted a ballot measure to amend the constitution and require unanimity in recommending pardons and commutations to the governor for individuals sentenced to life in prison. The measure passed. In a case called *PA Prison Society v. Cortes*, a group of state prisoners and advocacy groups filed suit in federal court arguing that the amendment violated the US Constitution because it increased the punishment applied to life-sentenced inmates with no possibility of parole.[232] Clemency was their only option. In 2010, the US Court of Appeals for the Third Circuit found the law constitutional, as it did not increase punishment but merely created a disadvantage.

Each state varies in the scope and effect of a pardon as well. In Massachusetts, once a pardon is granted, the governor orders the record of the conviction sealed so that the public cannot access the information and the conviction's existence may be denied.[233] In Arkansas, expungement of a criminal record is automatic except in cases involving serious violence, and the right to possess firearms does not automatically accompany a grant of clemency—it must explicitly be restored through the pardon.[234] Under other states' laws, a separate legal process for expunging an individual's criminal record is the only way for a legal disability to be removed despite receiving a pardon.

(Federal law has no process for expungement, so repercussions from a criminal conviction may linger.)

In Alabama, full pardons are rare, with the extent and scope of each pardon specified in the actual pardon grant.[235] Delaware's pardon relieves the recipient of disabilities except for the constitutional prohibition against holding state office for a so-called "infamous crime," such as embezzlement of public money, bribery, and perjury, which call into question the individual's character.[236] In South Carolina, pardons restore all civil rights, gun rights, and the right to be licensed for any profession, and a pardoned conviction cannot be used as a predicate offense in future criminal proceedings.[237] Prior to 2005, a pardon removed an individual from the state's sex offender registry, too, but now only pardons based on innocence have that effect.[238] In Texas, a pardon restores civil rights and removes barriers "to some, but not all, types of employment and professional licensing."[239] In South Carolina, a pardoned conviction must still be reported on job applications.[240]

...AND WHY?

States vary widely on the effect of pardons—from restoring all civil rights to banning people from holding public office. Should the federal pardon system have similar nuances?

A handful of state governors have lost their jobs as a result of pardons that the public considered corrupt. Jeff Davis, Arkansas governor from 1901 to 1913, quipped: "If I did not show mercy, I would not expect mercy when I bow down before the judgment seat."[241] Davis lived by this personal creed, averaging one pardon per day throughout his six-year term as governor. In 1979, by contrast, newly elected governor of Tennessee Lamar Alexander was secretly sworn in three days early in order to prevent his predecessor, Ray

Blanton, who was under investigation for selling pardons, from issuing any in the waning hours of his term.[242]

4

Global Approaches to
the Pardon Power

At least 183 national constitutions explicitly provide for a clemency process, while others recognize clemency through unwritten conventions or by statute.[243] Although the legal frameworks for exercising the pardon power vary significantly among different countries, the US Constitution's monarch-like approach to the presidential pardon power is hardly universal.[244] Like in many American states, most Western countries diversify the decision-making authority of pardons across a number of branches of government or delegate clemency power to independent commissions. The factors that bear on whether to grant a pardon, the frequency with which the power is used, and the accompanying restrictions and processes also vary across the globe.

148

In the majority of countries, the authority to grant pardons is held by the head of state, a tradition that adheres to the historical vesting of the pardon power in the monarch. In countries such as the United States, Russia, Spain, and Nigeria, the head of state wields the pardon power directly. In other places, such as in Zimbabwe, Malta, and Singapore, the power to grant pardons is delegated to a ministerial cabinet with the head of state maintaining the final decision-making authority. In some countries where the pardon power is particularly broad, steps have been taken to prevent self-dealing. For example, the constitution of Kenya prohibits outgoing executives from issuing pardons, while Malaysia's constitution limits self-pardons or pardons for family members.

. . . AND WHY?
**Kenya prohibits pardons on the last days in office.
Malaysia limits self-pardons and pardons for family members.
Is the United States behind the curve?**

Only seven out of twenty-two European republics have a relatively unlimited pardon power, with most requiring some involvement of other individuals—such as consultation or approval from a cabinet, council, or committee, or a recommendation from a parole board or other independent body. In Greece, for example, the president must follow the recommendation of the justice minister and confer with a council of judges before issuing a pardon. Portugal, Finland, and Indonesia all require that pardons conform to the opinions of the country's supreme court. The King of Sweden has no pardon power, which belongs to the chancellor of justice, an elected official. In Japan, wardens of penal institutions must petition a national commission on behalf of a prisoner, which then makes a recommendation to the Japanese cabinet for a final decision. The constitutions of New Zealand, Singapore, South Africa, and Sri Lanka all likewise contain restrictions on the executive pardon power. In Cyprus, Slovakia, Romania, Portugal, Latvia, Italy, and Ireland, the law requires that executive pardon decisions obtain a countersignature from another official or body to ensure that the power is exercised in a transparent and accountable manner.

In other parts of the world, the legislature participates in pardon decisions. Under the constitutions of Nicaragua, Switzerland, Turkey, and Uruguay, the pardon power belongs to the legislature or is shared between branches. Denmark requires that Parliament consent to a pardon. Although emperors Napoleon I and II both had the power to issue general pardons, after the French Revolution, the French legislature had the power to pardon. Outside the United States, pardons often take the form of bills that must be approved by a certain margin of the legislature. In Turkey, Uruguay, and to some extent in Nicaragua, the legislature holds the primary pardon power, with only supplementary powers granted to president. In Switzerland, a parliamentary commission vets applicants before advancing potential pardon recipients to the legislature. In many countries, such as Israel and France, mass pardons or amnesties require that the legislature make a broad determination as to a category of offenders—what some countries refer to as a "general pardon."

... AND WHY?

Some countries use nonpolitical mercy committees of experts. In Russia, a fifteen-member commission composed of artists, writers, and citizens has made pardon recommendations since 1992. If this were enacted in the United States, what perspectives would be important to include on this committee?

Some countries—such as Malaysia, Papua New Guinea, and the Solomon Islands—rely on mercy committees, which are typically independent and comprised of experts in corrections, law, medicine, or community relations—a structure that is more resistant to political influence. Mercy committees in Uganda, Kenya, Malaysia, Guyana, and Lesotho specifically exclude lawyers and government officials from membership. In Lesotho and Seychelles, appointments are vetted by judges. In Sierra Leone, the presidential cabinet makes appointments. In Gambia, the legislature approves appointees. In Uganda, Malaysia, Belize, Guyana, and Fiji, members of mercy committees have terms and mandatory retirement ages. Even in Russia, a country with a history of autocratic rule and a 1993 constitution that gives the president full and unlimited pardon power, a fifteen-member commission composed of artists, writers, and citizens has made pardon recommendations since 1992. None of these checks exist for the US presidency.

In addition, many countries offer some level of judicial review to limit the executive's unfettered discretion in granting pardons. In the late 1980s, a majority of the English House of Lords found that the royal prerogative of mercy (which is technically lodged in the British monarch, but is, in fact, delegated to other government ministers) was subject to review by the courts. India, Canada, and South Africa also allow for judicial review of pardon decisions. In fact, the United States—along with countries like Singapore, Swaziland, and Malaysia—stands out for *not* allowing for judicial review of pardon decisions.

Overall, pardons have played a diminished role in criminal justice internationally as the death penalty has declined across the globe. As of the end of 2021, over two-thirds of the world's nations (or 108) had abolished the death penalty, with only 55 still utilizing it as a method of punishment.[245] The United States trails Iran, Egypt,

Saudi Arabia, Syria, and Somalia in carrying out the highest numbers of executions that year, with 314 in Iran and 11 in the United States, where twenty-seven states plus the federal government still use execution as a form of punishment. Most countries with capital punishment carry it out by hanging and shooting. Only the United States, China, and Vietnam use lethal injection. Saudi Arabia does it by beheading. The International Covenant on Civil and Political Rights (1977), which the United States ratified in 1992, and the American Convention on Human Rights (1969), which the United States signed but never ratified, both mandate the availability of pardons in death penalty cases.

If the goal of the pardon power is mercy, it would seem at its apex in "false positive" death penalty cases—that is, where the defendant is innocent and the criminal justice system got it horribly wrong. Given how few pardons are administered compared to the numbers sought, one thing is for certain: The power is not operating to prevent execution of innocent people in America. Which brings us to the question: Why have the pardon power at all?

...AND WHY?

If pardons are really about mercy, shouldn't every prisoner on death row be able to present definitive new evidence—and get an automatic pardon—if it exonerates them?

Part III
Why? Does the Pardon Power
Serve Justice?

Somewhat remarkably, despite the many debates over the proper purpose and fashioning of the US criminal justice system, deep or robust discussion around the benefits, scope, and abuses of the pardon power doesn't really happen. Like most things under the law, bright lines are hard to find. The kinds of factors that should bear upon whether to pardon are the very same factors that underlie everything from arrest, to conviction, to sentencing, even to what kinds of actions should be outlawed in the first place. These considerations collide with competing views of fairness, morality, justice, policy, theory, and religious doctrine. Oddly, unlike the criminal justice system, the pardon power lacks equivalently deep methodologies, concrete criteria, or established means of accountability and transparency.

The moment a person is stopped by a police officer, a series of legal rights kicks in under the Constitution and various other federal, state, and local laws. At the most rudimentary level, the Fourth Amendment to the US Constitution protects an individual against unreasonable searches and seizures, requiring that the government have probable cause to obtain a warrant from a judge before conducting a search or seizure. Any evidence obtained illegally cannot be used against a defendant in court.[246] The Due Process Clause gives defendants a right to have notice of the offense and an opportunity to be heard before their life (via execution), liberty (via incarceration), or property (via monetary forfeiture) can be taken away, even if the defendant in fact violated a law.

The Fifth Amendment protects individuals from having to provide information that could be used against them and from being prosecuted for the same crime more than once in the same court. The right to remain silent also means that the government cannot force a defendant to testify. The Sixth Amendment contains the right to legal representation, the right to a speedy trial, the right to a trial by a jury of one's peers in an open public forum, and a right to confront an accuser and any witnesses who testify against a criminal defendant. If a defendant cannot afford a lawyer, the court will appoint one. The Eighth Amendment prohibits cruel and unreasonable punishment and provides a right to reasonable bail. If judges and juries get things wrong, there is a right to appeal to a higher court and, separately, the ability to file a separate lawsuit challenging the government's ability to keep someone in custody under what is known as "habeas corpus," a concept that dates from the Magna Carta in thirteenth century England—or even earlier. And so on.

None of these protections existed in England when the pardon power first came on the scene in the seventh century. Today, the criminal laws aim to balance fair treatment of a defendant against society's broader need for safety and accountability, among other considerations. Nonetheless, the American criminal legal system remains far from perfect, with a multitude of systemic problems, *including those* associated with income inequality and racial injustice. However, if the system isn't working right, maybe the solution is to amend the criminal laws rather than give presidents—and in some (but not all) states, governors—a blank check to second-guess prosecutors, judges, and juries who made conviction and sentencing decisions under a complex system of existing laws. After all, clemency decisions are supposed to consider the very same information that the courts did. Yet unlike jury verdicts and judges' orders, a pardon decision cannot be appealed to a higher authority.

Moreover, while the information submitted to a criminal jury is subject to rigorous rules of evidence and the trial record is carefully preserved, no law requires presidents to reveal the reasons why one person received a pardon over others. For the most part, they can make those decisions based on considerations that the public might find objectionable or even offensive if they were made known. As it stands, there is no law clearly preventing a president from denying a pardon based on pure racial animus or granting one in order to hide their own criminal liability for serious wrongdoing committed in office.

... AND WHY?
Let's stop and think: Who should get pardons? Why?
What criteria would you apply if it were up to you?

With the rules for granting pardons largely unwritten, then, the public is left to hope that the awesome power of the pardon is used fairly and well. So, what *should* presidents and governors consider in deciding whether to issue pardons or commutations? Here's a starter list:

Why did the person commit the crime? Famously, the protagonist Jean Valjean in Victor Hugo's *Les Misérables* (1862) became ensnared in the criminal justice system for stealing a loaf of bread. The perceived injustice of his sentence—and the fallout from it—created one of the most compelling figures in literature. It's easy to conjure up similarly sympathetic figures in the modern day. Think about a domestic abuse victim who kills her abuser in a bid to save her life—or at least avoid another trip to the emergency room with broken bones and bleeding lacerations. Or consider a man who returns from a hunting trip, gear in hand, to find his spouse in bed with his best friend and shoots him. What about a juvenile who got

155

caught up in a schoolyard brawl that turned deadly, but had no idea that things would go sour until the lifeless victim lay on the ground?

These types of "gray area" scenarios should strike anyone as materially different from someone who engaged in a cold-blooded, premeditated murder spree. While it's the serial killer category that gets a disproportionate amount of media attention, most crimes are not committed by diagnosed psychopaths. The criminal laws accordingly create gradations of offenses. There are degrees of culpability for taking a life, for example, from premeditated homicide to negligent manslaughter. When acting as a de facto "second" judge or jury, should presidents and governors apply the same hierarchies of wrongdoing with the same level of careful attention to the facts and circumstances of every petitioner's case? As a practical matter, can they?

Have circumstances changed since the crime that materially altered the offender? Some people are imprisoned for decades for a nonviolent crime committed in their youth. Parole decisions might thus consider whether such individuals have "changed their ways" or "seen the light" and taken responsibility for a crime. Pardon determinations probably should too. Or maybe an inmate's health has declined substantially, either physically or mentally, rendering them incapable of threatening society anymore. A pardon would save taxpayer dollars and show some mercy for a person who might actually contribute to society once no longer incarcerated.

Has the offender already paid for the crime? Remember, pardons can be issued after someone has fully served a sentence. Once a person has "paid their debt" to society, should they have the specter of criminality around their neck for the rest of their lives? This debate wages across the country around people with felony convictions who did their time but nonetheless cannot vote. Critics of disenfranchising people who served their criminal sentences argue that the punishment has already been meted out, and losing a foundational element of citizenship is just overkill.[247] Others say it's a veiled form of racism, designed to *insidiously* keep Black men from the polls, as was the case for most of American history.[248] Felon disenfranchisement may even create political incentives to incarcerate categories of potential voters who tend to disagree with a certain political ideology.

Of course, access to the ballot can be addressed by state legislatures and, regarding federal elections, the US Congress. It probably shouldn't belong to governors through the fickle pardon process. If state legislators don't have the political will to change voting laws, maybe governors should respect that legislative judgment. On the other hand, if a judge issues a sentence on the rationale and assumption that once it is served, the offender will have suffered enough retribution for the crime, why shouldn't everyone be "pardoned" once they are out of prison? Of course, that idea seems infeasible, if not unwise; the existence of a criminal record is something that some members of the public want to know about to maintain public order and safety in their lives. So how should presidents and governors distinguish one candidate who has served a sentence from another when it comes to a pardon?

Can new technologies absolve the offender of guilt? If a reason for the pardon power is to absolve the innocent who were wrongly convicted, this should be an easy one—that is, if DNA evidence shows that an individual who is in prison did not commit the crime, a pardon should be automatic. Perhaps even more pointedly, in an ideal system, the mere possibility of innocence should incentivize presidents and governors to use their vast investigatory powers of law enforcement to apply modern technologies to *all* closed cases that wound up putting potentially innocent people in jail. If nothing else, such a policy would get presidents and governors out of the business of rendering pardons subjectively and maximize the possibility that nobody currently serving time is innocent of the crime charged—or that those who made it out of prison but were innocent the whole time can be free of the stain of the conviction. After all, if the pardon power is about mercy, and exclusive to presidents and governors, there are ways to use science to exercise that power in the most precise and accurate way possible: to free people wrongly imprisoned. Nevertheless, this logic hasn't been applied to pardon individuals who have been vindicated of criminal charges anywhere in the country.

Are there any facts about the offender's past—their childhood, IQ, or medical history—that distinguishes them from other people who found themselves in a similar situation? Here again, we can turn to Governor Pat Brown of California, who wrote about how these kinds of factors made a difference in his pardon calculus.[249] However, these issues already overlap with the criteria judges use at sentencing across the country. Indeed, Congress passed a statute that sets forth sentencing guidelines in an attempt to achieve balance and uniformity across the nation's federal courts.[250] Reams of pages have been devoted to analyzing whether the federal sentencing guidelines work. The Supreme Court even weighed in to tamp down on the guidelines' stringency, enabling greater discretion on the part of judges.[251]

And judges are often subject to critique for their criminal sentencing decisions. During Justice Ketanji Brown Jackson's 2022 Supreme Court confirmation hearings, Senate Republicans harshly criticized a handful of the sentences she applied as a lower court judge in cases involving perpetrators of child sex abuse imagery.[252] At the state level, voters elect many judges, so their sentencing decisions may likewise receive scrutiny when they are up for reelection. (Not so for federal judges, whose sentencing decisions instead are confined by the laws passed by Congress and the facts presented under the many rules that govern court proceedings.) Presidents and governors have no such constraints when it comes to clemency decisions.

Is there a broader public interest at stake in connection with a high-profile pardon or a mass pardon? President Gerald Ford reportedly pardoned Richard Nixon for a host of reasons, including his belief that it was time for the divided country to move on after the Watergate scandal, and that bypassing the trauma of a criminal trial was essential to achieving that.[253] This type of "amnesty" pardon is perhaps where a pardon may be most justified and least vulnerable to criticism. Presidents, in theory at least, pay for bad decisions in the next election—or their political party does. When it comes to decisions of national scope and importance, presidents operate alone under the Constitution precisely because, as President Harry Truman famously said, the buck needs to stop somewhere for the American people to know whom to hold accountable.[254]

Nonetheless, it's not hard to imagine a president who believes that their personal reelection, and thus their hold on power, is itself in the public interest because the specific individual in the White House is *that good* for America. Under those circumstances, would handing out pardons for political loyalists be justified as a means of hanging on to power—even if the other factors listed above do not favor a pardon for those folks? If the person in power is from the same political party as *you* at any point in time, maybe the answer is a hesitant yes.

The pardon power attaches to every president, however, so what flies for a president today will be the new normal for future presidents, including presidents whom you might not like as much. Surely, a system in which pardons go to friends and political pals but never to political critics sounds less like a democracy and more like a dictatorship, where loyalty to a single person is the definition of winners or losers in politics. The history of presidential pardons lays bare, moreover, that the rich and well-connected—people who already have access to privilege and power—have special access to the mercy of the pardon, too. Most people lack anything close to the means and influence to get before a president or governor and cannot pull strings to get to the top of the pardon list; they must pay the price charged by the routine criminal justice system and wait it out in prison or in the execution chamber, even if they are much more worthy of a pardon than those who ultimately receive one.

So, are some pardons still doled out to achieve compassion and mercy? The short answer is yes, although not with any consistency.

1

Mercy

Pardons for mercy are perhaps the most easily justifiable form of pardon, grounded in a belief that the criminal justice system often gets it wrong. They can also be among the most difficult. Pat Brown, former governor of California, shared why:

> [T]he longer I live, the larger loom those . . . decisions about justice and mercy that I had to make as governor. They didn't make me feel godlike then: far from it; I felt just the opposite. It was an awesome, ultimate power over the lives of others that no person or government should have, or crave. And looking back over their names and files now, despite the horrible crimes and the catalog of human weaknesses they

comprise, I realize that each decision took something out of me that nothing—not family or work or hope for the future—has ever been able to replace.

In the United States, commutations—or sentence reductions—are rare. Pardons are even rarer. The reasons why there are few winners and many losers in the quest for merciful pardons have to do in part with political volatility. As public opinion on crime reduction fluctuates, pardons can become a liability, particularly if a president or governor is up for reelection.

Consider the 1988 George W. Bush campaign's infamous use of a racially divisive television advertisement to stoke fear around the release of incarcerated individuals.[255] It featured photos of a Black man, Willie Horton, who was serving a life sentence without parole for murder. While on a weekend furlough from a Massachusetts prison, Horton raped a Maryland woman and stabbed her boyfriend. The Bush campaign used the episode to portray his Democratic opponent, Massachusetts governor Michael Dukakis, as soft on crime. The ads touted that while "Bush supports the death penalty for first-degree murderers," "Dukakis not only opposes the death penalty, he allowed first-degree murderers to have weekend passes from prison." The TV screen then showed photos of Horton with the words "kidnapping," "stabbing," and "raping."

The furlough program was in place when Dukakis took office, and a *New York Times* opinion writer noted at the time that "[m]any states and the Federal government give furloughs. Other prisoners on furlough have committed murder. Nevertheless, Mr. Bush has flogged Governor Dukakis with the case for months."[256] Marcia Chatelain, a University of Pennsylvania professor of Africana Studies told the *Times*'s Peter Baker in 2018 that the Willie Horton ad "wasn't just about a racist ad that misrepresented the furlough process. . . . [I]t also taught the Democrats that in order to win elections, they have to mirror some of the racially inflicted language of tough on crime." Baker also wrote that when Obama tried to form a bipartisan coalition to overhaul the criminal justice system to make sentencing fairer, "some lawmakers worried that any change that resulted in the release of someone who would then go on to commit another violent crime could be political suicide."

The Republican Party spearheaded a "tough on crime" platform in the 1980s, following Ronald Reagan's defeat of Jimmy Carter. By the 1990s, Democrats realized they had to join the anti-crime stance in order to win votes. Bill Clinton, then-governor of Arkansas, ran for president on a platform that emphasized tougher sentencing laws, telling an audience: "We cannot take our country back until we take our neighborhoods back."[257] What followed this period was a spike in death sentences, mandatory minimums, and "three strikes, you're out" laws.[258] All of these made issuing pardons a political liability for presidents and governors.

It also meant a surging prison population in the United States. In 2020, a study of 1.6 million prisoners conducted by a group of criminologists and sociologists from the State University of New York at Albany and the University of Pennsylvania found that the "tough on crime" era of the 1980s and early 1990s led to longer prison sentences than any generation before or after. Commentators have observed that "[t]he unprecedented rise in incarceration rates can be attributed to an increasingly punitive political climate surrounding criminal justice policy formed in a period of rising crime and rapid social change."[259] More disturbingly, a 2020 study found that those "sentencing shocks have been felt most acutely among the African American population."[260] *Moreover*, by 2020, there were 5.5 million Americans on probation, on parole, or incarcerated. The total prison population was 1.2 million, costing taxpayers $57 billion annually— not including municipal jails or military prisons. The United States has the second-largest number of prisoners worldwide, second only to China. A disproportionate number of them are Black.

To put it mildly, these numbers challenge the assumption that mercy-based pardons should be employed very conservatively. Arguably, they demand the very opposite. Pat Nolan, a former Republican leader in the California legislature who spent two years in federal prison in the 1990s on racketeering charges, told NBC News in 2015 that "I had a chance to see the impact of the policies I supported in the legislature. It wasn't protecting people [from criminals]. It was expensive, bureaucratic and wasteful. And we were locking up a lot of people who weren't dangerous."[261]

Exoneration Statistics

The University of Michigan's extensive and publicly accessible database, which is known as the National Registry of Exonerations (NRE), bears out Nolan's point. Since 1989, the NRE has tracked over 3,348 exonerations, representing over 29,971 years lost to incarceration, not counting pardons for political favor or amnesty (the longest time an exoneree was incarcerated was forty-seven years, two months).[262] Researchers designed the database to assess how often the criminal justice system gets it wrong—and who most often gets hurt as a result. Overall, the pardon statistics across the United States reflect incarceration statistics, which in turn disproportionately affect people of color, too often unfairly.[263]

Black people represent only 13.6 percent of the US population, but 53 percent of exonerations as of August 2022. During the period from 1989 to present, Black, Hispanic, and other minorities outpaced White exonerees in all categories but child sex crimes and white-collar crimes. Women account for only 8 percent of total known exonerees, which is consistent with their proportional prison populations in the United States. The data suggests that 63 percent of female exonerees were "convicted of crimes that never occurred."[264]

Data prior to 1989 is sparse. The NRE only identifies 456 exonerations occurring before then, with the earliest known pardon granted in 1820.[265] In that case, two brothers, Stephen and Jesse Boorn, were exonerated one year after being convicted and sentenced to death for the murder of their brother-in-law.[266] In a rather bizarre turn of luck for Stephen and Jesse, the purported victim, who had not been seen in some seven years, was found working on a farm in New Jersey.

... AND WHY?

As of 2021, nearly half of all exonerations involved wrongful convictions and hundreds of those involved police misconduct. Does this suggest that pardons should be used more often?

The Boorn brothers' case is no outlier. As of 2021, nearly half of all exonerations involved wrongful convictions. The database also identifies hundreds of cases of official misconduct, such as suppression of exculpatory evidence, inadequate investigation, witness tampering, and misstating facts to the jury. In 2021 alone, eighty-seven exonerations were tied to misconduct by government officials charged with upholding the law. For example, in Illinois—the state that often ranks number one in the total number of annual exonerees year after year—seventeen individuals were exonerated in connection with "misconduct of corrupt police officers led by Sgt. Ronald Watts of the Chicago Police Department, who planted drugs on people after they refused to pay when officers attempted to extort money from them." In November 2021, five additional drug convictions were vacated as a result of Sgt. Watts's bad behavior.

DOJ Pardon Criteria

At the federal level, the Justice Department has applied specific criteria to applications for pardons and commutations since 2014. The DOJ's eligibility criteria require that petitioners wait at least five years after conviction or release from confinement, whichever is later, before filing a pardon application. Presidents, including most recently Donald Trump, have been known to override it.[267]

Once a petition is filed with the DOJ, its staff takes into account the following "principal factors" in deciding whether to recommend to the president that a pardon be granted:[268]

A. **Post-conviction conduct, character, and reputation.** By this, the DOJ is referring to a "demonstrated ability to lead a responsible and productive life." The FBI conducts a background investigation into a petitioner's "financial and employment stability, responsibility toward family, reputation in the community, participation in community service, charitable or other meritorious activities and, if applicable, military record."

B. **Seriousness and relative recentness of the offense.** For "very serious" offenses (e.g., violent crime, major drug trafficking, breach of public trust, or white-collar fraud), more time should have elapsed, especially if "a prominent individual or notorious crime" is involved. If a crime is "very old and relatively minor," that matters too.

C. **Acceptance of responsibility, remorse, and atonement.** The DOJ says that "[a] petitioner should be genuinely desirous of forgiveness rather than vindication," and that any "attempt to minimize or rationalize culpability does not advance the case for a pardon." It goes so far as to say that statements like "Everybody was doing it" or "I didn't realize it was illegal" will be judged "in context." What's more, claims of flat-out "innocence or miscarriage of justice bear a formidable burden of persuasion." In other words, if you are truly innocent, think twice about using that as an argument for a pardon.

D. Need for Relief. The DOJ goes on to say that a pardon to lift "a variety of legal disabilities under state or federal law" can be "persuasive grounds for recommending a pardon." So, if a petitioner just wants a bar license reinstated—but is not asking for a criminal conviction to be wiped out, for example—that "may make an otherwise marginal case sufficiently compelling to warrant a grant" of the request.

On October 6, 2022, President Biden expanded on this list through a presidential proclamation granting pardons to "all current United States citizens and lawful permanent residents who committed the offense of simple possession of marijuana . . . which pardon shall restore to them full political, civil, and other rights."[269] Pardoned individuals still have to apply through the Office of the Pardon Attorney in order to obtain an official "certificate of pardon." At merely two pages, the application is simple, requiring basic contact and demographic information, citizenship and residency status, and conviction information such as the location, docket number, and criminal code section. In 2022 and 2023, he pardoned thousands of people for federal marijuana convictions.

Commutations are treated somewhat differently by the DOJ, as they merely reduce the period of incarceration rather than implying forgiveness of the underlying offense. Generally, a person must have started serving a sentence before filing a petition for a commutation, and all appeals of the underlying conviction should be finished. In deciding whether to recommend a commutation to the president, the DOJ considers "disparity or undue severity of sentence, critical illness or old age, and meritorious service rendered to the government by the petitioner, e.g., cooperation with investigative or prosecutive efforts that has not been adequately rewarded by other official action." The guidelines also mention "demonstrated rehabilitation while in custody or exigent circumstances unforeseen by the court at the time of sentencing." Accordingly, the DOJ may recommend pardons and commutations for individuals who have satisfactorily demonstrated they have seen the errors of their ways, and are "rehabilitated."

The criteria nonetheless pose a problem for people who are innocent or were otherwise wrongly convicted. Since the late 1980s, there have been 281 known exonerations based on DNA evidence, and as many as 570 more exonerations on other grounds.[270] Extrapolating from this data, researchers conservatively estimate that approximately 1 percent of the US prison population is innocent of the crimes for which they were convicted, which amounts to around 20,000 inmates. Even though a criminal jury must convict unanimously upon concluding that the government proved its case against a criminal defendant beyond a reasonable doubt—meaning, without a doubt for which the jury could give a reason—juries and judges make mistakes.

Researchers identify five common causes: 1) eyewitness misidentification; 2) false confessions; 3) bad lawyering; 4) unreliable informant testimony; and 5) unreliable forensic science.[271] Studies show that people are 1.5 times more likely to misidentify a stranger of another race.[272] Criminal defense lawyers can be overburdened, incompetent, or both. A good defense requires a host of lawyering techniques, including a thorough investigation of possible alibis; a strategy for undermining the government's evidence, including forensics on the part of the defense; the timely filing of important legal motions that could keep damaging evidence out of the trial; and diligent trial preparation and performance. The use of so-called "junk science" (assertions that lack actual scientific support) in criminal trials or testimony by witnesses lacking deep expertise in the underlying science can also be a serious problem. And once convicted, it's extremely hard to get a judgment overturned on any of these grounds. All of this may suggest that, for purposes of presidential pardons, the DOJ should generously consider evidence of a wrongful conviction.

That's even assuming mercy remains a legitimate rationale for the expansiveness of the president's power to pardon federal crimes in the modern age.

Obama, Biden, and (More) Trump Pardons

President Barack Obama received over 3,396 pardon requests and 33,149 commutation requests. He granted only 212 pardons and 1,715 commutations in eight years, a stunningly low rate (0.1 percent), although it was the highest number since President Harry Truman. His first commutation was for Eugenia Marie "Boobina" Jennings, who received a mandatory sentence of twenty-two years in prison for possessing fourteen ounces of crack cocaine. Given her history of arrests, the sentencing was mandatory, prompting federal judge G. Patrick Murphy to state: "Your whole life has been a life of deprivation, misery, whippings, and there is no way to unwind that, but the truth of the matter is, it's not in my hands. As I told you, Congress has determined that the best way to handle people who are troublesome is we just lock them up."[273] After serving ten years, Obama commuted her sentence but kept eight years of supervised release. One of twenty children, Jennings suffered from drug and alcohol addictions and sexual abuse. At the time of her commutation, she had three children and a cancer diagnosis. Mandatory minimum sentencings such as the one Jennings received are ripe candidates for clemency because they fail to account for individualized facts and circumstances that might justify a lighter sentence.

Like his predecessors, President Biden has used pardons as a way to right the wrongs of the criminal justice system. Beverly Ann Ibn-Tamas, now eighty years old, was convicted of killing her husband, a doctor in Washington, DC, during a heated argument in 1976.[274] During the trial, she testified that her husband regularly beat and verbally abused her and had threatened her in the moments before the shooting. She was also pregnant. If this case were brought today, battered woman syndrome would have been an available defense for Ibn-Tamas. But at the time, battered woman syndrome—also known as intimate partner violence—was not widely recognized. (A 2015 study of survey data collected from over 10,000 US adults found that approximately one-third of women had experienced contact sexual violence, physical violence, or stalking by at least one intimate partner.)[275] Ibn-Tamas was sentenced to up to five years in prison with credit for time served. After her release, she continued to raise her two children as a single mother and started working as the director of nursing and a case manager for a home-health agency. Biden's pardon of Ibn-Tamas is a classic example of using clemency to show mercy and accommodate for changes in how society views crimes.

Another category of mercy-related pardons involves war crimes. First Lieutenant Michael Behenna, US Army, was pardoned by President Donald Trump after his conviction of war crimes by a military court for unpremeditated murder of an Iraqi prisoner suspected of being a part of Al-Qaeda.[276] After a roadside explosion killed two soldiers, an intelligence report indicated that a then-Iraqi operative, Ali Mansur, could have participated in organizing the explosion. He was interrogated and released. Later, Behenna reportedly sought out Mansur to question him on his own, stripped him naked, and shot him twice. He left the body without telling anyone. It was found the next day by Iraqi police.

Behenna received a sentence of twenty-five years in prison. During his appeal, Behenna argued that the government had failed to disclose what's known as "*Brady* material"—an analysis of a forensic expert stating that the deceased's wounds indicated that the shooting that could have been in self-defense. The Army Clemency and Parole Board reduced his sentence to fifteen years and paroled him after five years. Trump granted him a full pardon in May of 2019. The director of the American Civil Liberties Union National Security Project called the pardon "a presidential endorsement of a murder that violated the military's code of justice."

Pardons and the War on Drugs

Clemency has also been used to address the effects of the drug wars.[277] The Jones family was caught up in a two-year investigation of crack cocaine users, dealers, and suppliers in Terrell, Texas, a town which had only one hundred Black residents at the time.[278] The Drug Enforcement Agency and local police leveraged arrests for low-level offenses into information on fellow users and higher-level dealers and suppliers. According to Sharanda Jones, a couple she knew "implicated me. Not as their main supplier but as someone who could just help out." The DEA recorded the couple pleading with Jones to front them drugs to be sold later. Jones ultimately told them any drug connections she had were "long gone, all gone." The couple later testified that she had previously provided them with forty kilograms of powder cocaine, and a Houston cocaine supplier testified that he provided her with cocaine to be sold as crack.

Jones was sentenced to life in prison after her conviction of one count of cocaine possession in 1999. It was her first criminal offense, and prosecutors offered no proof that Jones ever possessed, bought, or sold cocaine; her conviction rested on the testimony of drug dealers and users who received leniency in exchange for their cooperation. Jones received a harsh mandatory minimum sentence for her minimal role as a middle woman between a cocaine buyer and supplier. Pegged as part of a drug conspiracy, Jones also received multiple sentence enhancements, including that a concealed carry permit in her name showed that a firearm was present "in furtherance of a drug conspiracy," and that she committed perjury "for false denials of guilt on the stand."

When the judge read the verdict of "not guilty" for six of the seven counts, she felt relief. But that changed as she listened to prosecutors and the judge tally up the enhancements. "I remember him saying 'I'm sentencing you to life' and I was just numb," she later said. In shock, she was immediately taken into custody, despite having left her purse in the car after dropping her daughter at school and going to work at the diner she co-owned before attending the hearing. Her sister Sherena also served six years for a minor role in the alleged drug conspiracy. Her brother was sentenced to eighteen years. Her mother, a quadriplegic since a car accident at age twenty, was sentenced to seventeen years. She died a year before her release.

In 2014, then–attorney general Eric H. Holder started a "Smart on Crime Initiative" that prioritized prosecuting the most serious offenses, but provided no relief for individuals like Jones, who had already received extremely long sentences for nonviolent drug offenses. In 2009, Brittany K. Byrd, a second-year law student whose mother had been incarcerated, heard about Jones's situation and decided to write her final paper in her critical race theory seminar on Jones's story and the harsh realities of the sentencing disparity.[279] While working in private practice, Byrd filed a two-hundred-page clemency petition for Jones pro bono and obtained thousands of signatures and letters of support. It wasn't until Jones's daughter wrote to President Obama asking for her release that she finally received a commutation of her sentence in December of 2015, after having served seventeen years in prison.

...AND WHY?

Now consider this: Could pardons be a helpful tool for use in dealing with the drug addiction epidemic in America?

Posthumous Pardons

A final category of mercy-related clemency involves posthumous pardons.[280] Although they do nothing for the actual recipients, who are of course deceased, posthumous pardons have operated as a recognition that justice was denied—that the criminal process leading to a conviction was somehow unfair, flawed, or tainted, often by racial prejudice.

In 2020, for example, California governor Gavin Newsom posthumously pardoned Bayard Rustin, an associate of Martin Luther King Jr. and organizer of the 1963 March on Washington, DC. Rustin was convicted in 1953 of misdemeanor vagrancy and lewd conduct, jailed for sixty days, and compelled to register as a sex offender.[281] Black and gay, Rustin had been arrested for protesting World War II and segregation laws in the Jim Crow–era South. An arrest on a "morals charge" led segregationist senator Strom Thurmond to attack him from the Senate floor as a "sex-pervert" and "draft-dodger."[282] Newsom wrote in the pardon:

> Mr. Rustin was sentenced pursuant to a charge commonly used to punish gay men for engaging in consensual adult sexual conduct. His conviction is part of a long and reprehensible history of criminal prohibitions on the very existence of LGBTQ people and their intimate associations and relationships.[283]

In 2021, Virginia governor Ralph Northam pardoned seven Black men who were electrocuted over seventy years prior for the rape of a White woman.[284] The men were between the ages of eighteen and twenty-three, yet none had attorneys or parents present during their interrogations.[285] A number of them testified at trial, stating that the police had written the confessions they signed. Northam took no position on their guilt or innocence, stating that the pardons were about "recognition from the Commonwealth" that they were denied adequate due process, and that "[r]ace played an undeniable role during the identification, investigation, conviction, and the sentencing." From 1908 to 1951, all of the forty-five men who received the death sentence for rape in Virginia were Black.

...AND WHY?
Should posthumous pardons be in their own category?
After all, the pardoned individual cannot benefit from the pardon because they're dead.
Is this mercy? Amnesty? Or politics?

In 2019, the Florida Clemency Board unanimously, posthumously pardoned the so-called "Groveland Four," four Black youth who were falsely convicted of raping seventeen-year-old Norma Padgett, a White girl, in Lake County, Florida, in 1949.[286] One of the four, Ernest Thomas, escaped from custody only to be hunted down and shot a reported four hundred times by an angry mob of one thousand men, which also burned and shot at the homes of several Black families. The remaining three boys were beaten until they confessed, all later convicted by all-White juries.[287] Two, Walter Irvin and Samuel Shepherd—both World War II veterans—were sentenced to death.[288] Charles Greenlee, then only sixteen years old, got life in prison.

In 1951, the US Supreme Court overturned the convictions of Irvin and Shepherd, who were represented by future Supreme Court Justice Thurgood Marshall. Shortly thereafter, Lake County sheriff Willis V. McCall shot both men while they were handcuffed, on the way to a court appearance. McCall posed for a photograph in front of their lifeless bodies, but later argued he acted in self-defense.[289] Shepherd died, but Irvin survived by pretending he was dead until others arrived. Irvin was retried and sentenced to death by an all-White jury. Governor Thomas LeRoy Collins later commuted his sentence to life in prison. Two years before the posthumous pardon, the Florida House of Representatives passed a resolution stating that the Groveland Four "were the victims of gross injustices and that their abhorrent treatment by the criminal justice system is a shameful chapter in this state's history."[290]

A final prominent example of a posthumous pardon to address racist history is Oklahoma governor Frank Keating's posthumous pardon in 1996 of John the Baptist ("J.B.") Stradford for his involvement in the 1921 Tulsa Race Massacre.[291] Born enslaved in Kentucky, Stradford was a Black businessman and community activist.[292] His "owner's" daughter taught him to read. In 1863, he read about President Lincoln's Emancipation Proclamation and forged a travel permission slip with his owner's signature, escaping to Stratford, Ohio.[293] Lacking a surname, he changed the "t" in Stratford to a "d" and adopted the name Stradford. After earning enough money to secure legal documentation declaring his family in Kentucky free, he enrolled in Oberlin College in Ohio and, along with his new wife, was one of the first two Black students to graduate from there. He went on to law school at Indiana University, and later began investing in business ventures.

When his first hotel went out of business, Stradford moved to the Greenwood district of Tulsa, Oklahoma, one of several rapidly growing, all-Black towns that were popping up in what was known as Indian Territory. Stradford formed a partnership with O. W. Gurley and began investing in land. Over the next eighteen years, he built homes, rooming houses, a sixteen-room apartment building, a hotel, pool halls, shoeshine parlors, and bathhouses, becoming the richest Black man in the city.[294] On August 4, 1916, the City of Tulsa passed an ordinance banning people of one race from residing on any block in which three-quarters or more of the residents were of a different race.[295] Stradford led six hundred Black citizens in a protest two days later, petitioning the mayor that the ordinance "cast a stigma upon the colored race in the eyes of the world, and . . . sap[ped] the spirit of hope for justice before the law from the race itself." The mayor was unmoved, and housing segregation remained the law in Tulsa until 1963.[296]

On the morning of May 30, 1921, a nineteen-year-old Black man named Dick Rowland was arrested on rumors he had assaulted a White woman, and fear spread that he would be lynched.[297] Stradford gathered a meeting of other Black residents that evening. A White mob eventually descended on Greenwood. Stradford's group fled to his hotel, which was showered with machine-gun fire. The National Guard arrived by morning to evacuate the neighborhood, telling Stradford and the others that the building would not be damaged further if they would surrender, which they did. The National Guard took $2,000 of Stradford's money and burned the hotel to the ground, along with all thirty-five blocks of Greenwood.[298] The riot lasted two days, killing three hundred people, most of them Black, and injuring hundreds more. More than one thousand Black-owned businesses and homes were destroyed.

A week later, Stradford and nineteen other men were charged with inciting a riot, an offense that carried a life sentence or the death penalty. He fled to Independence, Kansas, where local police arrested and booked him. He fled again, this time to Chicago, where he succeeded in fighting extradition to Tulsa and opened a candy store, barbershop, and pool hall. He died in 1935, but Keating did not officially drop the charges against Stradford through a pardon until 1996.

Posthumous pardons have also followed proof of a deceased's innocence.[299] In 1987, Nebraska governor Bob Kerry pardoned William Jackson Marion on the centennial of his hanging for the murder of a man, John Cameron. Having gone to Mexico in 1872, Cameron turned up alive four years after Marion's execution, proving Marion's innocence.[300] And in 2019, Illinois governor Bruce Rauner posthumously pardoned Grover Thompson, a Black man with a history of mental health issues who had been convicted of stabbing a seventy-two-year-old woman in 1981.[301] Thompson had been napping on a bench at the time of the attack and was wearing different clothes than the suspect. He was offered a deal to avoid the death penalty.[302] Confined to a wheelchair, he died in prison in 1996.[303] Rauner denied Thompson's clemency request in 2015 but changed course as one of his last moves before leaving office. A serial killer serving time for other murders later confessed to the crime. Thompson was also exonerated by DNA evidence.

Another famous example occurred in 2013, when the Alabama pardon board approved posthumous pardons for three of the men known as the Scottsboro Boys—eighty years after their wrongful conviction for raping two White women in 1931.[304] Posthumous pardons were not allowed in Alabama until the legislature amended the law seven months earlier. Five other boys had their convictions overturned in 1937, and a sixth was pardoned before his death in 1976. Their ages ranged from thirteen to nineteen at the time of their arrest following a fight that broke out on a Southern Railroad freight train during the Great Depression.[305] Ruby Bates and Victoria Price accused all nine of raping them on the train; Bates ultimately retracted her story. Harper Lee reportedly based her iconic book, *To Kill a Mockingbird* (1960), on the case.

In 2010, Texas governor Rick Perry for the first time in the state's history posthumously pardoned someone based on DNA evidence.[306] Tim Cole, a Black military veteran who was a student at Texas Tech, was wrongfully convicted of rape in 1985, and died in prison four-teen years later. DNA evidence from the original rape kit implicated another man, Jerry Wayne Johnson, who had begun writing letters confessing to the crime in 1995.[307] The judge who ordered Cole's criminal record expunged called it "the saddest case" he'd ever seen. In

2009, the Texas legislature passed the Tim Cole Act, which increased compensation for people who have been wrongfully convicted from $50,000 to $80,000 per year of imprisonment.[308] The same year, the victim, Michele Mallin, urged Congress to create a federal agency tasked with enhancing forensic science nationwide.[309] "One of the most troubling things I've learned is that juries often hear evidence that is not as solid as it sounds," she said.

Sometimes posthumous pardons are issued to remedy wrongful executions—the notion being that the punishment did not fit the crime. In 2005, the Georgia Board of Pardons and Paroles formally pardoned Lena Baker, the only woman executed in Georgia in the twentieth century.[310] The same body had denied her parole request, allowing her execution by electric chair in 1945, a move it later called "a grievous error, as this case called out for mercy." Baker, a Black woman, was sentenced to death by an all-White, all-male jury and executed for the murder of her employer, a sixty-seven-year-old White man named Ernest Knight who hired her to care for him. Baker claimed she shot Knight in self-defense after he locked her in a gristmill and threatened to shoot her if she tried to leave. "I am ready to meet my God," she said immediately before her death.[311]

Another example occurred in 2001, when Maryland governor Parris Glendening pardoned John Snowden, a Black man who went to the gallows in 1919 for the rape and murder of a pregnant White woman who was also the wife of a prominent businessman.[312] "The more I looked into it," Glendening said, "the more I said, 'Something's just not right here,'" describing his pardon as an effort "to correct a past inequity." Snowden testified that the police had threatened and physically abused him, and that the judge did not permit defense attorneys to impeach the credibility (in other words, challenge their veracity in the eyes of the jury) of two key witnesses.[313] The all-White jury convicted Snowden in twenty minutes.[314]

On the day of the hanging, the state militia patrolled Black neighborhoods and the Baltimore police set up armed reinforcements near the execution site. Snowden's last words were: "I have been imprisoned one year and six months and now am about to shake hands with time and welcome eternity, for in a few hours from now, I shall step out of time into eternity to pay the penalty of a crime I am not guilty of." Shortly after his execution, an anonymous letter writer claimed responsibility for the murder. Maryland delegate William H. Cole IV said of the case: "It illustrates once again that there are problems with our penal system and the implications for the death penalty."

The vast majority of posthumous pardons have been granted at the state level, an estimated 175 as of 2021, nearly 40 percent of those to Black people. President Bill Clinton granted the first posthumous pardon by a president in 1999 to Lt. Henry Ossian Flipper, a formerly enslaved man who went on to become the first Black person to graduate from the United States Military Academy at West Point in 1877.[315] At the time, he was also the only Black commissioned officer in the US Army, and the first to command regular troops (before then, even all-Black regiments were commanded by White officers). In 1881, he was dismissed for "conduct unbecoming an officer and gentleman," based on an allegation that he embezzled government funds from a quartermaster's safe that his superior officer asked him to keep in his quarters.[316] At his descendants' urging, a review in 1976 found that his court-martial and dismissal were "unduly harsh and unjust." Flipper's pardon came 118 years after his conviction.

In 2018, President Trump granted a posthumous pardon to Jack Johnson, a Black boxer who was convicted more than a century ago under the White Slave Traffic Act after crossing a state line with his White girlfriend.[317] Trump said the pardon was granted because of "what many view as racially motivated injustice." Yet Johnson had previously been refused a pardon by both presidents George W. Bush

181

and Barack Obama. The reasons for the refusals are complex, but among them it seems that Trump's predecessors followed the advice of the US Office of the Pardon Attorney. Trump, who apparently had Johnson's case brought to his attention by actor Sylvester Stallone, broke with tradition by not seeking the DOJ's advice.

Bear in mind that no state constitution explicitly endorses post-humous pardons, which are not mentioned in the US Constitution, either. As in the United States, British kings used them both to remedy erroneous convictions and for political purposes. In 1966, for example, Britain posthumously pardoned Timothy Evans for the murder of his wife and daughter. Three years after his execution in 1950, one of the prosecution's witnesses confessed to the crime and was hanged. And in 2013, Queen Elizabeth pardoned Alan Turing, a famous mathematician and codebreaker during World War II who died by suicide two years after his conviction in 1952 for homosexual conduct. His probation was conditioned on his agreement to undergo chemical castration.[318] Turing also lost his security clearance and was denied entry into the United States. It was the fourth royal pardon granted since the end of World War II. In the Policing and Crime Act of 2017, the British Parliament retroactively pardoned all convictions under historical legislation outlawing homosexual acts. (Turing is portrayed by actor Benedict Cumberbatch in the 2014 film, *The Imitation Game*.)[319]

As purely symbolic acts, posthumous pardons may have less to do with mercy, and more to do with politics. In this way, they share the same basis for another broad category of pardons: amnesties.

2

Amnesty and Mass Pardons

The word *amnesty* comes from the ancient Greek word *amnestia*, which means "forgetfulness" or "passing over."[320] Amnesty is a form of pardon extended to an entire group of people in hopes that former transgressions can be "passed over," often for political reasons, often for political reasons, such as to incentivize rebels to accept a new government.

Amnesty has ancient roots. The oldest recorded was by Thrasybulus, an Athenian general who, in 403 BC, led the democratic resistance to a short-lived oligarchy in Athens.[321] Athens had been a democracy for approximately one hundred years when it became embroiled in a war with Sparta for dominance over the Greek world. After a coup, an oligarchy controlled by a number of elite and wealthy

Athenians took hold of the city. Thrasybulus led a resistance to the new government, ultimately reestablishing democracy in Athens. To prevent a bloody reprisal, he later pushed through a law that pardoned all but a few of the oligarchs involved in the coup.

... AND WHY?

Amnesty dates back to 403 BC when, after reestablishing democracy in Athens following a war, a general pardoned most of the oligarchs involved. Are there downsides to amnesty pardons? Perhaps individual pardons are the real problem?

Amnesty pardons were used in medieval England, as well. In 1660, the English Parliament passed the Indemnity and Oblivion Act, which pardoned everyone who had committed crimes during the English Civil War in order "to bury all seeds of future discords"; it excluded crimes such as murder, rape, witchcraft, and participation in Charles I's regicide.[322] As readers will recall, the English Civil War (1642–1651) had determined how England, Scotland, and Ireland would be governed.[323] During that time, King Charles I was overthrown, tried for treason, and executed in 1649. His son, Charles II, was exiled to Scotland and France. From 1649 to 1659, during a period known as the "Interregnum" (between reigns), the English monarchy was replaced with a republican political structure known as the Commonwealth of England.[324] In 1660, Charles II was restored as monarch to the thrones of England, Ireland, and Scotland.[325] Parliament gave him an annual income to run the government.[326]

Despite having restored the Church of England and religious freedom for Catholics, Charles II failed to persuade Parliament to pardon individuals who separated from the Church of England. In 1672, he issued his own pardon, known as the Royal Declaration of Indulgence, which suspended the penal code against all religious dissenters. With the backing of the Protestants, Parliament rescinded the pardon in 1679.

Following his ascent to power on the heels of the French Revolution, on April 28, 1802, Napoleon Bonaparte similarly granted general amnesty for opponents who fled France. After the French Revolution began, nobles, clergy, and commoners left the country to join the armies of the foreign nations at war with France. Some of the armies were created by brothers of King Louis XVI, the last king of France, who lost his head by guillotine in 1793.[327] Others joined the fight against the Revolution. Although the French Constitution of 1795 provided for the perpetual banishment of those who left France, Napoleon pardoned nearly all of the approximately 150,000 people who fled, penalizing only around 1,000 of the worst offenders.[328] Napoleon publicly stated that he respected their courage despite their rebellion against the king: "True . . . they were or should have been bound to the cause of their King. France gave death to their action, and tears to their courage. All devotion is heroic."

In the early days of the American republic, President George Washington pardoned a group known as the Whiskey Rebels in 1795. Upset by heavy taxes, distillers and farmers in western Pennsylvania rebelled, spurring Washington to mobilize 13,000 troops. Following ratification of the US Constitution in 1789, the country's Secretary of the Treasury, Alexander Hamilton, had taken steps to fund the new American government and repay its debt incurred to finance the Revolutionary War.[329] As a leader of the Federalist political party, he advocated a strong federal government—in sharp contrast to the anarchy of the French Revolution—and believed that a federal liquor tax would enhance the financial power of the national government relative to the states.[330]

In January of 1791, Hamilton proposed an excise tax "upon spirits distilled within the United States" (i.e., whiskey), and a duty on imported spirits. Congress enacted his proposal and Washington signed it into law in 1791. Because the tax was levied on whiskey producers rather than consumers, farmers who distilled whiskey from their surplus corn crops opposed the tax. It took months to put down the rebellion.[331] Although two insurgents were later convicted of treason, which carried a death sentence, Washington—along with his ally, the governor of Virginia—pardoned everyone who participated in the rebellion. The amnesty was the first instance in which the constitutional pardon power was used by a US president, and Washington was widely acclaimed for his action.

President John Adams's subsequent pardon of three leaders of the Fries's Rebellion wasn't so well received.[332] In 1799, hundreds of farmers in Pennsylvania took up arms to force the release of a group of prisoners who had protested a federal property tax imposed to raise money for an anticipated war with France. Adams called on federal troops to arrest the insurgents, including their leader, John Fries, who was later convicted of treason and sentenced to hang. Adams pardoned Fries before his execution and declared a general amnesty for everyone involved in the rebellion. The decision turned fellow Federalist Alexander Hamilton against Adams and helped enable Thomas Jefferson to defeat Adams in the 1800 presidential election.

Once in office, Jefferson himself pardoned anyone convicted under the Alien and Sedition Acts, a set of four laws enacted in 1798 with the support of the Federalist Party.[333] Together, the laws granted the president unilateral authority to imprison and deport non-citizens associated with enemy nations. They also criminalized false or malicious criticism of the government, a law that today would be banned under the First Amendment.

Subsequent presidents granted amnesty pardons, as well. James Madison pardoned deserters from the War of 1812. As detailed previously, President James Buchanan pardoned Mormons after a massacre in 1858. And during the Civil War, in which a huge number of soldiers were conscripted, President Lincoln pardoned deserters if they agreed to rejoin the fight. Lincoln and President Andrew Johnson after him also pardoned Confederates after the Civil War, and Congress restored their right to vote and hold office under the General Amnesty Act of 1872.[334] That same year, in *Armstrong v. United States*, the Supreme Court recognized the president's ability to confer amnesty as part of the constitutional pardon power. (Whether the Civil War pardons actually succeeded in restoring peace within the fractured nation is another question.)[335]

In the twentieth century, President Gerald Ford created a clemency board to evaluate conditional pardons related to the Vietnam War.[336] In 1977, his successor, President Jimmy Carter, pardoned all Americans who evaded the draft. Approximately 30 percent of those who fought were drafted, and draft "dodgers" often fled to Canada or came up with ruses (like mental health issues or physical hardships) to avoid service. President Bill Clinton and Republican House Speaker Newt Gingrich (who purported an intention to sign up for ROTC), President George W. Bush (who dubiously landed a coveted slot in the Air Force Reserve), and Donald Trump (who claimed to have "bone spurs" on his feet) were among many criticized for avoiding the Vietnam War draft. Carter's pardon did not include the nearly 500,000 members of the military who went AWOL or deserted (i.e., went AWOL for over thirty days). The move was extremely controversial in terms of those whom Carter did, and did not, pardon. He lost his bid for reelection in 1980.

...AND WHY?

President Jimmy Carter's pardon of Vietnam War draft evaders may have helped cost him reelection. Does that suggest that individual pardons should trigger political checks, too?

Across the globe, amnesty pardons have been granted in the interests of a nation, or when the peace and stability of the country are of greater public and political benefit than the punishment of an individual. In early 2018, for example, the president of Egypt issued a pardon via Twitter to over three hundred people, many of whom were arrested for taking part in "unauthorized" protests against the government. The lower house of the Russian Parliament—known as the State Duma—issued legislative amnesties for former Chechen rebels in the 1993 uprising and deserters from the Russian army, as well.

France uses amnesties to decrease prison overcrowding, and this has become an annual event, particularly during the summer when extreme heat can give rise to prison revolts.[337] Thailand, home to the eleventh-highest international incarceration rate and the largest prison population in Southeast Asia, uses twice-annual mass pardons routinely because the country lacks a Western-style parole system.[338] Brazil, home to the fourth-largest prison population in the world, also uses annual mass pardons to alleviate overcrowding.[339] These pardons typically apply to certain nonviolent offenders who have served part of their sentences and can affect around 2 percent of the prison population each year. Morocco, Romania, Vietnam, Zambia, and Zimbabwe also use mass pardons to address prison overcrowding.

The Russian State Duma has granted amnesty for thousands of prisoners living in squalid prison conditions; its actions are immune from presidential veto. After Communist rule took hold in East Germany following the fall of Adolf Hitler, mass amnesties were revived to resolve labor shortages and "brain drains" of skilled laborers; 20,000 prisoners were pardoned in 1951 alone. And in 1972, nearly half the number of detainees in the East German prison system was released. In addition to relieving prison overcrowding, these amnesties "served primary socialist goals such as showing the power and paternalism of the State."

188

Some countries use mass pardons as a grand gesture of mercy to celebrate special holidays or observances. The Japanese cabinet has historically issued pardons on special occasions for imperial family matters.[340] In 2019, it pardoned 550,000 individuals convicted of minor offenses in order to mark the new emperor's enthronement. In Morocco, national and religious celebrations are usually accompanied by royal pardons.[341] In Iran, as well, the Supreme Leader, acting at the request of the head of the judiciary, pardons a number of prisoners on important religious and national holidays every year.[342] Upon assuming the throne in 2016, the king of Thailand pardoned approximately 150,000 prisoners by either shortening their sentences or sanctioning their immediate release, including those who had been jailed for insulting the royal family. China's constitution enables the state president to grant special amnesty on instruction of the legislative body, known as the National People's Congress, but there exists no formal clemency system accessible to individual petitioners or any criteria for deciding individual cases.[343] As a result, China has seen only sporadic uses of the special pardon, such as grants of pardons in large batches to mark grandiose occasions.[344]

The US Constitution contains no mention of amnesty or mass pardons. However, the Supreme Court has recognized that amnesty pardons serve public policy goals under the constitutional scheme that are separate from the exercise of mercy toward a particular individual. In *Biddle v. Perovich*, the Court in 1927 rejected a defendant's argument that President William Howard Taft's commutation of his death sentence to life in prison for a murder conviction in Alaska was ineffective.[345] The defendant, Vuco Perovich, preferred execution to life imprisonment and argued that a president cannot substitute one form of punishment for another without his consent. Rather than relying on mercy as justification for the president's action, the Court asserted that the pardon power is an act of public welfare, not a gift: "A pardon in our days is not a private act of grace from an individual happening to possess power. It is a part of the Constitutional scheme. When granted, it is the determination of the ultimate authority that the public welfare will be better served by inflicting less than what the judgment fixed."

The Court went so far as to suggest that a public policy rationale for a pardon could actually outweigh the interests of an individual defendant. If a life sentence would have been authorized by law, it reasoned, the president could impose that sentence even if "it affects the judgment" imposed under the criminal justice system because "the public welfare, not [the defendant's] consent, determines what shall be done." The Court distinguished its holding in *Burdick*, in which it found that a newspaper editor's consent was required to override the Fifth Amendment.[346] The Court has accordingly painted an expansive picture of the president's power to pardon, both for mercy and for the sake of the public interest. Whether this dual rationale for the pardon power encompasses pardons for other reasons—possibly even corruption—is the subject of the next section.

3

Favoritism and Corruption

The pardon power comes with enormous risks of abuse.[347] Pardons have been used to curry favor with voters, threaten political rivals, and silence individuals who might otherwise testify against a president or governor. Pardons issued to secure power or evade accountability are the very definition of corruption. Yet to a large degree, they are perfectly legal in the United States.

... AND WHY?
Favoritism, self-preservation, and possible corruption are now universally accepted grounds for a presidential pardon. How on earth can that be okay?

In 1912, for example, South Carolina governor Coleman Blease stood in front of a crowd of supporters and committed to pardoning a convicted murderer who had been sentenced to life in prison.[348] Governor Blease's commitment came with a guarantee to pardon *any* convict whom "the people" wanted pardoned so long as they ensured that he won the election. He won the election.[349] In a show of gratitude, he did extend executive clemency to the convicted murderer, along with thirty-three other convicts, in response to the support he received from his voters. Blease was the "gold standard" when it came to currying political favors, rewarding his friends, and punishing those who didn't act as he demanded. At one point, he wagered that if the legislature did not act on his prison reform demands, he would be willing to pardon every prisoner in the system.

Lame-Duck Presidents

Lame-duck presidents often make their most controversial pardon decisions shortly before leaving office, when the possibility of political retaliation has become obsolete.[350] Rather than being granted for the sake of mercy or to heal the nation, the most disturbing of such pardons have gone to people with lots of money, power, fame, and influence, or those who otherwise have a close relationship with the president. Worse, presidents have used the pardon power to protect a president from public embarrassment or criminal liability.[351]

The first president to prominently use the pardon power for what appeared to be corrupt purposes was George H. W. Bush. Before leaving office, he pardoned a slew of senior officials involved in the Iran–Contra scandal, effectively immunizing—or "pardoning"—himself from subsequent investigations because key witnesses no longer had an incentive to cooperate.[352] Bill Clinton granted nearly two hundred pardons on his final day in office, including to a number of his biggest political donors.[353]

In his last hours in office, Trump pardoned seventy-three people and issued seventy commutations.[354] This was a month after he pardoned Charles Kushner, the father of his son-in-law, Jared Kushner; Paul Manafort, chairman of his 2016 campaign; and Roger J. Stone Jr., his close advisor whose sentence he had commuted over the prior summer. After Trump pardoned Stone, Federal District Court Judge Amy Berman Jackson stated: "He was not prosecuted, as some have complained, for standing up for the president. He was prosecuted for covering up for the president."[355] Trump's eleventh-hour pardon recipients included Stephen K. Bannon, his former chief strategist who was charged with defrauding donors to a private fund that was supposed to be used to build new sections of a wall along the Mexican border.[356] Bannon had not been tried or convicted; Trump pardoned him based on the indictment alone. Trump also pardoned Elliott

Broidy, a leading fund-raiser for his 2016 campaign who pleaded guilty to charges of conspiracy, having essentially created a plan to violate foreign lobbying laws by pushing the Trump administration to extradite a Chinese dissident and drop an embezzlement case related to a Malaysian financier who paid Broidy $9 million.[357] Talk about corruption.

Trump granted clemency to several other political figures, celebrities, and high-net-worth individuals.[358] Although the press coverage was moderately spare, Trump's pardons put in bold relief the distortions inherent in the presidential pardon power, with clemency doled out to moneyed political supporters with access and influence, as well as personal or familial cronies, and even some individuals with suspicious foreign ties—with no apparently legitimate basis. The underlying crimes are often heinous, and by all appearances the criminal justice system had functioned appropriately and diligently. Politically motivated pardons thus reveal presidential conflicts of interest, putting a president's self-interest over norms of fairness and justice, and squandering the public resources spent securing valid convictions.

Political pardons also exacerbate existing income disparities inherent in the criminal justice system. The Sixth Amendment to the US Constitution establishes a right to counsel in criminal prosecutions, and under the 1966 ruling in *Miranda v. Arizona*, the Fifth Amendment's protection against compelled self-incrimination includes the right to counsel if you are arrested and interrogated.[359] But lawyers for the indigent vary in quality, depending on attorney workload and funding for a particular state's public defense system.[360] By contrast, people with money can hire good private lawyers, build strong defenses, and—in the case of clemency—reach powerful influencers in high places. Low-income individuals caught up in the criminal justice system are often left to defend themselves alone or through overworked or low-performing court-appointed counsel.

Moreover, the right to counsel only extends to criminal prosecutions that carry a sentence of imprisonment. While the Supreme Court has never answered whether the Sixth Amendment right attaches to bail hearings, a 2023 study conducted by the RAND Corporation found that providing defendants with legal counsel during their initial bail hearing significantly decreases the likelihood that they will be required to post bail or be detained in jail prior to trial.[361] This is important for low-income individuals whose inability to pay money as a precondition to being released before trial could keep them behind bars for months—before the government is required to prove its case beyond a reasonable doubt—undermining the adage of "innocent until proven guilty." While that right is only really "guaranteed" for people with money, the same calculus holds true for executive clemency. Those with money and influence have a greater chance of receiving an act of "mercy" from the president of the United States, as well.

More Trump Pardons

Here's but a handful of examples from Trump's final rounds of clemency decisions.[362] The list gives a sense of the depth and breadth of the unfairness and apparent corruption that the presidential pardon power tolerates.

- **Anthony Levandowski**, a pioneer of self-driving car technology, was sentenced to eighteen months in prison for stealing trade secrets from Google. Trump pardoned him.

- **Robert "Robin" Hayes**, a former chairman of the North Carolina Republican Party, pleaded guilty in 2019 to bribery, conspiracy to commit wire fraud, and making false statements. He was sentenced to one year probation. Trump fully pardoned him.

- **Rick Renzi**, a former Republican congressman for Arizona, was sentenced in 2013 to thirty-six months in prison for seventeen felonies—including extortion, bribery, insurance fraud, money laundering, and racketeering—arising from a 2005 promise to use his legislative influence regarding a federal land exchange involving a co-defendant's property.[363] Trump pardoned Renzi.

- **Randall Cunningham**, another ex-Republican congressman from California, was sentenced to eight years and four months in prison in 2006 for taking $2.4 million in bribes from military contractors. Cunningham was a Navy "TOPGUN" fighter pilot in Vietnam who pleaded guilty to taking bribes to fund a lifestyle that included yachts, hunting trips, and a Rolls-Royce.[364] Trump granted him a pardon conditioned on his continued good behavior.

- **Rapper Kodak Black** was sentenced to nearly four years in prison in 2019 after pleading guilty to lying on background check forms in buying guns that were later found at crime scenes with his fingerprints.[365] Trump commuted his sentence, half of which he had served.

- **Desiree Perez**, chief executive of rapper Jay-Z's music empire, Roc Nation, was convicted of a drug conspiracy in 1994 and sentenced to five years' probation and later served nine months in prison for a parole violation. Trump granted her a full pardon. Roc Nation manages major artists like Rihanna, Mariah Carey, Alicia Keys, Shakira, J. Cole, Big Sean, and Megan Thee Stallion, as well as programs like the Super Bowl halftime show.[366] This pardon may explain why so few Roc Nation artists campaigned on behalf of Democrats in the 2020 presidential race and the contested Georgia election for two US Senate seats.[367]

- **Michael Harris**, known as Harry-O, served thirty years of a twenty-five-years-to-life sentence for drug trafficking and conspiracy to commit first-degree murder. While in prison, he helped found Death Row Records, which became a major force in hip-hop, producing hits for artists like Dr. Dre, Snoop Dog, and Tupac. Snoop and other rappers lobbied for clemency, and Trump commuted his sentence.

- **Ken Kurson** is a close friend of Jared Kushner and associate of Rudy Giuliani who was arrested in 2020 on cyberstalking charges.[368] After Trump offered him a seat on the board of the National Endowment for the Humanities, an FBI background check uncovered harassment allegations following Kurson's 2015 divorce, and he withdrew his name from consideration. In 2013, when Kushner owned a weekly newspaper called the *New York Observer*, he appointed Kurson editor in chief. Kurson helped write a speech for the 2016 Trump campaign. Seven months later, Kurson was charged with two state eavesdropping felonies based on his alleged installation of spyware on his then-wife's computer.[369] Trump pardoned Kurson.

- **Hillel Nahmad**, who is from a wealthy New York family of art dealers, served five months in federal prison in 2014 for leading a sports-gambling ring with alleged ties to Russian-American organized crime figures.[370] Trump issued Nahmad a full pardon.

- **Albert J. Pirro Jr.**, a Republican businessman and ex-husband of Fox News commentator and staunch Trump supporter, Jeanine F. Pirro, was convicted in 2000 of tax evasion and conspiracy charges. At that time, he was also a known friend of Donald Trump, who pardoned him an hour before leaving office.

- **Sholam Weiss** is a New York businessman who was sentenced in 2000 to 845 years in prison—the longest federal term ever imposed—for racketeering, wire fraud, and money laundering related to an insurance fraud scheme that siphoned $450 million from the National Heritage Life Insurance Company that sold annuities to retirees who mostly lived in Florida.[371] The company ultimately collapsed. Weiss vanished during jury deliberations in Orlando and wound up on the FBI's most wanted list. After a two-year legal battle that spanned three continents, federal authorities managed to have him extradited from Vienna, Austria, in 2002.[372] The FBI worked with Brazilian, German, and Austrian police forces to track his girlfriend to Vienna, at times sending investigators disguised as mail carriers to some of the hotels where he maintained an expensive lifestyle. At the time of his extradition, he was believed to have controlled at least $250 million of the stolen money. Trump commuted his sentence on January 19, 2021, releasing Weiss from prison.

- **Dr. Salomon E. Melgen** is an ophthalmologist whose chain of Florida clinics fraudulently billed the federal Medicare program approximately $42 million after Medicare patients were falsely told they had eye diseases. Melgen was sentenced to seventeen years in prison in 2018.[373] Trump commuted his sentence after three years.

Trump also specifically dangled pardons before Michael Flynn and Paul Manafort during Robert Mueller's investigation, which might well have had the effect of silencing material witnesses in an investigation of Trump's own conduct.[374] According to the *Washington Post*, when aides balked at the legality of some of the steps Trump intended to take to build his promised border wall, the former president told officials, "Don't worry, I'll pardon you."[375] The Mueller Report revealed that after Michael Flynn initially agreed to cooperate with the government, "the President's personal counsel left a message for Flynn's attorneys reminding them of the President's warm feeling towards Flynn, which he said 'still remains,' and asking for a 'heads up' if Flynn knew 'information that implicates the President.'"[376] Trump later told the press: "I don't want to talk about pardons for Michael Flynn yet. We'll see what happens. Let's see. I can say this: When you look at what's gone on with the FBI and with the Justice Department, people are very, very angry."

The Mueller Report added that, while the jury was deliberating on whether to convict Manafort on eight counts of bank and tax fraud, "the President praised Manafort in public, said that Manafort was being treated unfairly, and declined to rule out a pardon." After Manafort was convicted, "the President called Manafort 'a brave man' for refusing to 'break' and said that 'flipping' 'almost ought to be outlawed.'" Mueller concluded that "The President and his personal counsel made repeated statements suggesting that a pardon was a possibility for Manafort, while also making it clear that the President did not want Manafort to 'flip' and cooperate with the government." Then there's Roger Stone, who publicly refused to cooperate with the government's investigation. The Mueller Report recounted that Trump "called Stone 'very brave' and said he had 'guts!' for not 'testify[ing] against Trump.'" All three men were eventually pardoned. Only Manafort served any jail time.

4

From Presidents to Kings:
A Self-Pardon?

Donald Trump is the first president to realistically present the country with the possibility of a self-pardon.[377] It remains to be seen whether Trump issued himself a pardon for potential crimes committed in office, even if he claims he did nothing wrong. At the start of the 2024 election year, Trump faced four separate indictments: one in New York state court related to his alleged payment of hush money to porn star Stormy Daniels; a second in Florida related to his mishandling of classified documents after he left office; a third in Washington, DC, regarding his role in the plot to overturn the 2020 presidential election; and a fourth in Fulton County, Georgia, pertaining to his efforts to overturn Biden's 2020 win in the state.[378] (One or more of these cases might have gone to trial by the time this book is published.) These indictments present the possibility, at least in theory, that Trump could pull out the self-pardon to immunize himself from criminal liability. Whether a self-pardon during office would protect a president from criminal liability after leaving office has never been tested, although Richard Nixon reportedly considered it.[379] Governors have pardoned themselves, including the first governor of the Territory of Washington in the Pacific Northwest, Isaac Stevens, who had declared martial law and closed the courts after a judge questioned an executive order he issued.[380] Whether the Supreme Court would uphold a president's self-pardon is difficult to predict.

No court has considered the question of whether presidents can pardon themselves, even for crimes committed in the Oval Office. Article I, Section 3 of the Constitution states of impeachment, which is the most attainable remedy for presidential wrongdoing in office, that "the party convicted shall nevertheless be liable and subject to indictment, trial, judgment and punishment, according to law."[381] Given that impeachments cannot be pardoned under Article II, the impeachment language—which makes former presidents subject to the criminal laws for impeachable conduct—could be read to suggest that crimes related to impeachments cannot be pardoned, either. Trump was impeached for his role in the January 6th insurrection, with the House of Representatives charging him with "incitement of insurrection" against the US government and "lawless action at the Capitol."[382] Arguably, then, any crimes arising from the same conduct would be immune from a self-pardon.

In addition, Section 3 of the Fourteenth Amendment holds that "[n]o person shall . . . hold any office, civil or military, under the United States . . . who, having previously taken an oath . . . to support the Constitution of the United States, shall have engaged in insurrection or rebellion against the same, or given aid or comfort to the enemies thereof."[383] A self-pardon for Trump's actions listed in the January 6th indictment could clash with the Supreme Court's long-standing recognition that pardons cannot undermine other parts of the Constitution.[384] The Justice Department's Office of Legal Counsel opined in August of 1975—during Nixon's presidency—that "[u]nder the fundamental rule that no one may be a judge in his own case, the President cannot pardon himself." Constitutionally legitimizing a self-pardon for January 6th should therefore be unthinkable. (At least, one would hope.)

In justifying a broad pardon power for the president, Alexander Hamilton assuaged detractors in *Federalist* No. 69 by saying that the president's power would be "much inferior" to that of the despised King George III.[385] "The person of the King of Great Britain is sacred and inviolable," he explained, as "[t]here is no constitutional tribunal to which he is amenable; no punishment to which he can be subjected without involving the crisis of a national revolution." Whether Hamilton was correct, or whether modern presidents have in fact become kings, is a question that Trump's record of epic wrongdoing in office has forced the country to face head-on, once again.

It bears worth mentioning, too, that at the Constitutional Convention, the Framers debated adding "after conviction" as a condition to the pardon power, but decided against it on the rationale that pardons before conviction might be necessary to obtain the testimony of accomplices to a crime—something that is routinely accomplished today by prosecutorial grants of immunity to cooperating witnesses, without resorting to pardons. President Gerald Ford's famous preemptive pardon of Nixon before indictment or conviction was never tested in the courts. Nonetheless, it set a historical standard for pre-conviction pardons, which rarely occur outside the United States. No state constitution mentions self-pardons. Under state constitutions that require consultation with the legislature or another government body, a self-pardon is impossible. Self-pardons did not exist in England, either, because in theory the king could not commit a crime against himself. And while impeachment is a feasible response to a self-pardon, that assumes a president is still in office. Once he leaves, impeachment no longer applies. It would be up to the criminal justice system and the courts—versus Congress—to decide whether a presidential self-pardon is legally sound or whether the adage that "no one is above the law" holds true in America.

Part IV

Who Cares?
The Future of the Pardon Power

Because the pardon power is express in the Constitution, debating the question of whether it should continue to exist is an exercise in hypotheticals. It would take a constitutional amendment to abolish it. That said, given its implications for democracy, it's important to have a conversation around whether the president's pardon power serves any remaining purpose in the twenty-first century. One thing is for certain: It can ignite political controversy—in part because it's viewed as an outdated, archaic power, and also because it has repeatedly been abused. Increasingly, the pardon power has been used to stoke the flames of hyper-partisanship that threaten the country's stability.

As a matter of logic, an unlimited pardon power makes little sense in a system of laws.[386] If a pardon is needed, it means the law or procedures underlying the conviction got things wrong. If the law and procedures were fair and just, then the opposite must be true: Pardons that erase how that system operated to produce a particular conviction are wrong. It's either one or the other.

... AND WHY?
**If pardons are needed for mercy, why not change the law and
rules governing the criminal justice system to enhance fairness?
What legitimate role is the presidential pardon power
even playing anymore?**

204

Even in a system where certain pardons get it right as a matter of mercy and justice, because an individual fitting a certain profile—remorseful, able to contribute to society, maybe even convicted or sentenced unjustly—merits a pardon, then why shouldn't *everyone* fitting that profile get a pardon, too? DNA evidence has changed the game in this respect. If mercy were the animating rationale for modern-day pardons, shouldn't the government consider paying for DNA tests for every individual in prison—or on death row, at the very least—who could potentially be exonerated by DNA evidence? If exonerated by DNA evidence, folks should get automatic pardons. But that's not how the system works anywhere in the United States.

Does a pardon forgive the offender or the offense? The pardon power offers no answer. If the pardon power is about mercy, it's the person who is pardoned. On that theory, every person in similar circumstances should get one. If a pardon is for amnesty, then maybe it's the offense that gets pardoned. But even so, that's something that legislators can probably address by changing the underlying criminal laws to heal a national wound. The president does not need to have that power, except perhaps during times of war. Congress could make that clear in the federal criminal code.

What if it's sheer power, influence, or favoritism that motivates a pardon? Consider former California governor Jerry Brown's 2015 pardon of actor Robert Downey Jr., who served a one-year prison sentence for charges related to a traffic stop that included possession of narcotics and the unlicensed possession of a concealed firearm.[387] Downey Jr. went on to play the Marvel megastar, Ironman. Brown's stated reason for the pardon was the actor's "'good conduct' since leaving prison more than fifteen years ago." Lots of inmates across the country can make the same claim, but they have no prayer of seeing a pardon. Whether Downey Jr.'s was done to remedy some injustice, or whether his privileged status as an A-List movie star contributed to Brown's decision, is impossible to know.

More troubling is the tale of Ben Pogue, owner of a Texas construction company who lent his private jet to Donald Trump's reelection campaign in the fall of 2019.[388] Months later, Trump pardoned Pogue's father, Paul Pogue, who pleaded guilty to filing false tax returns in 2010 and received a sentence of three years' probation. Ben Pogue donated over $385,000 to Trump's reelection bid, including $100,000 worth of private air travel. There is no law expressly banning pardons for money. Although they could conceivably qualify as a bribe, establishing that precedent would require a prosecutor willing to bring that charge, which is virtually impossible to fathom given the broad assumption that the president's power to pardon is unlimited. Few prosecutors would want to take on that challenge only to be potentially defeated in the US Supreme Court on a theory of broad constitutional immunity for presidential pardons (although immunity should not apply to pardons used for bribes).

In May 2023, a former director of business development for Rudy Giuliani, Noelle Dunphy, filed suit against Giuliani in New York state court, seeking $10 million in damages for sexual assault, harassment, and wage theft, among other claims.[389] In her seventy-page complaint, Dunphy alleges that Giuliani told her he could break the law because "I have immunity."[390] She then asserts:

> He also asked Ms. Dunphy if she knew anyone in need of a pardon, telling her that he was selling pardons for $2 million, which he and President Trump would split. He told Ms. Dunphy that she could refer individuals seeking pardons to him, so long as they did not go through "the normal channels" of the Office of the Pardon Attorney, because correspondence going to that office would be subject to disclosure under the Freedom of Information Act.

Although Dunphy does not claim to have information that Giuliani managed to sell pardons, the allegations are serious, particularly given Giuliani's suggestion that Trump would "split" the profits from the sale of pardons. Giuliani reportedly said of the Mueller investigation, "When the whole thing is over, things might get cleaned up with some presidential pardons."[391]

During Trump's final months in office, his son-in-law Jared Kushner (whose father also got a pardon from Trump) reportedly managed an "avalanche" of clemency requests coming into the White House.[392] A source told the *Huffington Post*, "The ones who are going to get pardoned and get to the top of the list are the ones who have representatives, staff or counsel that were loyal to the president." Only a small fraction of Trump's pardons came with the recommendation of the DOJ's pardon attorney (a different source denied that Kushner played a key role in Trump's final round of pardons). Pay-to-play pardons have no legitimate role in our constitutional structure, which assumes some measure of accountability for office holders, whether that comes through the courts or the ballot box. If presidents can easily secure money and favors in exchange for pardoning criminal acts, the Constitution's pardon clause is merely a tool of corruption and abuse—certainly not what the Framers had in mind in rejecting the unlimited monarchy of King George III.[393]

These days, the pardon power may be taking on a different but equally sinister role as the country leans toward authoritarianism. Take Texas, for example. On July 25, 2020, Daniel Perry killed Black Lives Matter (BLM) protester Garrett Foster at a demonstration in Austin, Texas.[394] Foster, who was White, attended the protest with his fiancée, Whitney Mitchell, a Black woman and quadruple amputee.[395] He was carrying an AK-47 rifle, as allowed under Texas law.[396] Reportedly, Perry accelerated his car toward a crowd of protesters, including Foster, who then approached the vehicle in an effort to get him to stop. Perry shot Foster and was later indicted on murder charges. At trial, Perry's attorneys argued that he acted in self-defense under Texas's "stand your ground" law, which says there is no duty to retreat from an attacker before resorting to lethal force in perceived self-defense.[397] According to Perry's attorneys, after motioning for Perry to roll his window down, Foster raised his assault rifle. However, at least three witnesses testified at trial that Foster was pointing his rifle down toward the ground when he approached Perry's vehicle.[398] Perry was convicted of murdering Foster on April 7, 2023, and sentenced to twenty-five years in prison.

Almost immediately after Perry's conviction, and before sentencing, Texas governor Greg Abbott announced his intention to pardon Perry. After requesting that the state Board of Pardons and Paroles expedite a review of the case, Abbott took to Twitter to say that he would approve a pardon from the Board "as soon as it hits [his] desk." Under the Texas constitution, the governor may pardon someone only if the seven-member board first recommends it. (Abbott appointed all seven members of the current board.) Travis County District Attorney José Garza called Abbott's intervention "deeply troubling" and vowed to "continue to fight to uphold the rule of law." At Perry's May 10, 2023, sentencing, the board was continuing to investigate. As of December that year, no pardon had issued.

Abbott is not the only one unhappy about the jury's verdict. Prominent conservatives expressed their outrage and pressured Abbott to interfere.[399] Former Fox News host Tucker Carlson called Perry's conviction a "legal atrocity," and Matt Rinaldi, the chairman of the Texas Republican Party, believes Perry should never have been prosecuted. Carlson similarly backed Kyle Rittenhouse, the seventeen-year-old who killed two BLM protesters in Kenosha, Wisconsin, on August 25, 2020. Rittenhouse was later acquitted, saying he "had to maintain order when no one else would."[400] Then-candidate for the House of Representatives Marjorie Taylor Green (R-GA) called him an "innocent child." *New York Times* columnist Jamelle Bouie wrote that one of "the most troubling aspects of the shooting was the almost jubilant reaction of conservative media to the news that someone had taken the law into his own hands and meted out lethal force."

Given the conservative base's response to Kyle Rittenhouse's actions, Abbott's instinct to announce a pardon immediately upon Perry's conviction for murdering a BLM protester should come as no surprise. It suggests that the next decade could unveil a new, regular use for the pardon power as a tool for winning votes by freeing people convicted of crimes that conform to a certain political ideology.

Former president Donald Trump has also discussed the possibility of pardoning the January 6th insurrectionists since the final days of his presidency.[401] As of January 6, 2024, over 1,265 people have been charged in connection with the January 6th attack, including 452 individuals whose charges include "assaulting, resisting, or impeding officers or employees."[402] According to two former advisors, between January 6th and President Joe Biden's inauguration in January 2021, Trump considered issuing a blanket pardon for all rioters. Trump has repeated this idea numerous times since.

On September 1, 2022, Trump told conservative radio host Wendy Bell that he would "very, very strongly" consider issuing "full pardons with an apology to many [of the rioters]" if he won the 2024 presidential election.[403] He also told Bell that he is financially supporting some of the defendants, although he declined to provide details about how. In late December 2022, the House committee investigating January 6th released transcripts detailing how Trump continued to discuss blanket pardons for those charged in relation to January 6th.[404] Trump's director of personnel, Johnny McEntee, said in an interview with the House committee that in his final days in office, Trump discussed pardoning "the people that weren't violent," who "just walked in the building."

During CNN's town hall on May 10, 2023, Trump again said that he would pardon "a large portion" of the rioters, but that he would need to look at individual cases, because "a couple of them . . . got out of control."[405] He has claimed that the rioters are being treated unfairly and that it is impossible for them to receive a fair trial. In a 2021 interview, he said that the January 6th rioters are "great people." On CNN he said they "were there with love in their heart," and that it was "a beautiful day."

Trump undoubtedly knows that the denial of the legitimacy of the 2020 presidential election (what people call "The Big Lie") prompted the January 6th insurrection. He also knows that it's an important piece of his presidential platform for 2024.[406] In the 2022 midterms, numerous Republican candidates who embraced the lie that the 2020 election was rigged to favor Joe Biden were reelected at the state and federal levels.[407] In some cases, they ascended to a higher office, including former House Speaker Kevin McCarthy, one of 147 House Republicans who voted to discard the Electoral College vote in January of 2021.

Republican consultant Alex Conant told *Politico*, of Florida governor Ron DeSantis's chances of winning the GOP nomination in lieu of Trump, "If a candidate can't dispose of a fake issue like who won the election, how can voters expect them to handle the real issues?"[408] Trump's promise to pardon those convicted of crimes around January 6th is meant to rally voters to remedy the perceived injustice of 2020, thrusting the pardon power onto center stage for the 2024 presidential election cycle, with enormous implications for democratic governance.

As Gabriel Schoenfeld, a senior fellow at the Niskanen Center, wrote for *The Bulwark*:

> If Trump were to pardon ... many of the ... roughly one thousand January 6th defendants, Trump will be in a position to forge what amounts to a personal militia, whose members, grateful and loyal to him, will have license to work his will outside of the law, secure in the knowledge that they will be pardoned, including for felonies as serious as sedition.[409]

1

Protect the Pardon Power?

Traditionally, the pardon power existed as a responsible way to correct errors in the criminal justice system, and its use as a means of showing mercy to the deserving is arguably a reason that it should be preserved. In medieval England, however, Naomi D. Hurnard has explained, "[i]t was scarcely ever available to those condemned to death in error, but in other respects it was grossly overemployed," mainly out of political necessity.[410] The king obtained military recruits in exchange for a pardon. The monarch also granted pardons to those who deserved mercy, but only if they realized they needed a pardon and took steps to secure one.

In 1249, for example, a four-year-old girl named Katherine Passeavant was imprisoned in the abbot of St. Albans's jail after opening a door and accidentally pushing a younger child into a vat of hot water. The child later died. Katherine's father immediately brought the matter to the king, who directed the sheriff to deliver her a pardon. Although Katherine might have obtained the same outcome through the justice system, her father was one of "many people who found themselves in this situation and could afford to pay something for it, [and] sought clemency at once" because "they did not care to bank on the court[s]."

In 1272, by comparison, two men sat together on a bench that collapsed under their weight. One man's knife slipped from its sheath and fatally cut his companion. The man fled, and the king's justices ordered him outlawed. Had he not fled in panic, he might have been spared a life of outlawry by seeking a pardon.

Today, the pardon power works in much the same way. It can literally mean the difference between liberty or imprisonment, or life versus death, in a system that does not always produce fair or just outcomes. But it works much better for people who have money, power, and access to good advocates than it does for low-income or otherwise disenfranchised individuals, however deserving they may be of mercy. This blind spot is a problem, and one that the Supreme Court has almost cynically overlooked in addressing another stopgap in the criminal justice system: the writ of habeas corpus, which gives courts (versus the president) the power to show mercy in certain criminal cases.

In medieval Latin, *habeas corpus* literally means "to have the body." Whereas a criminal trial assesses whether the government has enough evidence to prove beyond a reasonable doubt that a defendant committed a crime, and the process of appealing a conviction determines whether the evidence was sufficient, and the law and trial procedures were properly followed, habeas corpus is available as a *separate* civil action. It does not address the conviction; rather, it challenges the government's ability to detain a person against their will. The notion is that the police cannot sweep people off the street for no reason and with no evidence simply "because."

The Constitution does not expressly establish a right to habeas corpus, but it does assume it exists, providing in Article I, Section 9, Clause 2 that "The Privilege of the Writ of Habeas Corpus shall not be suspended, unless when in Cases of Rebellion or Invasion the public Safety may require it." Although it's generally believed that only Congress can constitutionally take that action, President Lincoln suspended the writ during the Civil War in order to maintain order after declaring martial law; Congress later enacted a statute permitting his action.[411] The writ has been suspended three additional times in the history of the nation—in certain counties in South Carolina that were overrun by the Ku Klux Klan during the post–Civil War period of Reconstruction; in two provinces in the Philippines that were under American rule during an insurrection in 1905; and in Hawaii after the Japanese bombed Pearl Harbor.[412]

Congress has passed a number of federal statutes creating a complex scheme governing prisoner claims of unlawful detention, with the Supreme Court following up with a dizzying series of opinions interpreting the scope and availability of habeas corpus. In a case called *Harris v. Nelson*, the Court explained that the "writ of habeas corpus is the fundamental instrument for safeguarding individual freedom against arbitrary and lawless state action" and must be "administered with the initiative and flexibility essential to ensure that miscarriages of justice within its reach are surfaced and corrected."[413]

Reading this statement, one might wonder why the pardon power is simultaneously necessary as a means of showing mercy. If the arrest, indictment, trial, and appeal processes all have numerous constitutional and other safeguards, and the "Great Writ" exists as an added measure to ensure that no prisoner is being unlawfully detained, isn't the pardon power redundant? But this critique of the pardon power assumes that habeas corpus is a viable mechanism for relief, when in fact numerous procedural and evidentiary hurdles have been erected that make it very difficult for prisoners to win their claims.

In a case called *Herrera v. Collins*, the Supreme Court in 1993 minimized the availability of habeas corpus to catch things that fall through the cracks in criminal cases. Why? Somewhat remarkably, it reasoned that the pardon power exists to fill in gaps that the writ of habeas corpus—as interpreted by the Court—leaves unaddressed. The case involved Leonel Torres Herrera, who was convicted of murder and sentenced to death in January 1982. He appealed his conviction and lost. He also filed a habeas petition in federal court and lost that, too. Then, ten years after his conviction, Herrera filed a second federal habeas petition arguing that he was actually innocent of the murder. He cited the Eighth Amendment's ban on cruel and unusual punishment and the Fourteenth Amendment's Due Process Clause, claiming that they forbade the execution of an innocent man. As proof, he submitted sworn statements from an eyewitness to the crime and a number of witnesses who said that Herrera's brother, now dead, confessed to the murder. Writing for the Supreme Court, the late Chief Justice William Rehnquist flatly stated that Herrera "urges us to hold that this showing of innocence entitles him to relief in this federal habeas petition. We hold that it does not."[414]

The Court did not assess the veracity of the affidavits or decide that, as a matter of fact, Herrera did commit the murder and thus was not actually innocent—despite acknowledging that "the central purpose of any system of criminal justice is to convict the guilty and free the innocent." Instead, Rehnquist wrote that "claims of actual innocence based on newly discovered evidence have never been held to state a ground for federal habeas relief absent an independent constitutional violation occurring in the underlying state criminal proceeding." In other words, being innocent is not enough to evade the death chamber. Herrera had to show that his constitutional rights were somehow *also* violated by the process. "Once a defendant has been afforded a fair trial and convicted of the offense for which he is charged," Rehnquist wrote, "the presumption of innocence disappears." The government proved its case beyond a reasonable doubt. If it turns out that it didn't have the facts right, so long as the government presented its case in a manner consistent with the Constitution, Herrera is out of luck. The death sentence stands.

The Court acknowledged Herrera's argument that "this case is different because he has been sentenced to death." But the fact that he could be executed for a crime he did not commit makes no difference as a matter of federal habeas law, it concluded. The answer instead, Rehnquist wrote, is that "under Texas law, petitioner may file a request for executive clemency," which is "rooted in our Anglo-American tradition of law, and is the historic remedy for preventing miscarriages of justice where judicial process has been exhausted." He went on to proclaim that "Executive clemency has provided the 'fail safe' in our criminal justice system," despite the "unalterable fact that our judicial system, like the human beings that administer it, is fallible. But history is replete with examples of wrongfully convicted persons who have been pardoned in the wake of after-discovered evidence establishing their innocence."

Justice Harry Blackmun wrote a dissenting opinion, in which Justices John Paul Stevens and David Souter joined. "The Eighth Amendment prohibits 'cruel and unusual punishments,'" he responded. "This proscription is not static but rather reflects evolving standards of decency. . . . I think it is crystal clear that the execution of an innocent person is at odds with contemporary standards of fairness and decency." And because "[a] pardon is an act of grace," Blackmun added, "one thing is certain: The possibility of executive clemency is *not* sufficient to satisfy the requirements of the Eighth and Fourteenth Amendments. . . . The vindication of rights guaranteed by the Constitution has never been made to turn on the unreviewable discretion of an executive official or administrative tribunal."

Blackmun hit the nail on the head. The pardon power is discretionary, unpredictable, lacking in procedures and transparency, and its exercise is not subject to any review or oversight. The president is utterly unaccountable if he grants unfair, corrupt, or possibly even illegal pardons. Wrote Blackmun: "The execution of a person who can show that he is innocent comes perilously close to simple murder."

Recall that the Texas governor makes pardon decisions based on recommendations by a board whose members serve six-year terms and are appointed by the governor. Pardons for innocence are allowed, but in order to be considered, a person must provide the board with "either evidence of actual innocence from at least two trial officials, or the findings of fact and conclusions of law from a district judge indicating actual innocence."[415] Likewise, the standards for commuting a sentence from death to life in prison in Texas require a "written recommendation of a majority of the applicant's trial officials in the county of conviction, stating that the penalty now appears to be excessive and recommending a definite term, based on new information not before the judge or jury at trial or a statutory change in the penalty."[416]

With his witness affidavits, Herrera had none of what Texas now requires in order to file a pardon application. By presenting evidence of innocence by "trial officials," the State of Texas is referring to the current prosecuting attorney, judge, sheriff, or chief of police of the agency from the county and court that arrested the person seeking clemency. As a practical matter, it means the prisoner must persuade the agency that arrested, tried, and convicted him that they were wrong, and that they should take the time to say so in writing just so the clemency application can be submitted. Even then, there's no guarantee that the board, let alone the governor, will grant it. Of course, these hurdles are insurmountable without money for high-profile lawyers and access to influential people in Washington, DC, or close to the state governor's office. For Herrera, because the

216

trial was over and he had exhausted all appeals, he had no way of alternatively obtaining a written decision by a district judge stating he was innocent based on the newly discovered evidence about his brother's confession.

The Supreme Court's rationale for tolerating the possibility of an innocent man's execution falls apart with one glance at facts on the ground about the feasibility of obtaining a pardon. Given the barriers to obtaining a pardon for people without money and powerful friends, the mercy justification for a pardon holds no water. It may not have done so in medieval England. It certainly does not do so now.

2

Narrow the Pardon Power?

Mercy-based pardons are also problematic because they lack the procedural mechanisms binding the criminal justice systems that landed an individual in jail. Those prosecutions were initiated by individuals within the executive branch of government who enforce the law (police and prosecutors) pursuant to criminal statutes enacted by legislatures. Judges oversaw the convictions before juries, assessed and accepted plea agreements, and issued sentences. In many states, those sentences were reassessed by parole boards, which may be entities that are autonomous, or separate from the executive branch with support from a department of corrections, or they may be part of the executive branch of government. Parole boards follow procedures for assessing whether inmates should be released from prison and

218

providing for supervision post-release. The name comes from the French word *parole*, meaning "word," or "word of honor"—as if a parolee gives his promise to abide by the law in exchange for release.

In contrast to parole and probation, which are awarded by judges, often within the confines of statutory provisions, a pardon can be granted by the executive alone and has much fewer limitations. A pardon represents an exit from the judicial system, which was responsible for the conviction and the appeals, and circles back to the power of the executive branch, which is headed by governors.

But is a pardon actually an executive function, given that the arrest, indictment, prosecution, and maybe even parole proceedings are long over? Or is it a judicial one? If it's a president or governor exercising the pardon power, it involves a single decision-maker weighing the facts and the law and rendering a judgment. Ideally, judges are politically and ideologically neutral (federal judges are appointed for life for that reason, while many state judges are elected). And judges are bound by the rules of civil and criminal procedure, as well as rules of evidence. They don't often get to make decisions as to criminal guilt or innocence; those are made by jurors from the accused's community. If it's a quasi-judicial power, shouldn't pardons be bound by some sort of rules to ensure fairness and evenhandedness? Alternatively, one could argue that a pardon functions like legislation, because it reflects a policy judgment that a certain law should not take effect.

In 1916, the Supreme Court took aim at judges' ability to suspend a sentence as a measure of mercy and justice, suggesting that such powers belong exclusively to the executive under the pardon power. In *Ex parte U.S.*, a federal prosecutor challenged a district judge's "permanent suspension" of a criminal sentence for embezzlement of money from a bank.[417] The defendant had pleaded guilty and was sentenced to five years in prison. The judge suspended the sentence "during the good behavior of the sentence" permanently, and "absolutely removed the accused from the operation of the punishment provided by the statute," which amounted to "a refusal to carry out the statute" underlying the conviction. The prosecutor argued that the judge could temporarily suspend the sentence pending other judicial proceedings, but not altogether. The defendant's option was to apply for a pardon.

The Court agreed with the government, holding that what the lower court did "amounts to a refusal by the judicial power to perform a duty resting upon it." It nonetheless stayed any action on the lower court's decision "so as to afford ample time for executive clemency . . . to meet the situation." Thus, as with the writ of habeas corpus, the Supreme Court took the position that clemency operates as an essential mechanism "to cure wrongs" that caused "misery and anguish and miscarriage of justice . . . to many innocent persons." Courts are, by comparison, restrained from helping to cure those situations.

But it's odd that the executive would have greater powers to address "the mistaken exercise of power" in connection with execution and adjudication of the laws under the criminal justice system. With pardons, there's a fundamental conflict with the notion that the same person who executes the law is the person to make final decisions as to whether an accused should be punished for the crime charged, and how severely. The president is the head of the Department of Justice. He appoints the attorney general and many people serving in deputy positions. The DOJ houses numerous subagencies, including agencies with law enforcement power, meaning they operate as the federal government's police force. They include the Bureau of Alcohol, Tobacco, Firearms and Explosives; the Drug Enforcement Administration; the Federal Bureau of Investigation; the Federal Bureau of Prisons (which has its own federal officers with arrest authority); and the US Marshals Service. And of course, the DOJ has federal prosecutors whose job it is to charge people and organizations with federal crimes. So the president, through his subordinates, can arrest people and prosecute them before judges and juries, sending many to jail—or even death row. The pardon power gives the prosecutor the power to step into the shoes of the judge or jury and change the outcome of the criminal case that he, through his employees, brought in the first place. It feels like a conflict of interest, doesn't it?

Remember, too, that the Supreme Court has relied heavily on English common law in interpreting US law, including the pardon power under the US Constitution. In a famous case known as Dr. Bonham's case, the English Court of Common Pleas decided in 1610 that the College of Physicians could not wear both hats—it could not act as a prosecutor and a court in the same case. Thomas Bonham was a trained medical doctor who was rejected from the College of Physicians, a professional membership organization founded by royal charter from King Henry VII in 1518. He applied again. This time, the College's rejection came with a fine and a threat of imprisonment if he continued to practice. Dr. Bonham kept practicing and was arrested and put in prison. The College sued him to collect a fine, claiming that, as part of its royal charter as the medical licensing authority, it was free to decide who could practice medicine and to punish those who practiced without a license. The majority of the court sided with Dr. Bonham, condemning the statutes that gave the College the power to act as both a party and a judge.

With a pardon, that's precisely what happens: The president, or a governor, is both the party to the underlying criminal case—that is, the state prosecution—and the ultimate "judge" of whether the conviction and punishment will stand. Of course, England also had a pardon power. But that was for kings and queens, which a president is most definitely not. Rejection of an unlimited hereditary monarchy was the very basis of the American Revolution. During the Constitutional Convention, George Mason took issue with the fact that the proposed Constitution "would give the President . . . the unrestrained power of granting pardons for treason, which may be sometimes exercised to screen from punishment those whom he had secretly instigated to commit the crime, and thereby prevent a discovery of his own guilt."[418] Mason's statement showed an apprehension about the potential for the executive branch to misuse the pardon power for personal or political reasons.

While there is no singular legal definition of a "corrupt" pardon, it would presumably include one that is self-serving, shows favoritism, or interferes with a criminal investigation, particularly one that could implicate the president. Many of President Trump's pardons meet this definition. There was speculation that Paul Manafort and Mike Flynn were offered pardons in exchange for loyalty to Trump in connection with Special Counsel Robert Mueller's probe into Russia's assistance to the Trump campaign in the 2016 presidential election. In his report, Mueller wrote: "Many of the president's acts directed at witnesses, including discouragement of cooperation with the government and suggestions of possible future pardons, occurred in public view."[419]

When asked by Vermont Senator Patrick Leahy, a Democrat, whether "a president can lawfully issue a pardon in exchange for the recipient's promise not to incriminate him," former attorney general Bill Barr, who served in the Trump administration, replied, "No, that would be a crime."[420] He repeated that sentiment three times during his 2019 confirmation hearings. Then-Republican Senator Ben Sasse of Nebraska called Trump's pardons of such loyalists "rotten to the core," and referred to Roger Stone and Paul Manafort as "felons" who "flagrantly and repeatedly violated the law and harmed Americans." Adam Schiff of California, the Democratic member of the House of Representatives who led the first impeachment trial of Trump, said: "During the Mueller investigation, Trump's lawyer floated a pardon to Manafort. Manafort withdrew his cooperation with prosecutors, lied, was convicted, and then Trump praised him for not 'ratting.' Trump's pardon now completes the corrupt scheme." Schiff tweeted: "Lawless until the bitter end." Instead of pardoning more individuals in federal prisons serving long sentences for nonviolent crimes, Schiff said, "who does Trump pardon? Those who lie, cheat or steal for him and his family."

In addition to pardoning his own brother, President Bill Clinton pardoned four Hasidic Jews whose communities voted unanimously for Hillary Clinton in the 2000 Senate elections, as well as Susan McDougal, who served time in jail for contempt after being convicted of four felonies in connection with Independent Counsel Kenneth Starr's Whitewater investigation. She later returned to jail for contempt for refusing to answer questions before Starr's grand jury. Clinton also pardoned Marc Rich and his partner Pincus Green, who were indicted on sixty-five criminal counts for tax evasion, wire fraud, racketeering, and trading with Iran at a time when Iranian revolutionaries were still holding American citizens hostage. (Rudy Giuliani was the federal prosecutor behind that indictment.) Rich's former wife, Denise, made contributions to the Clinton Library foundation. The pardon was later investigated by the US Attorney in Manhattan. Said one Washington lawyer who succeeded in securing a pardon for a client: "Clearly, there has to be a voice there pushing for your person, or you have absolutely no chance."[421] Still, Clinton's pardons were mostly made on the recommendation of the DOJ's pardon attorney, making Trump an outlier.

Former President Jimmy Carter said of the controversial Clinton pardons: "I don't think there is any doubt that some of the factors in his pardon were attributable to his large gifts. In my opinion, that was disgraceful."[422] Clinton wrote an opinion column for the *New York Times* defending his pardons of Rich and Pincus.[423] He later admitted that the decision to pardon Rich and Pincus "wasn't worth the damage to my reputation."[424] A "common ingredient" in Clinton's pardons, the *New York Times* reported, was access, either to the president himself or his White House counsel. Third-party intermediaries such as Hugh Rodham, Hillary Clinton's brother, were paid six-figure fees for lobbying assistance. Other so-called "Friends of Bill" with special access included Rev. Jesse Jackson and Terry McAuliffe, a Clinton fund-raiser and subsequent governor of Virginia.

Clinton's column cited President George H. W. Bush's pardoning of six people involved in the Reagan-era Iran–Contra scandal, including former secretary of defense Caspar Weinberger. As noted previously, all six men pardoned had been charged with, convicted of, or pled guilty to lying to or withholding information from Congress. As Clinton noted, Bush's pardons "assured the end of that investigation," and thus his own liability in connection with a scandal involving senior officials in Ronald Reagan's administration who secretly facilitated the sale of arms to Iran, which was under an arms embargo. The administration sought to use the money from the arms sale to fund an insurgent group in Nicaragua called the Contras, which was engaged in a guerrilla war against the anti-American government. Congress had banned further funding of the Contras. Reagan took "full responsibility" for the actions of his administration but claimed activities were "undertaken without my knowledge" and that he was "disappointed" in those who served him.[425]

A congressional report issued on November 18, 1987, stated that "If the president did not know what his national security advisers were doing, he should have," and that his administration engaged in "secrecy, deception, and disdain for the law."[426] Bush, who denied having any knowledge of the Iran–Contra affair while serving as Reagan's vice president, pardoned Weinberger before his trial for two counts of perjury and one count of obstruction of justice. He also pardoned Elliott Abrams, the assistant secretary of state; Duane Clarridge, a former CIA official; Clair George, chief of CIA covert operations who had yet to be sentenced; and Alan Fiers, chief of the CIA's Central American Task Force. Bush wrote in his diaries that he was "one of the few people that knew fully the details. This is one operation that has been held very, very tight, and I hope it will not leak."[427] Independent Counsel Lawrence Walsh reportedly considered indicting Bush for covering up the contents of his diaries—which Walsh had requested in 1987, but were only turned over in 1992, after Bush lost reelection to Clinton. Bush also refused Walsh's request to take his deposition. Walsh considered taking the matter involving Bush before a grand jury.

... AND WHY?
**Could presidents tap people to commit crimes on their behalf
and just pardon them all and get away with it?
If yes, is this the only way the Supreme Court could
legitimately read the Constitution's pardon power?
(Of course not.)**

It takes little imagination, then, to think of a realistic scenario in which a president, in full possession of the powers of the office—including the commander-in-chief authority over the entire US military, control of the DOJ and the entire federal law enforcement apparatus, and command authority over national security and immigration—taps people to commit crimes on his behalf in exchange for pardons. Or he sells pardons to the highest bidder, making millions off the presidency, aware that pardons are perceived of as "absolute," and that immunity protects presidents from liability for actions taken in an official capacity as president. (Trump is pushing that argument beyond its logical boundaries, too, in claiming that the January 6th indictment should be dismissed on absolute immunity grounds.[428]) Bill Barr told Congress that promising a pardon in exchange for silence about presidential wrongdoing would be a crime. Presumably, Barr was referring to obstruction of justice, as silencing fact witnesses in a possible criminal probe would obstruct or interfere with that investigation.

Barr was also the person who infamously doused the Mueller Report's conclusions that Trump engaged in multiple acts of obstruction relating to his probe of the 2016 election. Barr's four-page memo, released weeks before the actual Mueller Report, took issue with the "law and fact concerning whether the President's actions and intent could be viewed as obstruction."[429] The president, after all, is in charge of the DOJ. He appoints the attorney general who is removable by the president at will. The attorney general is the nation's top prosecutor, who decides whether to initiate and proceed with a criminal investigation, and at the conclusion of that investigation, whether to bring charges against anyone. Those decisions are largely discretionary; the executive branch gets lots of leeway to say "yes" or "no" to an investigative step or a prosecution.

The theory implicit in Barr's four-page memo is that presidents cannot obstruct justice because they are in charge of the Department of Justice. Trump fired FBI director James Comey, and the Mueller Report detailed evidence showing that he did so in order to kill the Russia probe, which implicated him. He also made efforts to fire Mueller himself. These men served at the pleasure of the president. Was firing them the exercise of his lawful discretion as the head of the executive branch? Or was it obstruction, because he was trying to thwart a criminal probe that could implicate him? If it's the former, as Barr suggests, then presidents *never* can obstruct justice. They *are* justice at the federal level for the time that they are president. That can't be correct.

This is very close to the argument attorney Alan Dershowitz made on Trump's behalf during his first impeachment trial: "If a president does something which he believes will help him get elected in the public interest, that cannot be the kind of quid pro quo that results in impeachment," Dershowitz said.[430] Dershowitz was renowned for his "willingness to pull a range of levers" to obtain clemency for clients during the Trump administration, the *New York Times* reported, and "he emerged as a highly sought-after and often influential inter-mediary as Mr. Trump decided who would benefit from his pardon powers."[431] Dershowitz "played a role" in at least two pardons and ten commutations, "while also helping to win a temporary reprieve from sanctions for an Israeli mining billionaire." One client for whom Dershowitz was unsuccessful in securing a pardon, George Nader, pleaded guilty to possessing child sex abuse imagery and sex-traf-ficking a minor. He also cooperated with Mueller. Nader's defense lawyer, Jonathan S. Jeffress, paid Dershowitz an hourly rate for his services. "We understood that Mr. Dershowitz was seeking clemency on behalf of Mr. Nader," Jeffress told the *New York Times*, "and that he was rejected for the sole reason that Mr. Nader had cooperated in the Mueller investigation."

Dershowitz is not alone in collecting thousands of dollars in clemency-related lobbying. In March of 2021, the *New York Times* reported on interviews with over three dozen lobbyists and lawyers who reported a "lucrative market" for collecting fees from wealthy people with federal felony convictions in order to push for clemency from the Trump White House. One top advisor for the Trump cam-paign received $50,000 for helping former CIA officer John Kiriakou obtain a pardon for a conviction for illegally disclosing classified information, plus a $50,000 bonus if he received one. Kiriakou connected with Rudy Giuliani, as well, whose associate told him that a presidential pardon is "going to cost $2 million."[432] A friend of Kiriakou's who heard the story filed a whistleblower report with the FBI. (There's no law prohibiting lobbying the White House for clemency, although an actual "quid pro quo" attempt could violate bribery laws.)

It's thus hard to deny that, on balance, presidential pardons do not function to achieve the lofty goal of doling out mercy and justice to the worthiest who somehow became embroiled in the criminal justice system. In fact, the presidential pardon system has become rife with corruption and abuse—including at the highest levels of office and involving some of the most sensitive aspects of the presidency (such as secret foreign arms sales in defiance of Congress or attempts to thwart an investigation into Russia's influence on a presidential campaign to the incumbent's benefit).

The pardon power simply isn't working. It is hurting democracy and undermining basic notions of due process and fairness. It exacerbates income and race inequalities. It defiles the office of the presidency and the legitimacy of the criminal justice system. And to the extent amnesty pardons remain important, Congress can pass legislation to achieve similar ends. Although the presidential pardon power simply makes no sense anymore, and can't reasonably be eradicated, Congress and the DOJ could take steps to minimize its flaws.

3

Reforming the Pardon Power

The president's pardon power should be checked. How to do that depends in part on the objectives of reform, which fall into two broad categories.

The first category is for legitimate pardons—those that actually operate to show mercy or remedy an injustice, such as an excessive sentence for aiding a nonviolent drug offense (particularly if the underlying fact pattern has racist overtones, as with many posthumous pardons). Reforms to the pardon power should incentivize more of those types of pardons and make the system for granting them fairer and more consistent.

The second category is for illegitimate pardons—those that are about doling out favors for wealthy donors, cronies, family members, or allies in a criminal enterprise. Pardons in this category serve no valid purpose in a democracy specifically created to reject the unlimited powers of a hereditary monarch. Worse, they exacerbate flaws in our system that already reward the rich and powerful at the expense of the poor and disenfranchised, and foster corruption at the highest echelons of the executive branch.

... AND WHY?

Pardons fall into two categories: the proper ones that serve mercy and amnesty, and the improper ones that disserve the rule of law. How could lawmakers figure out ways to enhance the former and disincentivize the latter? Should they?

It is hard to imagine that mechanisms aimed at encouraging legitimate pardons could also enable illegitimate ones. If Congress were to pass a law requiring and funding DNA testing for all capital offenses to weed out false positives, for example—that is, convictions that happen either by jury verdict or guilty pleas despite the defendants' innocence—that law would not somehow produce more *corrupt* pardons for the undeserving. Congress would not necessarily need the president's pardon to help free people on death row for other reasons, either. It could make appropriate adjustments to the underlying criminal laws. Fixing the system to maximize mercy-based pardons could be costly—both in terms of taxpayer dollars and political fallout—but it would not produce more improper pardons.

The reciprocal calculus is less satisfying. Mechanisms aimed at discouraging illegitimate pardons could also tamp down legitimate ones. If presidents were required by Congress to follow fairer and more consistent procedures of transparency and accountability, fewer legitimate pardons might result, along with fewer illegitimate pardons. This is because there would be greater political accountability for pardon decisions, and possibly even due process protections that could produce tricky litigation that presidents might prefer to avoid. (Recall that due process attaches if there is an expectation that adherence to certain procedures will produce a favorable outcome; so long as the pardon process remains relatively vague, unsuccessful applicants, oddly, have fewer grounds to raise a constitutional complaint.)

This book nonetheless proceeds from the premise that such a price is worth paying. The pardon system is already out of balance at the federal level, where presidents are more likely to pardon people who can "pay" for pardons through expensive lawyers and insiders with access. For the bulk of applicants, there are evidentiary barriers that make it difficult even to apply for a pardon in the first place. As a result, the underlying facts bearing on an individual's worthiness for a mercy-based pardon do not regularly carry the day anyway. This is no doubt due in part to an overriding public sentiment favoring harsh treatment for disfavored categories of criminals. (White-collar criminals would not qualify.)

This book posits generally that Congress should pass a series of laws mandating transparency, constraining lobbying for pardons, and establishing legislative criteria to guide the exercise of the president's discretion by identifying pardons that would clearly violate bribery and obstruction-of-justice laws. Any attempt at legislative reform would undoubtedly wind up before the US Supreme Court, which could conceivably strike all or part of it down as unconstitutional.

But this possibility is hardly a good reason to avoid reforms altogether. For that to happen, a person with "standing" to sue would have to bring a case challenging the law; presumably, this would have to be a sitting president who believed their discretion was being curtailed by the pardon law. But that would require a president to air in a public lawsuit how the pardon power is operating behind closed doors, which is politically risky, if not just embarrassing. And in any event, the judicial system might not resolve the scope of a president's power to issue pardons before the end of a particular president's term, making it less likely that a president would bother with litigation in the first place.

If a president did file suit, it could raise questions around why that president is so invested in an unlimited pardon power that it's worth expending the political and legal capital necessary to follow through on planned pardons. The lawsuit could therefore bring scrutiny to the real possibility that the president is actually invested in rewarding donors and loyalists, which is not a legitimate basis for issuing pardons. All this is to say that legislation regarding the pardon process could take effect by virtue of timing and inertia—or at least, set expectations through robust debate and transparency.

This book doesn't take on the task of proposing thorough or detailed policy recommendations, let alone analyze how they would fare as a matter of existing constitutional precedent. Rather, borrowing from state and international clemency alternatives, it offers this starter list of reforms for federal pardons:

- The creation of a **clemency board** comprised of presidential appointees with a range of experience that would have meaningful input into pardon decisions.
- Mandatory public **transparency** of the record of decisions in every clemency case and an explanation of the reasons for granting or denying each petition.
- **Stricter limits on outside lobbying for pardons.**
- **A ban on pardons that would otherwise amount to a bribe or obstruction of justice** under existing federal criminal laws.
- Establishment of **public standards for mass pardons** for prison overcrowding, innovations in DNA evidence and other technologies, or to address a national crisis.

The primary aim of these modest suggestions is to disincentivize presidents from using pardons corruptly—i.e., for their own financial or political profit, or to cover up or insulate their own wrongdoing. Second, they attempt to level the playing field so that the "haves" do not have such an advantage in pardon applications. Third, by keeping a certain number of innocent people out of prison (which costs federal taxpayers upward of $85 billion a year) and enacting standards for pardons in the broader interests of the country, such as for postwar amnesty, these reforms could serve broader public interests, consistent with the president's constitutional role and obligations.

Clemency Board

Congress should establish a federal clemency board comprised of presidential appointees from a range of relevant backgrounds to make initial recommendations based on established criteria and procedures that are transparent to the public.

Critics might argue that such a move is unconstitutional, citing *Schick v. Reed*, in which the Supreme Court stated that the president's pardon power "flows from the Constitution alone, not any legislative enactments," and "cannot be modified, abridged, or diminished by the Congress."[433] And in *Ex parte Garland*, it wrote that the pardon power "is not subject to legislative control. Congress can neither limit the effect of his pardon, nor exclude from its exercise any class of offenders. The benign prerogative of mercy reposed in him cannot be fettered by any legislative restrictions."[434]

But a restriction on the exercise of the pardon power is different from establishing an executive branch agency designed to assist in implementing the president's Article II powers. Moreover, the vast administrative state, which consists of hundreds of executive branch agencies, already makes plain that the president does *not* exercise unlimited, unaccountable, nontransparent power to enforce the laws, to enact regulations, or even to exercise his commander-in-chief power. Although the Supreme Court would have to grapple with Civil War–era cases describing the pardon power as unlimited, it could borrow from modern jurisprudence under Article II to justify similar guardrails around the pardon power.

For example, the Supreme Court has endorsed Congress's ability to create "independent agencies" (such as the Securities Exchange Commission and the Federal Election Commission), whose leadership consists of board members with staggered terms. Despite the president's constitutional power to appoint and remove executive branch officers, the Supreme Court has endorsed this structure even though it denies any one president the ability to hire or fire members all at once and thus control their regulatory and enforcement agendas. Many independent agency heads cannot be fired by the president except for "cause," either, on the rationale that they should be insulated from pure politics in doing the important work of government. Legislation establishing a pardon board at the federal level could be developed against this backdrop of tolerance for independence within the executive branch—even though all employees, in theory, ultimately answer to the president.

There is historical precedent for having executive branch appointees exercise pardon authority, as well. In 1789, at the time when the Constitution was ratified, the president exercised the pardon power in consultation with the secretary of state, who could issue pardons on the president's behalf, a role that ended by executive order in 1893.

Many nations also include committees in the pardon process, either under the constitution or by statute. In some instances, their recommendations are advisory only. In others, they are binding. The same holds true for US states. Independently appointed boards, which hold hearings under established procedures, grant more clemency requests than governors acting without having to account for their input. Alabama, Connecticut, Georgia, and Idaho, which all have clemency boards with final decision-making authority, grant between 30 to 60 percent of the petitions received annually.[435]

Clemency boards also tend to have members with widely diverse backgrounds. In Kentucky, the clemency board includes experts in law, education, mental health, corrections, and child and adult protective services. In Ohio, members include experts in victims' rights, rehabilitation, and drug and alcohol services. In Delaware, Nebraska, and Nevada, all members must hold public office, making them directly accountable to the public. These states also tend to have high rates of granting clemency requests and include open applications, public hearings, and binding recommendations. In Colorado, the board must include corrections officers and at least one crime victim.

A pardon board would also reinforce the DOJ's tradition of making prosecutorial decisions independent of presidential influence. Although a requirement of prosecutorial independence is not in the Constitution, control of criminal prosecutions by a chief executive is not part of this country's "received tradition" from England. Before the American Revolution, most prosecutions in England were conducted by private individuals and prosecuting societies. Likewise, colonial prosecutions were largely initiated by private individuals with little interference from the president. Although early presidents also occasionally directed federal district attorneys to initiate or dismiss prosecutions, by the end of the twentieth century, prosecutorial independence had become a central principle of federal prosecution.

Today, the Department of Justice acts independently of the president's direct control, with its decisions and investigations largely unaffected by political interference. Prosecutorial independence helps to foster a just administration of the criminal laws rather than the sacrifice of justice to further specific political ends. It also ensures that prosecutions are based solely on the merits of the individual case. Attorney General Merrick Garland has thus affirmed publicly that "political or other improper considerations must play no role in any investigative or other prosecutorial decisions."[436] Presidential pardons to donors, friends, and cronies upend this tradition and undermine public confidence in the criminal justice system.

Transparency

Increased transparency around presidential pardons and commutations would decrease the role of political connections, lawyers, and money. This could come in the form of congressional oversight hearings, which occurred after President Clinton's controversial pardons, or through legislation mandating a record of pardon decisions. Congress could also amend the Freedom of Information Act (FOIA) to make the reasons for pardons available to the public. With proper transparency, corrupt presidential pardons could impact on state prosecutions, civil lawsuits, and congressional investigations. Although presidential pardons only apply to federal offenses, they do not erase the underlying facts or evidence of the crimes. Therefore, state authorities could still pursue charges based on state laws, civil plaintiffs could still seek damages or injunctions, and congressional committees could still subpoena witnesses or documents.

In a majority of states, the victim or the victim's representative or the prosecutor must be notified of a pardon request. Some states allow for hearings. Others process applications through the parole system. The typical procedure includes a formal petition to the board or governor; notice in the newspaper or to victims' families, the judge, the police, or the prosecutor; input from a corrections' official or parole authority; and investigative hearings. In twenty-seven states, governors must report their clemency decisions to the state legislature.[437] In Massachusetts, the governor need only report the pardons granted—not the denials—creating an incentive to ignore petitions to avoid any accountability. In Arkansas, by contrast, the governor must report every decision involving commutation, reprieve, or pardon, with reasons. Pennsylvania keeps public records.

Not so at the federal level. Established in 1865, the Office of Pardon Clerk evolved into the Office of the US Pardon Attorney in 1894.[438] In 1898, regulations were promulgated to establish a process for applying for federal pardons, but the system was optional and the recommendations advisory. Prior to 1931, the Justice Department disclosed reasons for pardon decisions, ranging from doubt about guilt or intellectual capacity to humanitarian concerns. These days, only the most controversial pardon decisions are accompanied by an explanation. In *Connecticut Board of Pardons v. Dumschat*, the US Supreme Court ruled in 1981 that state clemency authorities can deny clemency for any reason so long as it comports with the Constitution—or for no reason at all.[439]

Today, the DOJ's website explains that "Presidents in recent times have rarely announced their reasons for granting or denying clemency," and "if the President does not issue a public statement concerning his action in a clemency matter, no explanation is provided by the Department of Justice."[440] Under a ruling by a federal court in Washington, DC, the Office of the Pardon Attorney must release names of individuals who were denied clemency requests to the president. Otherwise, "deliberative communications pertaining to agency and presidential decision-making are confidential and not available under existing case law interpreting the [FOIA]." Congress could override that case law by changing the FOIA itself to mandate transparency.

The Pardon Attorney often asks the opinion of the victim and the US Attorney in the district where the conviction occurred before making a recommendation to the president, who can act entirely outside the process. Margaret Colgate Love, who served as Pardon Attorney under Bill Clinton, has observed that pardons decreased after federal prosecutors were given authority to advise on pardon applications. "By the time President Clinton entered office in 1993, the pardon program at Justice had lost whatever independence and integrity it once enjoyed within the Department, and was functioning primarily to ratify the results achieved by prosecutors, not to provide any real possibility of revising them."[441] Although "the pardon process was disciplined and regular," Love added, "it had no sense of mission

and produced very little." The office ceased to produce pardon recommendations by the end of Clinton's presidency.

... AND WHY?

**Margaret Colgate Love, who served as the DOJ's Pardon
Attorney under Bill Clinton, wrote that by the time
he took office in 1993, "the pardon program at Justice
had lost whatever independence and integrity
it once enjoyed within the Department."
Given the Trump pardons, have things improved?**

The system was replaced by an ad hoc process through the White
House Counsel's office, whose staff fielded calls from influential
supporters, compiled lists of petitioners, and debated the merits
in a series of meetings. Clinton made public announcements that
pardons were coming, but when he officially issued 177 pardons and
sentence commutations on the morning of January 20, 2001, his last
day in office, the move mushroomed into a huge scandal, tarnishing
his presidency. Love called the process "chaos," in part because the
DOJ resisted Clinton's pardon preferences and "in part because he
lacked a close relationship with his attorney general," Janet Reno,
who had authorized a number of independent counsel investigations
into the Clintons.[442]

Most presidents have relied on the established DOJ system in
making pardon and commutation decisions. Since President Jimmy
Carter, 95 percent of federal pardons were issued after the individuals
completed their full sentences and went on to live productive lives
for five or more years. These types of routine pardons enable folks to
regain their self-respect and some of the benefits of full citizenship
prospectively, such as the right to vote, carry a weapon, adopt a child,
obtain certain professional licenses, sell alcohol, and even race cars.

Prominent exceptions to presidents' compliance with the DOJ process include Ford's pardon of Nixon, Clinton's last-minute pardons, George H. W. Bush's pardon of prominent Iran–Contra figures, George W. Bush's commutation of Scooter Libby's sentence (Libby was convicted on four criminal counts relating to the leak of the covert identity of Central Intelligence Agency officer Valerie Plame Wilson, wife of a prominent critic of the Iraq war), and Donald Trump's pardon of numerous close aides. (Trump later gave Libby a full pardon.[443]) The Pardon Attorney has no say in politically motivated pardons.

Public disclosure of the reasons for pardon decisions would help enhance public confidence in the process and educate applicants who were denied pardons—as well as those who might apply in the future—as to the reasons for the denials. Lame-duck pardons issued between the time of an election and the time the next president takes office are particularly susceptible to abuse and corruption. If a president were required to provide an explanation containing certain information for each pardon at the time they are issued—particularly for donors, friends, family members, and political cronies—automatic public scrutiny could dissuade governors and presidents from issuing pardons for purely self-serving reasons. A legislative requirement of transparency could also motivate a fairer and more egalitarian approach to pardons that does not grossly favor the wealthy. During George W. Bush's two terms, only 13 people of color received a favorable pardon decision as compared to 176 White recipients. Those who had the support of a member of Congress were three times more likely to receive a pardon. If Bush had had to explain the reasons for these decisions, the more dubious pardons might have stalled.

On the other hand, too much transparency about an applicant could make it politically more difficult for a president or governor to justify a pardon or to spread negative information with no benefit to the applicant. There are already political disincentives to using clemency powers for fear that one decision could have catastrophic implications. From 1860 to 1900, before the development of systems of probation, presidents granted nearly half of all federal clemency petitions. This number has steadily declined with each successive president.[444]

From President Franklin D. Roosevelt through President Carter, approximately 200 people were pardoned each year. President Ronald Reagan pardoned only 200 per term. Clinton pardoned or commuted the sentences of only about 35 individuals per year. President Barack Obama issued 65 pardons by 2015, or about 12 per year, the lowest in presidential history. This is despite the fact that in April 2014, the DOJ announced a new clemency Initiative aimed at reinvigorating the process. If governors and presidents had to give reasons for their decisions, the frequency could likely decline even more. But given how few legitimate pardons are granted relative to the applicant pool and the unfairness and corruption that infects the process, the costs of transparency are probably worth it.

...AND WHY?

**President Barack Obama issued 65 pardons by 2015,
or about 12 per year—the lowest in presidential history.
If pardons are for mercy, is this surprising?**

Stricter Limits on Lobbying for Pardons

Federal judges pledge to operate under a judicial code of conduct banning them from having private communications with parties that have cases pending before them. Ethics rules bar lawyers from engaging in what are called "ex parte" communications with judges, on the rationale that it would be unfair to the other side of the dispute if the judge hears arguments behind closed doors that could influence the outcome, and the other party had no opportunity even to respond. Federal agency personnel within the executive branch, in general, are allowed to have ex parte communications with parties who are interested in a rule or regulation that an agency is considering, but the final outcome is subject to review by a judge under a statute called the Administrative Procedure Act. Moreover, there are limits on what gifts federal employees can accept and what kind of work they can legally do once they leave government service. Pardon decisions have no such constraints, and they are not subject to judicial review.

There is a panoply of legal requirements that apply to lobbying Congress, as well. In late 1995, President Clinton signed the Lobbying Disclosure Act into law, which requires that people or entities that qualify as a "lobbyist" (meaning they spend a certain amount of time engaged in lobbying efforts) under the law register with Congress and file regular reports.[445] Lobbying includes e-mails, calls, and in-person meetings with certain government officials on behalf of a company concerning any program, policy, legislation, regulation, contract, grant, loan, or nomination involving the federal government. Civil and criminal penalties can be imposed on people who fail to comply. Mick Mulvaney, former House member from South Carolina, director of the US Office of Management and Budget, and acting White House chief of staff for Donald Trump, said of the impact of lobbying, "We had a hierarchy in my office in Congress. If you're

242

a lobbyist who never gave us money, I didn't talk to you. If you're a lobbyist who gave us money, I might talk to you."[446]

Presidents, likewise, talk to pardon applicants with money. The historical record, exacerbated under Trump, makes that clear. Pay-to-play distorts democracy, and has no business being part of the Article II pardon power, which implicates liberty and even life for worthy—and unworthy—individuals, tilting the playing field away from justice toward corruption if money and influence are involved. Lobbying legislation is needed to correct this imbalance around the presidential pardon process.

Ban on Pardons that Equal Bribery or Obstruction of Justice

The federal bribery and obstruction-of-justice laws do not mention pardons, although a reasonable reading of them—as former attorney general Bill Barr assumed—would cover pardons for money or to silence potential witnesses who might testify against a president. But absent specificity and clarity in the law, few prosecutors would risk testing a theory that those laws apply to presidential pardons for fear of losing in court. Donald Trump's pardons—and the reporting that he was dangling the promise of pardons in order to secure loyalty, and even possibly selling pardons through Rudy Giuliani—probably warranted an investigation, but according to public information, to date, at least, President Biden's Justice Department has steered clear of scrutinizing his scheming around pardons. That sets a bad precedent for future presidents, especially Trump himself who, if reelected, would undoubtedly feel more emboldened to offer pardons for loyalty, thus insulating himself and his followers from accountability for any federal crimes committed while he is in office.

This massive constitutional loophole is totally out of step with the purposes of the pardon power, i.e., mercy and amnesty, and could be readily fixed by amending the bribery and obstruction statutes to make clear that pardons can be criminal. Of course, if a president were then ever indicted pursuant to one of these laws, a defense to the prosecution would undoubtedly include an argument that presidents can pardon whoever and however they want, regardless of the federal criminal laws. The Supreme Court would then decide who is right. But at this point, without some action from Congress, the option to use pardons to engage in criminal activity is "the law."

Establishing Public Standards
for Mass Pardons

Pardons are mostly debated in terms of whether clemency should or should not have been granted for a particular individual, based on that person's factual history and circumstances. Mass pardons, by contrast, are unusual in the United States—but they are not unprecedented. A handful of governors have emptied their death rows before leaving office. Notable historical examples include Terry Sanford of North Carolina in 1965, Winthrop Rockefeller of Arkansas in 1971, and Toney Anaya of New Mexico in 1986.[447]

In 2001, Ohio governor Richard Celeste commuted the prison sentences of 25 women who had killed or assaulted their domestic abusers. In 2012, Mississippi governor Haley Barbour pardoned over 200 individuals, clearing their criminal records. The state's attorney general challenged 21 in court for failing to comply with the state constitution's publication requirement. A judge upheld the governor's authority. California governor Jerry Brown repeatedly used mass grants of clemency to push for criminal justice reform, including 79 grants on Christmas Eve in 2012; 127 the same day in 2013; 63 on Good Friday in 2014; and 104 on Christmas Eve in 2014, mostly for low-level drug crimes. Over the prior twenty years, California governors had issued only 29 grants of clemency, combined.[448]

One of the most controversial mass pardons occurred in 2003, when Governor George Ryan pardoned four Black death row inmates, having concluded that they were innocent of the crimes for which they were convicted. Concerned with the state's system for capital sentencing, he appointed a commission to recommend changes, but the legislature refused to adopt any of the proposed reforms. Two days before leaving office, during a speech at Northwestern University, Ryan announced that he was commuting the death sentences of all 167 death row inmates, despite having campaigned on a pro–death sentence platform. It was the largest grant of clemency by a governor in American history. The death penalty was later abolished in Illinois. In a speech, Ryan recounted how a brutal murder had claimed the life of a family friend, but presented his decision as necessary to address the capriciousness of the state's criminal justice system rather than as an act of mercy.

Somewhat surprisingly, clemency is not used for death row inmates very often. During the 1990s, only between 1 and 8 death row inmates had their sentences commuted each year. During the same time period, there were 20 to 90 executions per year. Prior to that, governors granted approximately 25 percent of death row inmates' clemency requests, even in traditionally more progressive Northern states like Washington and Pennsylvania.

The pardon power, if used in a manner that serves its intended merciful aims, should arguably be used more frequently to administer justice on a mass scale, or even to save taxpayer dollars and modernize the criminal justice system by pardoning categories of prisoners whose incarceration is no longer serving the public good. Given the American "tough on crime" ethos, regular mass pardons of convicted individuals for the sake of mercy, prison overcrowding, advanced age, illness, or changes in notions of culpability—such as for victims of domestic abuse, for example—are virtually impossible to fathom. Nonetheless, legislative criteria or guidelines that draw from the history of amnesty decisions by past presidents would elevate the role of presidential clemency to its proper stature: to serve the public.

Conclusion

In *Federalist* No. 74, Alexander Hamilton wrote: "Humanity and good policy conspire to dictate, that the benign prerogative of pardoning should be as little as possible fettered or embarrassed." Hamilton's rationale was that "[t]he criminal code of every country partakes so much of necessary severity, that without an easy access to exceptions in favor of unfortunate guilt, justice would wear a countenance too sanguinary and cruel."[449] The Trump administration showed us that, in the wrong hands, the president's pardon power is poised to become a devastatingly sinister tool of corruption and abuse.

Imagine, again, a president who, on the first day of taking office, immunizes all of his aides from criminal prosecution for any actions they take on his behalf by promising to pardon them so long as they act with unwavering loyalty and in service of securing his unlimited power—including if that means committing crimes when he tells them to. In the wake of the Trump presidency, corrupt presidents can be expected to use the pardon power to shield themselves and their associates from prosecution or punishment, to influence or interfere with the judicial process, and to reward or influence political figures who are loyal to them or who can advance their agenda. A president might pardon state officials who are willing to manipulate election results, or federal officials who are willing to investigate or prosecute opponents. A president could also use the pardon power to appeal to his political base, to mobilize supporters for the next election, and to secure abject obedience from members of Congress. If a president were to muse publicly over social media or in interviews that something should happen, and then if someone went and did that thing, he could pardon that individual or individuals or group who followed his direction. Corrupt pardons also create expectations or demands from certain constituencies or interests for more pardons or favors from the president.

Corrupt presidential pardons undoubtedly have long-term consequences for the US political system and culture, as they undermine the norms and values of democracy—including a core system of checks and balances, the separation of powers between the branches, the long-term viability of the rule of law, actual political and legal accountability to the people, and a commitment to public transparency as a precondition to everything else. They could also polarize society and deepen the divisions and conflicts that already exist among different groups and ideologies. Other countries may view widespread use of corrupt presidential pardons as a sign of impunity, corruption, or authoritarianism. They may also question the credibility and legitimacy of the United States as a global leader and partner, damaging American alliances, interests, and values around the world.

Think these possibilities are too far-fetched to worry about? Consider Donald Trump's interview with NBC's Kristen Welker in September of 2023, in which he made clear that the question of pardoning himself was on the table:

FMR. PRES. DONALD TRUMP:

I could've pardoned myself. Do you know what? I was given an option to pardon myself. I could've pardoned myself when I left. People said, "Would you like to pardon yourself?" I had a couple of attorneys that said, "You can do it if you want." I had some people that said, "It would look bad, if you do." Because I think it would look terrible.

I said, "Here's the story. These people are thugs, horrible people, fascists, Marxists, sick people. They've been after me from the day I came down the escalator with Melania. And I did a great job as president." People are—great economy, great jobs, great this, great that, rebuilt the military, Space Force, everything. We—I could go on forever. Let me just tell you.

I said, "The last thing I'd ever do is give myself a pardon."

I could've given myself a pardon. Don't ask me about what I would do. I could've. The last day, I could've had a pardon done that would've saved me all of these lawyers, and all of these fake charges, these Biden indictments. They're all Biden indictments, political. They indicted—they want to arrest their political opponents. Only third-world countries do that, banana republics.

So, ready? I never said this to anybody. I was given the option. I could've done a pardon of myself.

You know what I said? "I have no interest in even thinking about it." I never even wanted to think about it. And I could've done it. And all of these questions you're asking me about, the fake charges, you wouldn't be asking me because it's a very powerful, it's a very powerful thing for a president. I was told by some people that these are sick lunatics that I'm dealing with.

"Give yourself a pardon. Your life will be a lot easier." I said, "I would never give myself a pardon."[450]

* * *

To suggest, as many seem to do, that there's absolutely nothing our system of laws could do about a presidential pardon to immunize crimes in the Oval Office short of a constitutional amendment cannot be correct. The president's textually unlimited constitutional powers are rendered accountable in many other ways. What it would take is a Congress willing to tackle this issue, knowing that any resulting legal framework would apply to future presidents of members' own political parties, as well. In light of today's acrid partisanship, that notion, of course, is fanciful. But the assumption that it would be patently illegal goes too far.

The constitutional objection to regulating the president's pardon process would inevitably center on Article II, and the Court's centuries-old pronouncements that pardons cannot be constrained. But the proper question is not about absolutes. It's about relativities—one that the Supreme Court in *Morrison v. Olson* raised in upholding a law that created an independent prosecutor capable of investigating the president himself.[451] The independent counsel could look into the conduct of a sitting president—as Kenneth Starr did with Bill Clinton, for example—without fear of termination. The legal question raised before the Supreme Court was this: Did the legislative endorsement of an independent prosecutor, who exercised executive authority belonging ultimately to the president himself, hamper the president's ability to carry out his other duties? In *Morrison*, the Court said "no." It held that even criminal prosecutions—which are at the apex of the president's power to execute the laws—are not *within the president's unlimited discretion* and could be constrained by legislation.

The pardon power is a cousin of that prosecutorial power. Both entail the discretionary exercise of mercy. *Morrison* suggests that the knee-jerk assumption that the pardon power is somehow more absolute than the power to execute the laws is wrong. Pardons can be placed within the reasonable boundaries of democracy itself.

Across the globe, the use of clemency is declining, on the perceived rationale that it can be overly lenient and contrary to the rule of law. In England, the "royal prerogative of mercy," on which the US president's power is based, is rarely used, and cannot abolish a criminal conviction. The king can only use it to reduce a prison sentence. A 2017 House of Commons briefing doesn't even count the pardon power as one of the powers reserved for the king over Parliament in the first place. One reason for the declining use of clemency in England is that the United Kingdom abolished the death penalty long ago. The collective disappearance of the death penalty and rise of parole boards help account for this trend in other parts of the world, too.

In the United States, of course, the death penalty is alive and well. Meanwhile, it is ruthlessness—not mercy—that increasingly defines the American spirit. That trend arguably justifies a different calculus— one that leans more heavily in favor of allowing presidents to exercise the prerogative of mercy as a counterweight to the miscarriages of the criminal justice system. The trouble is, despite being charged with acting in the best interests of the people they serve, US politicians are among the worst offenders of decency and fairness in modern America. Recent presidents have proven to be no exception. For this reason, among all the others, it's time for the pardon power to shrink, possibly into obscurity. Democracy will no doubt be better for it.

Acknowledgments

My deepest thanks to Brendan Duff, who took the lead on the Mormon pardons, and Caleb Thompson, who tackled the English history of the pardon power and its historical precursors.

Karen Cedeño and James Duffy did an outstanding job getting the manuscript and citations copy-edited and ready for publication.

Iyana Arrington, Anaum Cheema, Katelyn Keegan, Ahn-Thi Le, Kaitlyn Lyons, Palma Price, Kirsten Quinn, Rory Rightmyer, Adeiye Samura, Robert Taylor, and Sarah Williams also provided tremendously valuable research assistance for various chapters in this book.

And a special nod of appreciation to Dave Matchen and Adeen Postar for their expert support on many fronts.

References

The primary sources utilized in the researching and drafting of this book appear below. The author hopes that this reference list offers a resource for readers who wish to further understand the pardon power and its modern implications.

Introduction

On the Pat Brown Pardons:

1   MacKerron, J. A. (1990). A Talisman Against the Dark Forces [Review of the book *Public Justice, Private Mercy: A Governor's Education on Death Row*, by E. J. Brown]. *Journal of Criminal Law and Criminology*(1), 171–73.

2   Adler, D. & Brown, E. J. (1989). *Public Justice, Private Mercy: A Governor's Education on Death Row.* (pp. 3, 10, 53, 72, 83–85, 90–105, 110). New York: Weidenfeld & Nicolson.

On the History and Origins of the Pardon Power:

3   Duker, W. F. (1977). The President's Power to Pardon: A Constitutional History. *William & Mary L. Rev., 18*(3), 476, 486–87, 504–05, 525, 535–37.

4   Novak, A. (2016). *Comparative Executive Clemency: The Constitutional Pardon Power and the Prerogative of Mercy in Global Perspective* (pp. 1, 2–3, 4–15, 38–41, 81, 145–49, 188–89). Routledge.

5   Oaks, K. (2024, March). Pardon and Parole. *Corpus Juris Secundum 67A* (20).

6   *Marbury v. Madison*, 5 U.S. 137 (1803).

7   Blackstone, W. (3). *Commentaries on the Laws of England: Book 1, Of the Right of Persons* (p. 35) New York, Banks & Bros.

8   Blackstone, W. (3). *Commentaries on the Laws of England, in Four Books.* New York, Banks & Bros.

9   Robins, P. (2022, September 12). What is a constitutional monarchy? *New York Times.* https://www.nytimes.com/2022/09/12/world/europe/britain-constitutional-monarchy.html.

10   The Avalon Project. *English Bill of Rights 1689.* Yale Law School. https://avalon.law.yale.edu/17th_century/england.asp.

On Presidential Pardons in the Twenty-First Century:

11   Iredell, J. (1788, July 28). *Address in the North Carolina Ratifying Convention.* Founder's Constitution 4(17). http://press-pubs.uchicago.edu/founders/documents/a2_2_1s13.html.

12   Singh, M. (2020, December 23). Donald Trump's latest wave of pardons includes Paul Manafort and Charles Kushner. *The Guardian.* https://www.theguardian.com/us-news/2020/dec/23/donald-trumps-latest-wave-of-pardons-includes-paul-manafort-and-charles-kunsher.

13   Polantz, K. & Rabinowitz, H. (2022, February 5). *Trump's January 6 pardon pledge baffles some attorneys.* CNN. https://www.cnn.com/2022/02/05/politics/trump-pardon-us-capitol/index.html.

14   Feuer, A., Haberman, M. & Schmidt, M. S. (2022, June 23). Panel provides new evidence that G.O.P. members of Congress sought pardons. *New York Times.* https://www.nytimes.com/2022/06/23/us/politics/jan-6-pardons.html.

15   Curry, T. (2008, December 2). *As term ends, Bush faces historic pardon choice.* NBC News. https://www.nbcnews.com/id/wbna27996904.

16   Sawyer, W. & Wagner, P. (2023, March 14). *Mass Incarceration: The Whole Pie 2023.* Prison Policy Initiative. https://www.prisonpolicy.org/reports/pie2023.html.

17   Colgate Love, M. (2020). *50-State Comparison: Pardon Policy & Practice.* Restoration of Rights Project. https://ccresourcecenter.org/state-restoration-profiles/50-state-comparisoncharacteristics-of-pardon-authorities-2/.

On Justifications for the Pardon Power:

18   Novak, A. (2016). *Comparative Executive Clemency: The Constitutional Pardon Power and the Prerogative of Mercy in Global Perspective*. Routledge.

19   Matthew Flinders Girls Secondary College. (2022, May 19). *Medieval World: Crime and Punishment—Including Witchcraft*. https://mfgsc-vic.libguides.com/c.php?g=916765&p=6609523.

20   Bitesize History. (n.d.). *Crime and punishment in medieval England, c. 1000–c.1500*. BBC. https://www.bbc.co.uk/bitesize/guides/zqsqjsg/revision/2.

21   Renaud, J. (2018, November). *Eight Keys to Mercy: How to Shorten Excessive Prison Sentences*. Prison Policy Initiative. https://www.prisonpolicy.org/reports/longsentences.html.

22   National Constitution Center. (n.d.). The Amendments. https://constitutioncenter.org/the-constitution/amendments.

23   Justia. (n.d.). *U.S. Constitution Annotated: Fourteenth Amendment— Procedural Due Process Civil*. https://law.justia.com/constitution/us/amendment-14/05-procedural-due-process-civil.html.

24   U.S. Const. amend. 13, 14, 15.

25   Wehle, K. (2019). *How to Read the Constitution—and Why*. Harper Collins.

26   Duker, W. F. (1977). The President's Power to Pardon: A Constitutional History. *William & Mary L. Rev., 18*(3), 536.

27   Human Rights Watch. (2018, June 21). *US Criminal Justice System Fuels Poverty Cycle*. https://www.hrw.org/news/2018/06/21/us-criminal-justice-system-fuels-poverty-cycle.

28   NAACP. (n.d.). *Criminal Justice Fact Sheet*. https://naacp.org/resources/criminal-justice-fact-sheet.

29   Sawyer, W. (2022, January 11). *New Data: The Changes in Prisons, Jails, Probation, and Parole in the First Year of the Pandemic*. Prison Policy Initiative. https://www.prisonpolicy.org/blog/2022/01/11/bjs_update/.

Part I

1 Pardoning a Massacre: The Brigham Young Treason Pardons

30 Bowman, F. O. (2020, December 28). Purpose, Not Specificity, Limits the Pardon Power: A Rejoinder to Rappaport. *Just Security*. https://www.justsecurity.org/74010/purpose-not-specificity-limits-the-pardon-power-a-rejoinder-to-rappaport/.

31 Hoffstadt, B. M. (2001, February). Normalizing the Federal Clemency Power. *Texas Law Review 79*(3).

32 Ertman, M. M. (2010). Race Treason: The Untold Story of America's Ban on Polygamy. *Columbia Journal of Gender and Law, 19*(2), 296–302, 307, 326.

33 Miles, M. R. & Adkins, J. M. (2019). *Mormon Mobilization in Contemporary U.S. Politics.* Oxford Research Encyclopedia. https://www.oxfordreference.com/display/10.1093/acref/97801906143 79.001.0001/acref-9780190614379-e-871.

34 Marsh, J. W. (2001). *The Book of Mormon and the Message of the Four Gospels: The Second Coming of Jesus*. Provo, UT: Religious Studies Center, Brigham Young University.

35 The Nauvoo Expositor. (1844, June 7). *Nauvoo Expositor 1*(1).

36 Bentley, J. I. (2016). Road to Martyrdom: Joseph Smith's Last Legal Cases. *BYU Studies 55*(2), 22, 39–40, 46, 49–50, 52–53, 70, 71.

37 Richards, W., McEwan, J., & Bullock, T. (1844). *City Council Proceedings, 1844 February–1844 December*. The Church of Jesus Christ of Latter-day Saints, Church History Catalog. https://catalog.churchofjesuschrist.org/assets/779eb030-bf9e-4657-adfa-68d9b7d9e5f3/0/31#churchofjesuschrist.

38 Walker, R. W. (2011). *A Firm Foundation, Church Organization and Administration: Six Days in August: Brigham Young and the Succession Crisis of 1844*. (D. J. Whittaker & A. K. Garr, eds.). Brigham Young University. https://rsc.byu.edu/firm-foundation/six-days-august-brigham-young-succession-crisis-1844.

39   *The Mountain Meadows Massacre.* (n.d.). PBS. https://www.pbs.org/wgbh/americanexperience/features/mormons-massacre/.

40   National Archives. (1848). *Treaty of Guadalupe Hidalgo.* https://www.archives.gov/milestone-documents/treaty-of-guadalupe-hidalgo.

41   Ertman, M. M. (2010). Race Treason: The Untold Story of America's Ban on Polygamy. *Columbia Journal of Gender and Law 19*(2), 289-99.

42   PBS. (n.d.). *The Path to Utah Statehood.* https://www.pbs.org/wgbh/americanexperience/features/mormons-utah/.

43   Alexander, T. G. (2009). Thomas L. Kane and the Mormon Problem in National Politics. *BYU Studies 48*(4), 58–63. https://www.jstor.org/stable/43045091.

44   Miles, M. R. & Adkins, J. M. (2019). *Mormon Mobilization in Contemporary U.S. Politics.* Oxford Research Encyclopedia. https://www.oxfordreference.com/display/10.1093/acref/97801906143 79.001.0001/acref-9780190614379-e-871.

45   Walker, R. W. (2001). Thomas L. Kane and Utah's Quest for Self-Government, 1846–51. *Utah Historical Quarterly 69*(2). https://issuu.com/utah10/docs/uhq_volume69_2001_number2/s/10349591.

46   Scott, P. L. (n.d.). Fillmore. *Utah History Encyclopedia.* https://www.uen.org/utah_history_encyclopedia/f/FILLMORE.shtml.

47   Goodwin, K. S. (2019). The History of the Name of the Savior's Church. *BYU Studies Quarterly, 58*(3), 34–36.

48   H.R. Exec. Doc. No. 1, 48th Congress, 1st Session. (1851).

49   Roberts, David. (2008, June). The Brink of War. *Smithsonian.* https://www.smithsonianmag.com/history/the-brink-of-war-48447228/.

50   Jones, J. R. (2015). Mormonism, Originalism and Utah's Open Courts Clause, *BYU Law Review*, 2015-3, 810.

51   Linford, O. (1979). The Mormons, the Law, and the Territory of Utah. *American Journal of Legal History, 23*(3) 218–22.

52   The Church of Jesus Christ of Latter-day Saints. (n.d.). https://www.churchofjesuschrist.org/study/history/topics/deseret-alphabet?lang=eng.

53   A Mormon Saint in Town—Plurality of Wives. (1855, May 16). *Democratic Standard*. https://contentdm.lib.byu.edu/digital/collection/19CMNI/id/8215/rec/4.

54   Elwell, E. H. (1854, December 16). Mormon Life, p. 286. *The Portland Transcript: An Independent Family Journal of Literature, News, Etc., Vol. XVIII* (1854—55).

55   The Church of Jesus Christ Latter-day Saints. (n.d.). *Reformation of 1856–57*. https://www.churchofjesuschrist.org/study/history/topics/reformation-of-1856-57?lang=eng.

56   Worthen, B. W. (2012, May). *The runaway officials revisited: Remaking the Mormon image in antebellum America*. (1508805) [Master's Thesis, University of Utah]. ProQuest.

57   Linder, D. O. (n.d.). *The Mountain Massacre of 1857 and the Trials of John D. Lee*. Famous Trials. https://famous-trials.com/mountainmeadows/936-home.

58   Young, B. (1857, September 15). *Proclamation by the Governor*. University of Missouri-Kansas City Online. https://archive.org/details/GR_4449.

59   Associated Press. (2015, October 28). *Fraudulent documents jumpstarted "revolution" in LDS Church approach to history*. The Daily Universe. https://universe.byu.edu/2015/10/28/revolution-in-lds-church-approach-to-history1/.

60   Eldredge, J. (2008). The Utah War: A Photographic Essay of Some of Its Important Historic Sites. *Utah Historical Quarterly 76*(1). https://issuu.com/utah10/docs/uhq_volume76_2008_number1/s/10214898.

61   Davis, W. N. (1955). Western Justice: The Court at Fort Bridger, Utah Territory. *Utah Historical Quarterly 23*(1–4). https://issuu.com/utah10/docs/volume_23_1955/s/95260.

62   Buchanan, J. (1858, April 6). *Proclamation: Rebellion in the Territory of Utah*. The American Presidency Project. https://www.presidency.ucsb.edu/documents/proclamation-rebellion-the-territory-utah.

63   Poll, R. D. (n.d.). The Utah War. *Utah History Encyclopedia.* https://www.uen.org/utah_history_encyclopedia/u/UTAH_WAR.shtml.

64   MacKinnon, W. P. (2012). Prelude to Civil War: The Utah War's Impact and Legacy. *BYU Studies 21*(1). https://rsc.byu.edu/civil-war-saints/prelude-civil-war-utah-wars-impact-legacy.

65   Cumming, A. (1858, June 25). Proclamation of Governor Cumming. Available *in Report of the Secretary of War, Vol. 1,* at p. 113. https://play.google.com/store/books/details?id=3L1MAAAAYAAJ&rdid=book-3L1MAAAAYAAJ&rdot=1.

66   MacKinnon, W. P. (2016). *At Sword's Point, Part 2: A Documentary History of the Utah War, 1858–1859.* University of Oklahoma Press.

67   Twain, M. (1870–1871). *Roughing It* (ch. XIV).

68   Poll, R. D. (2016, April 20). *Deseret.* Utah Department of Cultural and Community Engagement. https://historytogo.utah.gov/deseret/.

69   The Monumentous. (n.d.). *A Monument and Memorial to the Mountain Meadows Massacre.* https://themonumentous.com/monument-memorial-mountain-meadows-massacre/.

70   *Mountain Meadows Massacre.* (n.d.). Historynet. https://www.atlasobscura.com/places/mountain-meadows-massacre-memorial.

71   Ravitz, J. (2007, September 11). LDS Church apologizes for Mountain Meadows Massacre. *Salt Lake Tribune.* https://archive.sltrib.com/story.php?ref=/lds/ci_6862682.

72   Layton, S. J. (2016, April 29). *Party Politics and Utah Statehood.* Utah Department of Cultural and Community Engagement. https://historytogo.utah.gov/party-politics-statehood/.

73   Davidson, L. (2021, January 14). Latter-day Saints are overrepresented in Utah's Legislature, holding 9 of every 10 seats. *Salt Lake Tribune.* https://www.sltrib.com/news/politics/2021/01/14/latter-day-saints-are/.

2 Pardoning Polygamy: The Mormon Pardons

74 Ertman, M. M. (2008). The Story of *Reynolds v. United States*: Federal "Hell Hounds" Punishing Mormon Treason. *University of Maryland Legal Studies*, 2008-5, 51.

75 Woodger, M. J. (2012). Abraham Lincoln and the Mormons. In Alford, K. L. (ed.), *Civil War Saints* (pp. 60, 66–67, 70). BYU Studies.

76 Morin, K. M. & Guelke, J. K. (1998). Strategies of Representation, Relationship, and Resistance: British Woman Travelers and Mormon Plural Wives, ca. 1870–1890. *Annals of the Association of American Geographers, 88*(3), 437, 438, 443, 448, 454.

77 *New York Times*. (1857, June 19). Highly Interesting from Utah: Graphic Narrative of Mormon Outrages. https://timesmachine.nytimes.com/timesmachine/1857/05/19/78498799.pdf.

78 Thatcher Ulrich, L. (2017). *A House Full of Females: Plural Marriage and Women's Rights in Early Mormonism, 1835–1870*. Knopf.

79 Gross, T. (Host). (2017, January 17). Author Interviews: How Mormon Polygamy in the 19th Century Fueled Women's Activism [Audio podcast]. In *Fresh Air*. NPR. https://www.npr.org/2017/01/17/510246850/how-mormon-polygamy-in-the-19th-century-fueled-womens-activism.

80 Ertman, M. M. (2010). Race Treason: The Untold Story of America's Ban on Polygamy. *Columbia Journal of Gender and Law, 19*(2), 294, 296–97, 314–15, 322.

81 PBS. (n.d.). *Polygamy and the Church: A History*. https://www.pbs.org/wgbh/americanexperience/features/mormons-polygamy/.

82 *Davis v. Beason*, 133 U.S. 333 (1890).

83 *Reynolds v. U.S.*, 98 U.S. 145 (1879).

84 Report, *Deseret News* [weekly], June 3, 1885, 316–17.

85 Cleveland, G. (1885, December 8). *First Annual Message*. The American Presidency Project. https://www.presidency.ucsb.edu/documents/first-annual-message-first-term.

86   Miles, M. & Adkins, J. (2019, February 25). Mormon Mobilization in Contemporary U.S Politics. *Oxford Research Encyclopedia*: Politics. https://doi.org/10.1093/acrefore/9780190228637.013.871.

87   *Mormon Church v. U.S.,* 136 U.S. 1 (1890).

88   Peterson, M. (2021, May 27). *Utah's Road to Statehood: The Obstacle of Polygamy.* Utah Division of Archives and Records Service. https://archivesnews.utah.gov/2021/05/27/utahs-road-to-statehood-the-obstacle-of-polygamy/.

89   *"The Manifesto and the End of Plural Marriage."* (n.d.). Church of Jesus Christ of Latter-day Saints. https://www.churchofjesuschrist.org/study/manual/gospel-topics-essays/the-manifesto-and-the-end-of-plural-marriage?lang=eng. (detailing the role of the 1890 Manifesto in the history of the LDS Church).

90   Glass, A. (2018). *President Cleveland pardons Mormon bigamists, September 25, 1894.* Politico. https://www.politico.com/story/2018/09/25/president-cleveland-pardons-mormon-bigamists-sept-25-1894-833579.

91   Utah Department of Cultural and Community Engagement. (n.d.). *Utah Statehood.* https://ilovehistory.utah.gov/utah-statehood/#:~:text=Tensions%20between%20Mormons%20and%20non%2DMormons%20grew.&text=A%20new%20political%20party%20was,made%20up%20of%20church%20members.

92   Lyman, E. L. (1998). Mormon Leaders in Politics: The Transition to Statehood in 1896. *Journal of Mormon History, 24*(2), 30–54. https://www.jstor.org/stable/23287599.

93   Harrison, B. (1893, January 4). *Proclamation 346—Granting Amnesty and Pardon for the Offense of Engaging in Polygamous or Plural Marriage to Members of the Church of Latter-day Saints.* The American Presidency Project. https://www.presidency.ucsb.edu/node/205484.

94   Cleveland, G. (1894, September). *Proclamation 369—Granting Amnesty and Pardon for the Offenses of Polygamy, Bigamy, Adultery, or Unlawful Cohabitation to Members of the Church of Latter-day Saints.* The American Presidency Project. https://www.presidency.ucsb.edu/node/206350.

95   Nielsen, C. (2021, October 31). *The Second Manifesto*. Prophets, Seers, and Revelators. https://prophetsseersandrevelators.wordpress.com/2021/10/31/the-second-manifesto/.

96   Edmunds–Tucker Act, 42 U.S.C. § 1461 (1887, repealed 1978).

97   Brown, E., & Adler, D. (1989). *Public Justice, Private Mercy: A Governor's Education on Death Row*. Grove Press.

98   Egelko, B. (2005, January 21). California: Governor sets high bar for clemency, Beardslee case indicates standard will be legal insanity. *SF Gate*. https://www.sfgate.com/health/article/CALIFORNIA-Governor-sets-high-bar-for-clemency-2736937.php.

99   Reinhold, R. (1986, November 27). Outgoing governor in New Mexico bars the execution of 5. *New York Times*. https://www.nytimes.com/1986/11/27/us/outgoing-governor-in-new-mexico-bars-the-execution-of-5.html.; Pierre, R. E. (2003, January 10). Governor to Pardon Four. *Washington Post*. https://www.washingtonpost.com/archive/politics/2003/01/10/ill-governor-to-pardon-four/41dd85cb-46c3-406f-979f-75d7a1f0a85a/; Fenton, J. (2014, December 18). O'Malley increases pardons, but remains stingy overall. *Baltimore Sun*. https://www.baltimoresun.com/politics/bs-md-omalley-pardons-20141213-story.html.

3   The Trump Pardons: A Short List of Notables

100   *The National Registry of Exonerations—Exoneration Registry*. (n.d.). https://www.law.umich.edu/special/exoneration/Pages/about.aspx.

101   Gerald R. Ford Presidential Library and Museum. (n.d.). *Nixon Pardon*. https://www.fordlibrarymuseum.gov/library/exhibits/pardon/pardon.asp.

102   Pincus, W. (1992, December 25). Bush pardons Weinberger in Iran–Contra Affair. *Washington Post*. https://www.washingtonpost.com/archive/politics/1992/12/25/bush-pardons-weinberger-in-iran-contra-affair/912743a7-026b-4134-b63d-4c1c57948673/.

103   *Clinton pardons McDougal, Hearst, others*. (2001, August 19). ABC News. https://abcnews.go.com/Politics/story?id=122001&page=1.

104 Kennedy, M. (2017, January 17). *President Obama commutes Chelsea Manning's prison sentence.* NPR. https://www.npr.org/sections/thetwo-way/2017/01/17/510307055/president-obama-commutes-chelsea-mannings-prison-sentence.

105 *New York Daily News.* (2016, January 18). Yankees owner George Steinbrenner is pardoned by Ronald Reagan in 1989 for his illegal contributions to Nixon. https://www.nydailynews.com/2016/01/18/yankees-owner-george-steinbrenner-is-pardoned-by-ronald-reagan-in-1989-for-his-illegal-contributions-to-nixon/.

106 Thomson-DeVeaux, A. (2021, January 21). *How Trump used his pardon power.* FiveThirtyEight. https://fivethirtyeight.com/features/how-trump-used-his-pardon-power/.

107 McCarthy, T. (2020, August 18). Trump to pardon women's suffrage leader Susan B Anthony. *The Guardian.* https://www.theguardian.com/us-news/2020/aug/18/susan-b-anthony-pardon-trump-19th-amendment.

108 Anthony, S. B. (1873, April 3). Is It a Crime for a Citizen of the United States to Vote? *Voices of Democracy.* https://voicesofdemocracy.umd.edu/anthony-is-it-a-crime-speech-text/#:~:text=SUSAN%20B.,%3F%E2%80%9D%20(3%20APRIL%201873).

109 *19th Amendment to the U.S. Constitution: Women's Right to Vote (1920).* (2021, September 21). National Archives. https://www.archives.gov/milestone-documents/19th-amendment.

110 *Susan B. Anthony Pro-Life America.* (2023, August 17). https://sbaprolife.org.

111 *Official Susan B. Anthony Museum & House.* (2022, December 6). https://susanb.org.

112 Schmidt, S. (2020, August 18). Susan B. Anthony was arrested for voting when women couldn't. Now Trump will pardon her. *Washington Post.* https://www.washingtonpost.com/history/2020/08/18/susan-b-anthony-trump-pardon/.

113 Anthony, S. B. (1872). *On Women's Right to Vote.* https://www.nolo.com/legal-encyclopedia/content/anthony-vote-speech.html.

114   Forgey, Q. (2020, August 28). *Trump pardons Alice Johnson after her RNC speech*. Politico. https://www.politico.com/news/2020/08/28/trump-pardons-alice-johnson-404470.

115   Torregano, T. (2023, June 20). *5 years free, Alice Johnson works to give others their 2nd chance*. Spectrum News. https://spectrumnews1.com/ca/la-west/human-interest/2023/06/20/5-years-free--alice-johnson-works-to-give-others-their-second-chance.

116   Timpf, K. (2018, June 7). President Trump was right to commute Alice Johnson's sentence. *National Review*. https://www.nationalreview.com/2018/06/president-trump-right-to-commute-alice-johnson-sentence/.

117   Mackelden, A. & Sanchez, C. (2020, August 27). *What to know about prison reform advocate Alice Marie Johnson*. Harper's Bazaar. https://www.harpersbazaar.com/celebrity/latest/a20968667/who-is-alice-marie-johnson-kim-kardashian-prison-reform/.

118   Kelly, A., Lucas, R., & Romo, V. (2020, December 24). *Trump pardons Roger Stone, Paul Manafort and Charles Kushner*. NPR. https://www.npr.org/2020/12/23/949820820/trump-pardons-roger-stone-paul-manafort-and-charles-kushner.

119   LaFraniere, S. & Benner, K. (2018, April 1). The Kushners saw redemption in the White House. It was a mirage. *New York Times*. https://www.nytimes.com/2018/04/01/us/charles-jared-kushner-white-house-real-estate.html.

120   Colvin, J. & Long, C. (2020, December 24). Kushner pardon revives "loathsome" tale of tax evasion, sex. *AP News*. https://apnews.com/article/donald-trump-charles-kushner-new-jersey-elections-crime-0155d15fa3110 8fd2c0e6360a3b597dd.

121   Lemire, J., Tucker, E., & Colvin, J. (2021, January 20). Trump pardons ex-strategist Steve Bannon, dozens of others. *AP News*. https://apnews.com/article/steve-bannon-trump-pardons-broidy-66c82f25134735e742b2 501c118723bb.

122   Wilson, M. (2023, August 19). Transcript: Steve Bannon's "War Room" Is Mobilizing. *Slate*. https://slate.com/transcripts/dkxWQlpNYkdBSnBXUmZ1NkYv NDB VOWtPOWtGbk9iWTZ0b2FXS3R3M21rYz0=.

123 *Lil Wayne and Kodak Black: Why did Donald Trump grant the rappers clemency?* (2021, January 20). BBC News. https://www.bbc.com/news/entertainment-arts-55730190.

124 Lil Wayne [@LilTunechi]. (2020, October 29). Just had a great meeting with @realdonaldtrump @potus besides what he's done so far with criminal reform, the platinum plan . . . [tweet]. *Twitter.* https://twitter.com/LilTunechi/status/1321941986174226432?lang=en.

125 Lock, S. (2021, January 20). Donald Trump pardons Tommaso Buti, Italian businessman charged with fraud. *Newsweek.* https://www.newsweek.com/tommaso-buti-italian1562970.

126 *Statement from the Press Secretary Regarding Executive Grants of Clemency* (2021, January 20). The White House. https://trumpwhitehouse.archives.gov/briefings-statements/statement-press-secretary-regarding-executive-grants-clemency-012021/.

127 *Kwame Kilpatrick, former Detroit mayor, sentenced to 28 years in prison for corruption.* (2013, October 10). CBS News. https://www.cbsnews.com/news/kwame-kilpatrick-former-detroit-mayor-sentenced-to-28-years-in-prison-for-corruption/.

128 United States Attorney's Office, Eastern District of Michigan. (2013, October 17). *Former Detroit Mayor Kwame Kilpatrick, Contractor Bobby Ferguson and Bernard Kilpatrick Sentenced on Racketeering, Extortion, Bribery, Fraud and Tax Charges.* U.S. Department of Justice. https://www.justice.gov/usao-edmi/pr/former-detroit-mayor-kwame-kilpatrick-contractor-bobby-ferguson-and-bernard-kilpatrick.

129 Williams, C., White, E., & Balsamo, M. (2021, January 20). US releases Detroit's disgraced former mayor from prison. *AP News.* https://apnews.com/article/donald-trump-kwame-kilpatrick-detroit-8441a18980a74aaa6503a5c098db25a1.

130 Kelly, A., Lucas, R., & Romo, V. (2020, December 24). *Trump pardons Roger Stone, Paul Manafort and Charles Kushner.* NPR. https://www.npr.org/2020/12/23/949820820/trump-pardons-roger-stone-paul-manafort-and-charles-kushner.

131 Hoffman, G. (2021). Trump pardons Aviem Sella, Jonathan Pollard's handler. *Jerusalem Post*. https://www.jpost.com/american-politics/trump-pardons-aviem-sella-jonathan-pollards-handler-656048.

132 Wamsley, L. (2020, December 23). *Shock and dismay after Trump pardons Blackwater guards who killed 14 Iraqi civilians*. NPR. https://www.npr.org/2020/12/23/949679837/shock-and-dismay-after-trump-pardons-blackwater-guards-who-killed-14-iraqi-civil.

133 Woolf, N. (2015, April 14). Former Blackwater guards sentenced for massacre of unarmed Iraqi civilians. *The Guardian*. http://www.theguardian.com/us-news/2015/apr/13/former-blackwater-guards-sentencing-baghdad-massacre.

134 Haltiwagner, J., Pickrell, R. (2020). *The former Blackwater guards Trump pardoned were convicted of killing 14 Iraqi civilians, including 2 children*. Business Insider Africa. https://africa.businessinsider.com/politics/the-former-blackwater-guards-trump-pardoned-were-convicted-of-killing-14-iraqi/g8kf4mk.

135 Mazzetti, M., & Goldman, A. (2020, March 7). Erik Prince recruits ex-spies to help infiltrate liberal groups. *New York Times*. https://www.nytimes.com/2020/03/07/us/politics/erik-prince-project-veritas.html.

136 Holland, S. (2020, December 22). *Trump grants full pardon to Russia probe figure George Papadopoulos*. Reuters. https://www.reuters.com/article/usa-trump-pardons-idINKBN28X06E.

137 *Trump pardons former campaign chairman Paul Manafort*. (2020, December 23). PBS NewsHour. https://www.pbs.org/newshour/politics/trump-pardons-former-campaign-chairman-paul-manafort.

138 Baker, P., Haberman, M., & LaFraniere, S. (2020, July 10). Trump Commutes Sentence of Roger Stone in Case He Long Denounced. *New York Times*. https://www.nytimes.com/2020/07/10/us/politics/trump-roger-stone-clemency.html.

139 Savage, C. (2020, November 25). Trump pardons Michael Flynn, ending case his justice dept. sought to shut down. *New York Times*. https://www.nytimes.com/2020/11/25/us/politics/michael-flynn-pardon.html.

140 Donald Trump, [@realDonaldTrump]. (2020, November 25). It is my Great Honor to announce that General Michael T. Flynn has been granted a Full Pardon [tweet]. *Twitter.* https://twitter.com/realDonaldTrump/status/1331706255212228608.

141 Litman, H. (2018, March 29). We may know why Paul Manafort has kept quiet. But his bet is still risky. *Washington Post.* https://www.washingtonpost.com/opinions/we-may-know-why-paul-manafort-has-kept-quiet-but-his-bet-is-still-risky/2018/03/28/ff1fa8a4-32cc-11e8-8bdd-cdb33a5eef83_story.html.

142 Myers, S. L., & Kramer, A. E. (2016, July 31). How Paul Manafort wielded power in Ukraine before advising Donald Trump. *New York Times.* https://www.nytimes.com/2016/08/01/us/paul-manafort-ukraine-donald-trump.html.

143 Mangan, D. (2021, April 15). *Trump campaign chief Manafort's associate Kilimnik gave Russia 2016 election strategy, polling, U.S. says.* CNBC. https://www.cnbc.com/2021/04/15/trump-campaign-chief-paul-manafort-employee-kilimnik-gave-russia-election-data.html.

144 Solomon, J. (2019, June 6). *Key figure that Mueller report linked to Russia was a State Department intel source.* The Hill. https://thehill.com/opinion/white-house/447394-key-figure-that-mueller-report-linked-to-russia-was-a-state-department/.

145 Breuninger, K. & Mangan, D. (2018, June 8). *Special counsel Robert Mueller files witness tampering indictment against Paul Manafort and Russian citizen Konstantin Kilimnik.* CNBC. https://www.cnbc.com/2018/06/08/special-counsel-robert-mueller-files-new-indictment-against-paul-manafort-nbc-news.html.

Part II

146 The Legal Aid Society of Cleveland. (n.d.). *What is a "pardon" and does it get rid of my criminal record?* https://lasclev.org/pardon/.

147   Texas Board of Pardons and Paroles Full Pardon Page. (n.d.). *What is the effect of a full pardon?* https://www.tdcj.texas.gov/bpp/exec_clem/Effects_of_a_Full_Pardon.html#:~:text=A%20full%20pardon%20restores%20certain,or%20administrator%20of%20an%20estate.

148   Conditional pardon. (n.d.). In *Encyclopedia Britannica.* https://www.britannica.com/topic/conditional-pardon.

149   Lempert, R. (2021, January 217). *Presidential pardons: Settled law, unsettled issues, and a downside for Trump.* Brookings. https://www.brookings.edu/articles/presidential-pardons-settled-law-unsettled-issues-and-a-downside-for-trump/.

150   U.S. Department of Justice. (n.d.) *Clemency recipients.* https://www.justice.gov/pardon/clemency-recipients.

151   Sample, B. (2018, December 30). *What does presidential clemency mean? Presidential pardon and reprieves explained.* Clemency. https://clemency.com/presidential-clemency-authority.

152   Washington State: Office of the Attorney General. (n.d.). *Reprieves, Pardons & Commutations.* https://www.atg.wa.gov/reprieves-pardons-commutations#:~:text=A%20commutation%20is%20generally%20defined,termination%20of%20the%20criminal%20penalty.

153   Czachor, E. M. (2024, January 26). *Kenneth Eugene Smith executed by nitrogen hypoxia in Alabama, marking a first for the death penalty.* CBS News. https://www.cbsnews.com/news/kenneth-eugene-smith-executed-by-nitrogen-hypoxia-in-alabama/.

154   *Office of the Pardon Attorney.* (2014, March 3). U.S. Department of Justice. https://www.justice.gov/pardon.

155   Colgate Love, M. (2020). *50-State Comparison: Pardon Policy & Practice.* Restoration of Rights Project. https://ccresourcecenter.org/state-restoration-profiles/50-state-comparisoncharacteristics-of-pardon-authorities-2/.

156 Reinhard, B., & Gearan, A. (2020, February 3). Most Trump clemency grants bypass Justice Dept. and go to well-connected offenders. *Washington Post.* https://www.washingtonpost.com/investigations/most-clemency-grants-bypass-doj-and-go-to-well-connected-offenders/2020/02/03/4e8f3eb2-21ce-11ea-9c2b-060477c13959_story.html.

157 Udofa, I. (2018). The Abuse of Presidential Power of Pardon and the Need for Restraints. *Beijing Law Review, 09*(02), 113–31. https://doi.org/10.4236/blr.2018.92008.

158 Malone, D. (2015, November 6). *The royal prerogative of mercy.* The Law Society Gazette. https://www.lawgazette.co.uk/practice-points/the-royal-prerogative-of-mercy/5052062.article.

159 Shogan, C. (2020, December 2). *The history of the pardon power: Executive unilateralism in the Constitution.* The White House Historical Association. https://www.whitehousehistory.org/the-history-of-the-pardon-power.

1 From Emperors to Kings

160 History.com Editors. Code of Hammurabi: Laws & Facts. (2009, November 9). *History.* https://www.history.com/topics/ancient-middle-east/hammurabi. Ellickson, Robert C. & Thorland, Charles D. (1995, October). *Ancient Land Law: Mesopotamia, Egypt, Israel.* Chicago-Kent Law Review, Vol. 71, Issue 1, Symposium on Ancient Law, Economics and Society Part II: Ancient Rights and Wrongs/Symposium on Ancient Law, Economics and Society Part II: Ancient Near Eastern Land Laws.

In addition to the specific citations referenced in footnotes, this section of the book drew heavily from the following additional sources:

Grupp, S. (1993, January). Some Historical Aspects of the Pardon in England. *The American Journal of Legal History 7*, no. 1.

Konig, D. T. & Zuckert, M. P., eds. (2019). *Jefferson's Legal Commonplace Book.* Princeton University Press.

Lacey, H. (2009). *The Royal Pardon: Access to Mercy in Fourteenth-Century England.* York: York Medieval Press.

Lacey, H. (2008, March) "Grace for the rebels": the role of the royal pardon in the Peasants' Revolt of 1381. *Journal of Medieval History, 34*(1).

Lévy, R. (2007). Pardons and Amnesties as Policy Instruments in Contemporary France. *Crime and Justice, 36*(1), 551-590, Crime, Punishment, and Politics in a Comparative Perspective.

Little, B. (2019, April 18). *Claiming 'Sanctuary' in a Medieval Church Could Save Your Life—But Lead to Exile.* History.

Morison, S. T. (2005, November) The Politics of Grace: On the Moral Justification of Executive Clemency. *Buffalo Criminal Law Review, 9*(1).

161 Amnesty and Pardon (n.d.). In *Encyclopedia.com.* https://www. encyclopedia.com/law/legal-and-political-magazines/amnesty-and-pardon.

162 Quran Reading. (2018, January 12). *Importance and Benefits of Forgiveness in Islam.* https://www.quranreading.com/blog/importance-and-benefits-of-forgiveness-in-islam-learn-from-quran-and-sunnah/.

163 Kamali, M. H. (2019, June 28). *Crime and Punishment in Islamic Law: A Fresh Interpretation.* Oxford University Press.

164 *Rights of the Accused under Shari'ah Law* (n.d.). In *Criminal Defense Wiki.* http://defensewiki.ibj.org/index.php/Rights_of_the_Accused_under_Shari'ah_Law.

165 Osanloo, A. (2006). The Measure of Mercy: Islamic Justice, Sovereign Power, and Human Rights in Iran. *Cultural Anthropology, 21*(4), 570–602. https://www.jstor.org/stable/4124723.

166 *Penalties of the Mosaic Law.* (n.d.). In McClintock and Strong Biblical Cyclopedia Online. https://www.biblicalcyclopedia.com/P/penalties-of-the-mosaic-law.html.

167 Torah (n.d.). In *Encyclopedia Britannica.* https://www.britannica.com/topic/Torah.

168   New International Version. (2011). Biblica. ESV Online.
       https://www.biblegateway.com/passage/?search=2%20Samuel%20
       16%3A5-22&version=NIV. *The Attorney General's Survey of Release
       Procedures: Pardon, Volume III*. Washington: United States Government
       Printing Office, 1939.

169   Bitesize History. (n.d.). *The death of Jesus*. BBC. https://www.bbc.co.uk/
       bitesize/guides/z6b96v4/revision/5.

170   Denova, R. (n.d.). Pontius Pilate. In *World History Encyclopedia*.
       https://www.worldhistory.org/Pontius_Pilate/.

171   Wilson, R. (n.d.). *Jesus before Pilate and Herod (Luke 23:1–25)*. JesusWalk
       Bible Study Series. https://www.jesuswalk.com/luke/103-pilate.htm.

172   Oresteia (n.d.). In *Encyclopedia Britannica*.
       https://www.britannica.com/topic/Oresteia.

173   2 Samuel 19 Commentary (n.d.). *Precept Austin*.
       https://www.preceptaustin.org/2-samuel-19-commentary.

174   Barnett, E. (2011). Family, feud, and the conduct of war in Anglo-Saxon
       England. [Master's thesis, University of Southern Mississippi]. Aquilla Digital.

175   Fletcher, Richard. *Bloodfeud: Murder and Revenge in Anglo-Saxon England*.
       New York: Oxford University Press, 2003.

176   Hurnard, N.D. (1969). *The King's Pardon for Homicide Before A.D. 1307*.
       Oxford University Press.

177   Kobil, D. T. (1991, February). The Quality of Mercy Strained: Wresting the
       Pardoning Power from the King. *Texas Law Review 69*(3), 569–642.; Lacey,
       H. (2005). *The Politics of Mercy: The Use of the Royal Pardon in Fourteenth
       Century England*. PhD Thesis, University of York.

178   Purkiss, D. (2006). *English Civil War: A People's History (1642–1651)*.
       Harper Press.

179   Hibbert, C. (2015). *Charles I: A Life of Religion, War and Treason*. St.
       Martin's Griffin.

180   Battle of Naseby. (2021, June 15). In *Encyclopedia Britannica*.
       https://www.britannica.com/event/Battle-of-Naseby.

181 Moore, K. D. (1989) Pardons: *Justice, mercy, and the public interest*. Oxford University Press.

182 Bowring, J. (1841). *The Works of Jeremy Bentham, Volume 1*. Simpkin, Marshall, & Co.; Barnett, J. D. (1927, February). The Grounds of Pardon. *Journal of the American Institute of Criminal Law and Criminology 17*(4), 490–530.

183 Bowman, F. O. (2020, December 28). *Purpose, Not Specificity, Limits the Pardon Power: A Rejoinder to Rappaport*. Just Security. https://www.justsecurity.org/74010/ purpose-not-specificity-limits-the-pardon-power-a-rejoinder-to-rappaport/.

184 Rakove, J. (1996). *Original Meanings: Politics and Ideas in the Making of the Constitution*. 244–87. Vintage.

185 Meyler, B. (2020, February 20). *Enlightening the pardon power*. The Hill. https://thehill.com/opinion/criminal-justice/483742-enlightening-the-pardon-power/.

186 U.S. Const. art. III, §3.

187 Hamilton, A. (1788, March 25). *The Federalist* No. 74. National Archives. https://founders.archives.gov/documents/Hamilton/01-04-02-0226. For a discussion of the Constitutional convention, see Buffa, D.W. "The pardon power and original intent." Brookings, July 25, 2018.

2   From Kings to Presidents

188 U.S. Const. art. II, §2.

189 *Marbury v. Madison*, 5 U.S. 137, 138 (1803).

190 *Ex parte Grossman*, 267 U.S. 87 (1925).

191 Novak, A. (2016). *Comparative Executive Clemency: The Constitutional Pardon Power and the Prerogative of Mercy in Global Perspective*. Routledge.

192 Hamilton, A. (1788, March 14). *The Federalist* No. 69. National Archives. https://founders.archives.gov/documents/ Hamilton/01-04-02-0220#ARHN-01-04-02-0220-fn-0001.

193 *Ex parte Garland*, 71 U.S. 333 (1866).

194 Dorris, J. T. (1953). *Pardon and Amnesty Under Lincoln and Johnson: The Restoration of the Confederates to their Rights and Privileges, 1861–1898.* University of North Carolina Press.

195 Broughton, Z. (2019). Constitutional law—I beg your pardon: *Ex parte Garland* overruled; The presidential pardon power is no longer unlimited. *Western New England Law Review, 41*(1), 183.

196 Johnson, A. (1866). *Presidential pardon for John Shelton.* Document Bank of Virginia. https://edu.lva.virginia.gov/dbva/items/show/149.

197 *U.S. v. Klein,* 80 U.S. 128 (1871).

198 *Knote v. U.S.,* 95 U.S. 149 (1877).

199 U.S. Const. art. I, §9.

200 *Carlesi v. New York,* 32 F. Supp. 479 (E.D. N.Y. 1940).

201 *U.S. v. Wilson,* 32 U.S. 150 (1833).

202 *Burdick v. U.S.,* 236 U.S. 79 (1915).

203 *Bjerkan v. United States,* 529 F.2d 125, 128 n.2 (7th Cir. 1975) (reading *Burdick* as holding that acceptance of a pardon is admission of guilt).

Conditional Pardons

204 Cowlishaw, P. (1975, November). The Conditional Presidential Pardon. *Stanford Law Review 28*(1).

205 *Ex parte Wells,* 59 U.S. 307 (1855).

206 *Schick v. Reed,* 419 U.S. 256 (1974).

207 *Furman v. Georgia,* 408 U.S. 238 (1972).

208 *Hoffa v. Saxbe,* 378 F. Supp. 1221 (D.D.C. 1974).

209 The President's Conditional Pardon Power (2021, June 10). *Harvard Law Review, 134*(8), 2833–54.

Due Process Protections for Pardons

210 *Ohio Adult Parole Authority v. Woodard*, 523 U.S. 272 (1998).

211 National Archives and Records Administration. (n.d.). *Magna Carta.* https://www.archives.gov/exhibits/featured-documents/magna-carta.

212 *Sandin v. Conner*, 515 U.S. 472, 482 (1995).

213 Johnson, L. F. (1916). *Famous Kentucky Trials and Tragedies.* The Baldwin Law Book Company, Inc.

214 Stout, D. (2001, January 20). Clinton pardons McDougal, Cisneros. *New York Times.* https://www.nytimes.com/2001/01/20/politics/clinton-pardons-mcdougal-cisneros.html?searchResultPosition=7.

215 Blinder, A. (2014, November 14). Arkansas: Governor will pardon son. *New York Times*, A14.

216 *Young v. Hayes*, 218 F.3d 850 (8th Cir. 2000).

217 *Ex parte Garland*, 71 U.S. 333, 334 (1866).

218 Ford, G. (1974, September 08). *Proclamation 4311, Granting pardon to Richard Nixon.* Ford Library and Museum. https://www.fordlibrarymuseum.gov/library/speeches/740061.asp.

219 *Burdick v. United States*, 236 U.S. 79 (1915).

220 Gerstein, J. & Cheney, K. (2020, November 30). *"Any and all possible offenses": Trump pardon grants Flynn a sweeping reprieve.* Politico. https://www.politico.com/news/2020/11/30/trump-flynn-pardon-reprieve-441527#:~:text=President%20Donald%20Tru'p's%20pardon%20of,interference%20in%20the%202016%20election.

221 Death Penalty Information Center. (n.d.). *Clemency.* Retrieved 2023, October 27. https://deathpenaltyinfo.org/facts-and-research/clemency.

3 From Presidents to Governors

222 Colgate Love, M. (2020). *50-State Comparison: Pardon Policy & Practice*. Restoration of Rights Project. https://ccresourcecenter.org/state-restoration-profiles/50-state-comparisoncharacteristics-of-pardon-authorities-2/.

223 Federal Bureau of Investigation (2020). *National Incident-Based Reporting System, 2020*. https://crime-data-explorer.app.cloud.gov/pages/downloads.

224 Pennsylvania Constitution, Article IV, § 9(a).

225 South Carolina Constitution, Article IV, § 14.

226 Clemency in other cases, South Carolina Code § 24-21-920.

227 Louisiana Constitution, Article IV, § 5I(1).

228 Robertson, C. (2012, January 11). Mississippi: Some pardons by Barbour are halted. *New York Times*. https://www.nytimes.com/2012/01/12/us/mississippi-some-pardons-by-barbour-are-halted.html?searchResultPosition=3.

229 Mississippi Constitution, Article V, § 124.

230 *In re Hooker*, 87 So.3d 401, 414 (2012).

231 Liptak, A. (2005, October 2). To more inmates, life term means dying behind bars. *New York Times*, A1.

232 *Pennsylvania Prison Society v. Cortes*, 622 F.3d 215 (3d. Cir. 2010).

233 Pardons by Governor, Mass. Gen. Laws § 18-127-152 (2010).

234 Felony convictions eligible for sealing, Ark. Code Ann. § 16-90-1406 (2023); Sealing of records for a pardoned person, Ark. Code Ann. § 16-90-1411 (2014).

235 Authority to grant pardons and paroles, remit fines and forfeitures, etc., Ala. Code § 15-22-36 (2019).

236 Effect of pardon, restoration of civil rights, 11 Del. Code § 4364 (2003). *State ex rel. Wier v. Peterson*, 369 A.2d 1076 (1976).

237   Civil rights restored upon pardon, S.C. Code Ann. § 24-21-990 (1976).

238   Sex offender registry, S.C. Code Ann. § 23-3-430 (2022).

239   Texas Board of Pardons and Paroles. (2017, February 2017). *What is the effect of a full pardon?* https://www.tdcj.texas.gov/bpp/exec_clem/Effects_of_a_Full_Pardon.html.

240   South Carolina Department of Probation, Parole, and Pardons. (n.d.). *Frequently Asked Questions.* https://www.dppps.sc.gov/FAQ#parole_pardon_hearings.

241   Barnett, J. (1927). The Grounds of Pardon. *Journal of Criminal Law and Criminology, 17*(4), 490–530. https://scholarlycommons.law.northwestern.edu/cgi/viewcontent.cgi?article=2037&context=jclc.

242   Raines, H. (1979, January 18). Gov. Blanton of Tennessee is Replaced 3 Days Early in Pardons Dispute. *New York Times*, A16.

4   Global Approaches to the Pardon Power:

243   Novak, A. & Pascoe, D. (2022). Executive Clemency during the Coronavirus Pandemic: A Global Analysis of Law and Practice. *International Criminology 2*(1), pp. 84–97. https://ssrn.com/abstract=4034054.

244   Novak, A. (2016). *Comparative Executive Clemency: The Constitutional Pardon Power and the Prerogative of Mercy in Global Perspective.* Routledge.

245   Bandera, G. (2022, July 31). *The surge in death penalty use and the road to abolition.* Fair Planet. https://www.fairplanet.org/story/which-countries-have-the-death-penalty/#:~:text=By%20the%20end%20of%202021,the%20Democratic%20Republic%20of%20Congo.

Part III

246   *Mapp v. Ohio*, 367 U.S. 643 (1961).

247 Bouie, J. (2019, April 11). Tell me again why prisoners can't vote. *New York Times*. https://www.nytimes.com/2019/04/11/opinion/voting-prisoners-felon-disenfranchisement.html.

248 Kelley, E. (2017, May 9). *Racism & Felony Disenfranchisement: An Intertwined History*. Brennan Center for Justice. https://www.brennancenter.org/our-work/research-reports/racism-felony-disenfranchisement-intertwined-history.

249 Brown, E., & Adler, D. (1989). *Public Justice, Private Mercy: A Governor's Education on Death Row*. Grove Press (p. 163).

250 Imposition of a sentence, 18 U.S.C. § 3553 (2018).

251 *United States v. Booker*, 543 U.S. 220 (2005).

252 Davis, A., & Hsu, S. (2022, March 24). The child pornography case at the center of Ketanji Brown Jackson's hearing. *Washington Post*. https://www.washingtonpost.com/investigations/2022/03/24/hawkins-brown-jackson-pornography-sentence/.

253 Ford, G. (1974, September 08). *Proclamation 4311, Granting pardon to Richard Nixon*. Ford Library and Museum. https://www.fordlibrarymuseum.gov/library/speeches/740061.asp.

254 Whitman, A. (1972, December 27). Harry S. Truman: Decisive president. *New York Times*, 46–47.

1 Mercy

255 Baker, P. (2018, December 3). Bush made Willie Horton an issue in 1988, and the racial scars are still fresh. *New York Times*. https://www.nytimes.com/2018/12/03/us/politics/bush-willie-horton.html.

256 George Bush and Willie Horton (1988, November 4). *New York Times*, 34A.

257 Ifill, G. (1992, July 24). Clinton, in Houston speech, assails Bush on crime issue. *New York Times*, A13.

258 Butterfield, F. (1995, March 23). "3 Strikes" law in California is clogging courts and jails. *New York Times*, A1.

259   Travis, J., Western, B., & Redburn, S. (eds.). (2014). *The Growth of Incarceration in the United States: Exploring Causes and Consequences*, 4. The National Academies Press.

260   Shen, Y., Bushway, S., Sorensen, L. C., & Smith, H. L. (2020). Locking up my generation: Cohort differences in prison spells over the life course. *Criminology, 58*(4), 645–77. https://doi.org/10.1111/1745-9125.12256.

261   *How the political ground shifted on criminal justice reform.* (2015, February 24). NBC News. https://www.nbcnews.com/politics/politics-news/how-politicians-came-support-criminal-justice-reform-n309966.

262   National Registry of Exonerations (n.d.). *Exonerations before 1989.* Retrieved on September 03, 2023. https://www.law.umich.edu/special/exoneration/Pages/ExonerationsBefore1989.aspx?View={43e04d15-8918-459f-bb8f-dddc168edf0d}&SortField=Exonerated&SortDir=Asc.

263   Gross, S. R., Possley, M., Otterbourg, K., Stephens, K., Paredes, J. W., & O'Brien, B. (2022, September). *Race and Wrongful Convictions in the United States.* National Registry of Exonerations. https://www.law.umich.edu/special/exoneration/Documents/Race%20Report%20Preview.pdf.

264   Jackson, K. & Gross, S. (2014). *Female exonerees: Trends and patterns.* National Registry of Exonerations. Retrieved on September 03, 2023. https://www.law.umich.edu/special/exoneration/Pages/Features. Female.Exonerees.aspx#:~:text=No%2Dcrime%20cases%3A%20 63%25,%25%2C%20271%2F1313).

265   National Registry of Exonerations (n.d.). *Exonerations before 1989.* Retrieved on September 03, 2023. https://www.law.umich.edu/special/exoneration/Pages/ExonerationsBefore1989.aspx?View={43e04d15-8918-459f-bb8f-dddc168edf0d}&SortField=Exonerated&SortDir=Asc.

266   Warden, B. (n.d.). *Stephen Boorn.* National Registry of Exonerations. Retrieved September 03, 2023. https://www.law.umich.edu/special/exoneration/pages/casedetailpre1989.aspx?caseid=24.

267   Wehle, K. (2022, June 6). *Trump's pardon abuses expose the myth of unlimited presidential power.* Politico. https://www.politico.com/news/magazine/2022/06/22/trump-pardon-abuse-00041372.

268 U.S. Department of Justice (2018, April). *Justice Manual* § 9-140.112. https://www.justice.gov/jm/jm-9-140000-pardon-attorney#9-140.112.

269 Biden, J. (2022, October 6). *Proclamation 10467, Granting pardons for the offense of simple possession of marijuana*. https://uscode.house.gov/view.xhtml?req=granuleid:USC-prelim-title21-section844&num=0&edition=prelim#:~:text=Biden%20Jr.%2C%20do%20hereby%20grant,currently%20codified%20at%2021%20U.S.C.

270 Schwartzapfel, B. & Levintova, H. (2011, December 12). *How many innocent people are in prison?* Mother Jones. https://www.motherjones.com/politics/2011/12/innocent-people-us-prisons.

271 LaPorte, G. M. (2017, September 7). *Wrongful convictions and DNA exonerations: Understanding the role of forensic science*. National Institute of Justice. https://www.ojp.gov/pdffiles1/nij/250705.pdf.

272 Southall, A. (2017, December 16). To curb bad verdicts, court adds a lesson for jurors on racial bias in identifications. *New York Times*, A18.

273 Fuchs, E. (2013, September 3). *The vast majority of America's prisoners won't get the mercy Obama gave this single mom*. Insider. https://www.businessinsider.com/eugenia-jennings-sentence-commuted-2013-9.

274 Kanno-Youngs, Z. & Tankersley, J. (2022, December 31). Biden issues six pardons, most for minor drug offenses. *New York Times*, A15.

275 Smith, S. G., Zhang, X., Basile, K. C., Merrick, M. T., Wang, J., Kresnow, M., Chen, J. (2018). *The National Intimate Partner and Sexual Violence Survey (NISVS): 2015 data brief—updated release*. National Center for Injury Prevention and Control, Centers for Disease Control and Prevention. https://www.cdc.gov/violenceprevention/pdf/2015data-brief508.pdf.

276 Zaveri, M. (2019, May 7). Trump pardons ex-soldier convicted in Iraqi man's murder. *New York Times*, A16.

277 Novak, A. (2016). *Comparative Executive Clemency: The Constitutional Pardon Power and the Prerogative of Mercy in Global Perspective*. Routledge.

278 Bruer, W. (2016, September 1). *From a life sentence to clemency from Obama.* CNN. https://www.cnn.com/2016/09/01/politics/clemency-sharanda-jones/index.html.

279 Horwitz, S. (2015, July 15). How a first crack cocaine offense led to a life sentence. *Washington Post.* http://www.washingtonpost.com/sf/national/2015/07/15/from-a-first-arrest-to-a-life-sentence/.

Posthumous Pardons

280 Novak, A. (2016). *Comparative Executive Clemency: The Constitutional Pardon Power and the Prerogative of Mercy in Global Perspective.* Routledge.

281 Kaur, H. (2020, February 5). *Bayard Rustin, a gay civil rights leader arrested for having sex with men, is pardoned 67 years later.* CNN. https://www.cnn.com/2020/02/05/us/bayard-rustin-california-posthumous-pardon-trnd/index.html.

282 Abdelfatah, R. (2021, February 25). *Remembering Bayard Rustin: The man behind the march on Washington.* NPR. https://www.npr.org/2021/02/22/970292302/remembering-bayard-rustin-the-man-behind-the-march-on-washington.

283 *Bayard Rustin, gay Civil Rights leader, posthumously pardoned by Gov. Newsom.* (2020, February 5). CBS San Francisco. https://www.cbsnews.com/sanfrancisco/news/bayard-rustin-gay-civil-rights-leader-pardoned-gov-gavin-newsom/.

284 Vigdor, N. (2021, August 31). 70 years after being executed for rape, 7 black men are pardoned in Virginia. *New York Times.* https://www.nytimes.com/2021/08/31/us/martinsville-seven-posthumous-pardons.html.

285 Franklin, J. (2021, August 31). *These 7 black men were executed for an alleged rape. Now, they have been pardoned.* NPR. https://www.npr.org/2021/08/31/1032859243/virginia-history-pardons-execution-civil-rights-martinsville-seven.

286 Lipscomb, J. (2021, November 23). Four Black men were accused of rape in Jim Crow Florida. 72 years later, they've been exonerated. *Washington Post.* https://www.washingtonpost.com/nation/2021/11/23/groveland-four-exonerated-rape/.

287   Ortiz, E. (2021, November 23). *Groveland Four, the Black men accused in a 1949 rape, get case dismissed.* NBC News. https://www.nbcnews.com/news/us-news/groveland-four-black-men-accused-1949-rape-get-case-dismissed-rcna6016; Weisfeldt, S. (2021, November 22). *4 Black men exonerated more than 70 years after being wrongly accused of raping a White teen girl.* CNN. https://www.cnn.com/2021/11/22/us/groveland-four-exonerated-florida/index.html.

288   Stewart, I. (2019, January 11). *Accused of Florida rape 70 years ago, 4 Black men get posthumous pardons.* NPR. https://www.npr.org/2019/01/11/684540515/accused-of-florida-rape-70-years-ago-4-black-men-get-posthumous-pardons.

289   Fortin, J. (2017, April 27). Florida apologizes for "gross injustices" to Groveland Four, decades later. *New York Times.* https://www.nytimes.com/2017/04/27/us/groveland-four-apology-florida.html.

290   Rado, D. (2019, January 11). Righting a Florida wrong: Groveland Four pardoned after nearly 70 years. *Florida Phoenix.* https://floridaphoenix.com/2019/01/11/righting-a-florida-wrong-groveland-four-pardoned-after-nearly-70-years/.

291   Oklahoma clears Black in deadly 1921 race riot. (1996, October 26). *New York Times.* https://www.nytimes.com/1996/10/26/us/oklahoma-clears-black-in-deadly-1921-race-riot.html.

292   J. B. Stradford. (n.d.). *Black Wall Street USA.* https://blackwallstreet.org/jbstradford.

293   *The victory of Greenwood: J. B. Stradford.* (2021, May 26). The Victory of Greenwood. https://thevictoryofgreenwood.com/2020/07/13/the-victory-of-greenwood-j-b-stradford/.

294   Gara, A. (n.d.). *The Baron of Black Wall Street.* Forbes. https://www.forbes.com/sites/antoinegara/2020/06/18/the-bezos-of-black-wall-street-tulsa-race-riots-1921/.

295   *Tulsa race massacre.* (n.d.). Oklahoma Historic Society. https://www.okhistory.org/learn/trm.

296 Moreno, C. (2021, June 2). *Decades after the Tulsa Race Massacre, urban "renewal" sparked Black Wall Street's second destruction.* Smithsonian. https://www.smithsonianmag.com/history/ black-wall-streets-second-destruction-180977871/.

297 Toole, T. C. (2021, May 28). *Thousands lost everything in the Tulsa Race Massacre—including my family.* National Geographic. https://www.nationalgeographic.com/history/article/ thousands-lost-everything-tulsa-race-massacre-including-my-family.

298 Madigan, T. (2021, April). *Looking Back at the Tulsa Race Massacre, 100 Years Later.* Smithsonian. https://www.smithsonianmag.com/history/ tulsa-race-massacre-century-later-180977145/.

299 Seligman, S. D. (2021, October 26). *Justice for the dead.* The Atlantic. https://www.theatlantic.com/ideas/archive/2021/10/ posthumous-pardons-justice-dead/620485/.

300 Cousino, M. B. (n.d.). *William Jackson Marion.* National Registry of Exonerations Pre-1989. Retrieved August 3, 2023, from https://www.law. umich.edu/special/exoneration/Pages/casedetailpre1989.aspx?caseid=212.

301 Possley, M. (2022, October 28). *Grover Thompson.* National Registry of Exonerations. https://www.law.umich.edu/special/exoneration/Pages/ casedetail.aspx?caseid=5488.

302 *Gov. Rauner grants Grover Thompson first posthumous exoneration in state history; "Uncle Grover was a very good man."* (2019, January 15). CBS News. https://www.cbsnews.com/chicago/news/grover-thompson-wrongful- conviction-illinois-innocence-project-bruce-rauner/.

303 *Illinois' first posthumous clemency granted to man who died behind bars.* (2019, January 16). CBS News. https://www.cbsnews.com/news/grover- thompson-illinois-1st-posthumous-clemency-granted-to-man-who-died- behind-bars/.

304 *Eighty years later, Scottsboro Boys pardoned.* (2013, November 21). Innocence Project. https://innocenceproject.org/news/ eighty-years-later-scottsboro-boys-pardoned/.

305 *Scottsboro Boys: Trial, case, Harper Lee & names.* (2022, August 30). History. https://www.history.com/topics/great-depression/scottsboro-boys.

306 *Judge clears dead Texas man of rape conviction.* (2009, February 7). NBC News. https://www.nbcnews.com/id/wbna29065906.

307 Goodwyn, W. (2009, February 5). *Family of man cleared by DNA still seeks justice.* NPR. https://www.npr.org/2009/02/05/100249923/family-of-man-cleared-by-dna-still-seeks-justice.

308 Possley, M., & The Innocence Project. (2015, March 10). *Timothy B. Cole.* National Registry of Exonerations. https://www.law.umich.edu/special/exoneration/Pages/casedetail.aspx?caseid=3114.

309 Mallin, M. (2009, July 31). Forensic science institute could spare future victims. *Houston Chronicle.* https://www.chron.com/opinion/outlook/article/forensic-science-institute-could-spare-future-1736206.php.

310 *Pardon set for woman executed in Georgia.* (2005, August 15). NBC News. https://www.nbcnews.com/id/wbna8963656.

311 Phillips, L., & College, A. (2020). Lena Baker case. *New Georgia Encyclopedia.* https://www.georgiaencyclopedia.org/articles/history-archaeology/lena-baker-case/.

312 Apperson, J., & Siegel, A. F. (2001, June 1). Glendening pardons black in 1919 murder. *Baltimore Sun.* https://www.baltimoresun.com/news/bs-xpm-2001-06-01-0106010310-story.html.

313 Seligman, S. D. (2021, October). *A Second Reckoning: Race, Injustice, and the Last Hanging in Annapolis.* University of Nebraska Press.

314 Price, L. (2021, October 3). New book details posthumous pardon of John Snowden, a Black Annapolitan accused of killing a white woman, hanged after trial. *Capital Gazette.* https://www.capitalgazette.com/news/ac-cn-annapolis-second-reckoning-john-snowden-20211003-sqoxuxp2ljfh3hvvsapjahxr3u-story.html.

315 Willmes, M. (n.d.). *Henry Flipper.* National Museum of the U.S. Army. https://www.thenmusa.org/biographies/henry-flipper/.

316 *Lieutenant Henry Ossian Flipper.* (2021, January 31). U.S. Army Center of Military History. https://history.army.mil/html/topics/afam/flipper.html.

317 McMillan, A. (n.d.). *The Pardon: Politics or mercy?* International Bar Association. https://www.ibanet.org/article/465431E6-8846 -4A89-BA0A-6A8B85E5ED1D.

318 *Alan Turing.* (2013, September 30). Stanford Encyclopedia of Philosophy. https://plato.stanford.edu/entries/turing/.

319 Dockterman, E. (2014, November 28). *The true story of The Imitation Game.* TIME. https://time.com/3609585/the-true-story-of-the-imitation-game/.

2   Amnesty and Mass Pardons

320 Etymonline. (n.d.). Amnesia. In *Online Etymology Dictionary.* https://www. etymonline.com/word/amnesia.

321 Westlake, H. D. & Hornblower, S. (2016, March 7). *Thrasybulus.* In *Oxford Classical Dictionary.* https://oxfordre.com/classics/ display/10.1093/acrefore/9780199381135.001.0001/ acrefore-9780199381135-e-6420?rskey=ZL6xcL&result=1.

322 Cannon, J. A. (n.d.). Indemnity and Oblivion, Act of. In *Encylopedia.com.* https://www.encyclopedia.com/history/encyclopedias-almanacs- transcripts-and-maps/indemnity-and-oblivion-act.

323 Ohlmeyer, J. H. (n.d.). *English Civil Wars.* In *Britannica.* https://www.britannica.com/event/English-Civil-Wars.

324 *Interregnum* (1649-1660). (n.d.). The Royal Household. https://www.royal. uk/interregnum-1649-1660.

325 Dan, M. (2019, April 26). 5 *Famous or infamous grants of amnesty.* History & Headlines. https://www.historyandheadlines. com/5-famous-or-infamous-grants-of-amnesty/.

326 Partridge, J. (2022, September 14). The sovereign's wealth: UK royal family's finances – explained. *The Guardian.* https://www.theguardian.com/uk-news/2022/sep/14/ the-sovereigns-wealth-uk-royal-familys-finances-explained.

327 Holmberg, T. (n.d.). *Decree on Émigrés.* The Napoleon Series. https://www. napoleon-series.org/research/government/diplomatic/c_emigres.html.

328 Constitution of the Year III (1795). In *John Hall Stewart, A Documentary Survey of the French Revolution* (New York: Macmillan, 1951), 588–91, 610–12. https://revolution.chnm.org/d/450.

329 *Whiskey Rebellion.* (2023, June 21). History. https://www.history.com/topics/early-us/whiskey-rebellion.

330 Kotowski, P. (n.d.). *Whiskey Rebellion.* George Washington's Mount Vernon. https://www.mountvernon.org/library/digitalhistory/digital-encyclopedia/article/whiskey-rebellion/.

331 *Whiskey Rebellion.* (n.d.). American History Central. https://www.americanhistorycentral.com/entries/whiskey-rebellion/.

332 Grubbs, P. (n.d.). Fries Rebellion. *Encyclopedia of Greater Philadelphia.* https://philadelphiaencyclopedia.org/essays/fries-rebellion/.

333 *The Alien and Sedition Acts (1798).* (n.d.). National Constitution Center. Retrieved August 13, 2023, from https://constitutioncenter.org/the-constitution/historic-document-library/detail/the-alien-and-sedition-acts-1798.

334 *See Cawthorn v. Amalfi*, 35 F.4th 435 (4th Cir. 2024) (discussing General Amnesty Act of 1872).

335 *Armstrong v. United States*, 364 U.S. 40 (1960).

336 Ford to create Clemency Board. (1974, September 7). *New York Times.* https://www.nytimes.com/1974/09/07/archives/ford-to-create-clemency-board.html.

337 Lévy, R. (2007). Pardons and Amnesties as Policy Instruments in Contemporary France. *Crime, Punishment, and Politics in a Comparative Perspective*, 36(1), 551–90. https://doi.org/10.1086/592811.

338 For prisoners in Thailand, the Royal Pardon is key to freedom. (2022, February 4). *RICE.* https://www.ricemedia.co/thailand-prisoners-royal-pardon/; Mellen, R. (2021, January 20). Most world leaders have pardon power. Few use it the way Trump has. *Washington Post.* https://www.washingtonpost.com/world/2021/01/19/trump-world-pardons-history/.

339 Glickhouse, R. (2014, December 24). Why some Brazilian jailbirds can sing "I'll Be Home for Christmas." *Christian Science Monitor.* https://www.csmonitor.com/World/Americas/Latin-America-Monitor/2014/1224/Why-some-Brazilian-jailbirds-can-sing-I-ll-be-home-for-Christmas.

340 Zhang, L. (2019, November 5). *In Japan: Pardon system debated.* The Library of Congress. https://blogs.loc.gov/law/2019/11/in-japan-pardon-system-debated.

341 Aamari, O. (2023, July 29). Throne day: King Mohammed VI grants Royal Pardon to 2,052 convicts. *Morocco World News.* https://www.moroccoworldnews.com/2023/07/356744/throne-day-king-mohammed-vi-grants-royal-pardon-to-2-052-convicts.

342 *Iran grants nearly two thousand prisoners amnesty, reduction in sentences.* (2023, April 20). Rudaw. https://www.rudaw.net/english/middleeast/iran/200420232.

343 *Constitution of the People's Republic of China.* (n.d.). The National People's Congress of the People's Republic of China. http://www.npc.gov.cn/englishnpc/constitution2019/201911/1f65146fb6104dd3a2793875d19b5b29.shtml.

344 Chen, Q. (2021, January 2). US presidents regularly issue pardons, Chinese presidents don't—But could that change? *South China Morning Post.* https://www.scmp.com/lifestyle/article/3116085/us-presidents-regularly-issue-pardons-chinese-presidents-dont-could.

345 *Biddle v. Perovich*, 274 U.S. 480 (1927).

346 *Burdick v. United States*, 236 U.S. 79 (1915).

3   Favoritism and Corruption

347 Sisk, G. C. (2007). Suspending the Pardon Power during the Twilight of a Presidential Term. *Missouri Law Review, 67*(1), 13–27.

348 Wood, A. L., & Ring, N. J. (2019). Cole Blease's pardoning pen: State power and penal reform in South Carolina. In *Crime and Punishment in the Jim Crow South* (pp. 147–69). University of Illinois Press. https://doi.org/10.5406/j.ctvgs0c92.

349 Stone, C. N. (1963, January). Bleasism and the 1912 Election in South Carolina. *The North Carolina Historical Review 40*(1).

350 Novak, A. (2016). *Comparative Executive Clemency: The Constitutional Pardon Power and the Prerogative of Mercy in Global Perspective.* Routledge.

351 Janovsky, D. (2019, April 11). *No excuse for corrupt pardons.* Project On Government Oversight. https://www.pogo.org/analysis/2019/04/no-excuse-for-corrupt-pardons.

352 Pincus, W. (1992, December 25). Bush pardons Weinberger in Iran-Contra affair. *Washington Post.* https://www.washingtonpost.com/archive/politics/1992/12/25/bush-pardons-weinberger-in-iran-contra-affair/912743a7-026b-4134-b63d-4c1c57948673/.

353 Goldstein, A., & Schmidt, S. (2001, January 21). Clinton's last-Day clemency benefits 176. *Washington Post.* https://www.washingtonpost.com/archive/politics/2001/01/21/clintons-last-day-clemency-benefits-176/d7e3ed9b-853f-4cdd-a5d4-4f9037f832c3/.

354 Johnson, K., Jackson, D., & Wagner, D. (2021, January 20). Donald Trump grants clemency to 144 people (not himself or family members) in final hours. *USA Today.* https://www.usatoday.com/story/news/politics/2021/01/19/donald-trump-pardons-steve-bannon-white-house/4209763001/.

355 Berman, D., & Polantz, K. (2020, February 21). *"The American people cared. And I care." Top lines from Judge Amy Berman Jackson during the Roger Stone sentencing.* CNN. https://www.cnn.com/2020/02/20/politics/amy-berman-jackson-quotes/index.html.

356 Jackson, D., Johnson, K., & Phillips, K. (2021, January 20). Trump pardons former adviser Stephen Bannon. *USA Today.* https://www.usatoday.com/story/news/politics/2021/01/19/trump-adviser-stephen-bannon-receives-pardon/3811128001/.

357 Haberman, M., Vogel, K. P., Lipton, E., & Schmidt, M. S. (2021, January 20). With hours left in office, Trump grants clemency to Bannon and other allies. *New York Times.* https://www.nytimes.com/2021/01/20/us/politics/trump-pardons.html.

358 Helderman, R. S., Fahrenthold, D. A., Reinhard, B., & Dawsey, J. (2021, January 21). In one of his final acts, Trump showered clemency on people with connections to him and his allies. *Washington Post*. https://www. washingtonpost.com/politics/trump-pardons/2021/01/20/dfc79216-5b49-11eb-8bcf-3877871c819d_story.html.

359 *Miranda v. Arizona*, 384 U.S. 436 (1966); U.S. Const. amend. VI.

360 Brunt, A. V. (2015, June 17). Poor people rely on public defenders who are too overworked to defend them. *The Guardian*. https://www.theguardian.com/commentisfree/2015/jun/17/poor-rely-public-defenders-too-overworked.

361 Anwar, S., Bushway, S. D., & Engberg, J. (2023). *The impact of defense counsel at bail hearings*. RAND Corporation. https://www.rand.org/pubs/research_briefs/RBA1960-1.html; *Providing legal counsel at initial bail hearings reduces use of cash bail, lowers incarceration*. (2023, May 5). RAND Corporation. https://www.rand.org/news/press/2023/05/05.html.

362 Here are some of the people Trump pardoned. (2021, January 26). *New York Times*. https://www.nytimes.com/article/who-did-trump-pardon.html.

363 Office of Public Affairs. (2013, October 28). *Former Congressman Richard G. Renzi sentenced for extortion and bribery in illegal federal land swap*. US Department of Justice. https://www.justice.gov/opa/pr/former-congressman-richard-g-renzi-sentenced-extortion-and-bribery-illegal-federal-land-swap.

364 Babcock, C. R., & Weisman, J. (2005, November 29). Congressman admits taking bribes, resigns. *Washington Post*. https://www.washingtonpost.com/archive/politics/2005/11/29/congressman-admits-taking-bribes-resigns/eec84374-abd3-4e00-b6c4-8a5ecf402e9d/.

365 Coscarelli, J. (2019, November 13). Kodak Black sentenced to nearly 4 years in prison. *New York Times*. https://www.nytimes.com/2019/11/13/arts/music/kodak-black-jail-sentencing.html.

366 Rao, S. (2021, January 20). Lil Wayne, Kodak Black among pop culture figures granted clemency on Trump's final day in office. *Washington Post*. https://www.washingtonpost.com/arts-entertainment/2021/01/20/lil-wayne-kodak-black-celebrity-trump-pardons/.

367   Aswad, J., & Halperin, S. (2021, January 21). *Why did Roc Nation CEO Desiree Perez receive a Trump pardon?* Variety. https://variety.com/2021/music/news/roc-nation-desiree-perez-trump-pardon-1234888885/.

368   Jacobs, S. (2020, October 23). Trump family friend Ken Kurson charged in New York stalking case. *Washington Post*. https://www.washingtonpost.com/national-security/ken-kurson-arrested-jared-kushner-rudy-giuliani/2020/10/23/e046fda6-1564-11eb-ba42-ec6a580836ed_story.html.

369   Mangan, D. (2022, February 16). *Jared Kushner's friend Ken Kurson pleads guilty in stalking case involving ex-wife, earlier got Trump pardon.* CNBC. https://www.cnbc.com/2022/02/16/ken-kurson-friend-of-trump-aide-jared-kushner-guilty-in-stalking-case-.html.

370   Glanz, J., Kennedy, R., & Rashbaum, W. K. (2013, May 17). Case casts harsh light on family art business. *New York Times*. https://www.nytimes.com/2013/05/17/arts/design/helly-nahmad-gallery-owner-indicted-in-gambling-case.html.

371   Rashbaum, W. K. (2000a, March 9). 845 years in prison, if the authorities can catch him: F.B.I. says fugitive has a flair for fraud and hiding stolen cash. *New York Times*. https://www.nytimes.com/2000/03/09/nyregion/845-years-prison-if-authorities-can-catch-him-fbi-says-fugitive-has-flair-for.html.

372   Rashbaum, W. K. (2000b, October 26). Fugitive arrested in Austria after a year on the run. *New York Times*. https://www.nytimes.com/2000/10/26/nyregion/fugitive-arrested-in-austria-after-a-year-on-the-run.html.

373   Anderson, C. (2021, January 21). Florida eye doctor gets clemency from Trump in health fraud. *AP News*. https://apnews.com/general-news-f3b24 69f62be5e0dc6b132ae06731ef0.

374   Schoenfeld, G. (2023, March 31). *Trump and the abuse of the pardon power.* The Bulwark. https://plus.thebulwark.com/p/trump-and-the-abuse-of-the-pardon-power.

375 Miroff, N., & Dawsey, J. (2019, August 29). "Take the land": President Trump wants a border wall. He wants it black. And he wants it by Election Day. *Washington Post*. https://www.washingtonpost.com/immigration/ take-the-land-president-trump-wants-a-border-wall-he-wants-it-black- and-he-wants-it-by-election-day/2019/08/27/37b80018-c821-11e9-a4f3- c081a126de70_story.html.

376 Mueller, III, Robert S. (2019). *Report on the Investigation into Russian Interference in The 2016 Presidential Election* (1). U.S. Department of Justice. https://www.justice.gov/archives/sco/file/1373816/download.

4   From Presidents to Kings: A Self-Pardon?

377 Totenberg, N. (2021, January 9). *Can Trump pardon himself?* NPR. https://www.npr.org/2021/01/09/955087860/can-trump-pardon-himself.

378 Zhou, L., & Prokop, A. (2023, August 16). *Trump's 4 indictments, ranked by the stakes*. Vox. https://www.vox.com/trump-investigations/23832341/ trump-charges-prison-time-sentence-indictments.

379 Novak, A. (2016). *Comparative Executive Clemency: The Constitutional Pardon Power and the Prerogative of Mercy in Global Perspective*. Routledge.

380 Kutner, M. (2017, July 24). No president has pardoned himself, but governors and a drunk mayor may have. *Newsweek*. https://www.newsweek. com/trump-granting-himself-pardon-governors-641150.

381 Lawton, M. C. (1974, August 5). *Presidential or legislative pardon of the President: Memorandum Opinion for the Deputy Attorney General*. U.S. Department of Justice, Office of Public Affairs. https://www.justice.gov/ olc/opinion/presidential-or-legislative-pardon-president.

382 Naylor, B. (2021, February 9). *Article of Impeachment cites Trump's "incitement" of Capitol insurrection*. NPR. https://www.npr.org/sections/ trump-impeachment-effort-live-updates/2021/01/11/955631105/ impeachment-resolution-cites-trumps-incitement-of-capitol-insurrection.

383 U.S. Const. amend. XIV, § 3.

384 Rebellion or insurrection, 18 U.S.C. § 2383 (1948). The President's Conditional Pardon Power. (2021). *Harvard Law Review, 134*(8), 2833–54.

385 Hamilton, A. (1788, March 14). *The Federalist* No. 69. National Archives. https://founders.archives.gov/documents/Hamilton/01-04-02-0220.

Part IV

386 The President's Conditional Pardon Power. (2021). *Harvard Law Review, 134*(8), 2833–54.

387 Dobuzinskis, A. (2015, December 25). California governor pardons Robert Downey Jr. for '90s drug case. *Reuters*. https://www.reuters.com/article/people-robertdowneyjr-idINKBN0U71F420151225.

388 Friendly skies: Jet-owning donors reap Trump-era rewards. (2020, October 1). *AP News*. https://apnews.com/article/virus-outbreak-donald-trump-business-kimberly-guilfoyle-elections-d6a2c54227b7acbf36360c5c07630419

389 Habeshian, S. (2023, May 16). *Lawsuit alleges Rudy Giuliani plotted to sell Trump presidential pardons for $2 million each.* Axios. https://www.axios.com/2023/05/16/rudy-giuliani-noelle-dunphy-sexual-assault-lawsuit.

390 Brown, H. (2023, May 18). *What to make of Giuliani's alleged cash-for-pardons pitch.* MSNBC. https://www.msnbc.com/opinion/msnbc-opinion/rudy-giuliani-lawsuit-trump-pardon-scheme-rcna84894.

391 Stewart, E. (2018, June 15). *Rudy Giuliani says the Russia investigation could get "cleaned up" with pardons hours after Paul Manafort was jailed.* Vox. https://www.vox.com/policy-and-politics/2018/6/15/17469004/rudy-giuliani-pardon-paul-manafort.

392 Walker, H. (2020, December 24). *Jared Kushner played key role in White House pardon "free-for-all."* Huffington Post. https://www.huffpost.com/entry/kushner-pardon-free-for-all_n_5fe51a42c5b64e442102e617.

393 Dembart, L., & Tribune, I. H. (2001, February 20). Meanwhile: The U.S. Founding Fathers worried about pardons. *New York Times*. https://www.nytimes.com/2001/02/20/opinion/IHT-meanwhile-the-us-founding-fathers-worried-about-pardons.html.

394 Dickinson, E. J. (2020, July 27). *28-year-old veteran shot dead at Black Lives Matter protest in Austin, Texas.* Rolling Stone. https://www.rollingstone.com/culture/culture-news/garrett-foster-austin-shooting-protest-1034507/

395 Montgomery, D., & Fernandez, M. (2020, July 31). Motorist who shot a protester in Austin claims self-defense. *New York Times.* https://www.nytimes.com/2020/07/31/us/austin-protest-shooting-foster-perry.html.

396 Levenson, E., Kafanov, L., & Salahieh, N. (2023, May 10). *Army sergeant who killed a Black Lives Matter protester in Texas sentenced to 25 years in prison.* CNN. https://www.cnn.com/2023/05/10/us/daniel-perry-texas-sentencing-wednesday/index.html.

397 Ebrahimji, A. (2023, April 18). *In two recent cases, homeowners have been charged with shooting people on their property. Here's what the law says.* CNN. https://www.cnn.com/2023/04/18/us/stand-your-ground-laws-explainer/index.html.

398 Burga, S. (2023, April 14). *Texas Gov. Greg Abbott is trying to pardon a man convicted of murdering a BLM protester. Here's what to know.* TIME. https://time.com/6272117/greg-abbott-blm-protester-murder-pardon/.

399 Weber, P. J., & Bleiberg, J. (2023, April 10). Abbott's fast-track to pardon in protest killing "unusual." *AP News.* https://apnews.com/article/texas-abbott-shooting-protest-army-murder-719c3ecf0d3247324dc077903eaf4a5d.

400 Bouie, J. (2023, May 16). The Republican embrace of vigilantism is no accident. *New York Times.* https://www.nytimes.com/2023/05/16/opinion/neely-penny-perry-rittenhouse-desantis.html; Elfrink, T. (2020, August 27). Tucker Carlson suggests teen charged in Kenosha protester killings had to "maintain order when no one else would." *Washington Post.* https://www.washingtonpost.com/nation/2020/08/27/tucker-rittenhouse-carlson-kenosha-shooting/.

401 Palmeri, T. (2022, February 2). *Trump considered blanket pardons for Jan. 6 rioters before he left office.* Politico. https://www.politico.com/news/2022/02/02/trump-considered-blanket-pardons-for-jan-6-rioters-before-he-left-office-00004738.

402 Anderson, M., & McMillan, N. (2023, March 25). *1,000 people have been charged for the Capitol riot. Here's where their cases stand.* NPR. https://www.npr.org/2023/03/25/1165022885/1000-defendants-january-6-capitol-riot.

403 Alfaro, M. (2022, September 2). Trump vows pardons, government apology to Capitol rioters if elected. *Washington Post.* https://www.washingtonpost.com/national-security/2022/09/01/trump-jan-6-rioters-pardon/.

404 Broadwater, L., Edmondson, C., & Lai, S. (2022, December 27). Jan. 6 Transcripts Shed New Light on How Trump Considered Blanket Pardons. *New York Times.* https://www.nytimes.com/2022/12/27/us/politics/jan-6-transcripts-trump-pardons.html.

405 Dorn, S. (2023, May 10). *Trump Town Hall: Trump open to pardoning Proud Boys for seditious conspiracy—and calls Jan. 6 "beautiful day."* Forbes. https://www.forbes.com/sites/saradorn/2023/05/10/trump-open-to-pardoning-proud-boys-for-seditious-conspiracy-and-calls-jan-6-beautiful-day-in-cnn-town-hall/; Quarshie, M. (2023, May 10). Trump says he would pardon Jan. 6 Capitol protesters. *Washington Examiner.* https://www.washingtonexaminer.com/news/campaigns/donald-trump-would-pardon-jan-6-capitol-protesters.

406 US Attorney's Office, District of Columbia (2024, January 5). *Three years since the Jan. 6 attack on the Capitol.* U.S. Department of Justice. https://www.justice.gov/usao-dc/36-months-jan-6-attack-capitol-0.; Patterson, S. (2023, September 24). For Donald Trump, "Stop the Steal" never gets old. *Wall Street Journal.* https://www.wsj.com/politics/elections/trump-2024-presidential-campaign-f5c64bf.

407 Herman, A. et al. (2023, March 9). The election-denying Republicans who aided Trump's "big lie" and got promoted. *The Guardian.* https://www.theguardian.com/us-news/ng-interactive/2023/mar/09/trump-big-lie-2020-election-republican-supporters-congress.

408 Goldenberg, S. (2023, May 15). *Trump puts DeSantis in a bind on 2020: Can he bring himself to say Trump lost?* Politico. https://www.politico.com/news/2023/05/15/trump-2020-election-desantis-bind-00096852.

409 Schoenfeld, G. (2023, May 30). *Trump and the abuse of the pardon power.* The Bulwark. https://plus.thebulwark.com/p/trump-and-the-abuse-of-the-pardon-power.

1 Protect the Pardon Power?

410 Hurnard, N. D. (1969). *The King's Pardon for Homicide Before A.D. 1307.* Oxford University Press.

411 Longley, R. (2020, June 3). *Why did Lincoln issue a proclamation suspending habeas corpus?* ThoughtCo. https://www.thoughtco.com/lincoln-issues-proclamation-suspending-habeas-corpus-3321581.

412 Barrett, A., & Katyal, N. (n.d.). *The Suspension Clause.* Constitution Center. https://constitutioncenter.org/the-constitution/articles/article-i/clauses/763.

413 *Harris v. Nelson*, 394 U.S. 286, 290–91 (1969).

414 *Herrera v. Collins*, 506 U.S. 390, 393 (1993).

415 Texas Board of Pardons and Paroles. (2019, January 22). *What is a pardon for innocence?* https://www.tdcj.texas.gov/bpp/exec_clem/Pardon_for_Innocence.html.

416 Texas Board of Pardons and Paroles. (2019, January 22). *What is a commutation of sentence?* https://www.tdcj.texas.gov/bpp/exec_clem/What_is_a_Commutation_of_Sentence.html.

2 Narrow the Pardon Power?

417 *Ex parte U.S.*, 242 U.S. 27, 37 (1916).

418 *The Records of the Federal Convention of 1787*, ed. Max Farrand (rev. ed. 1937). Oxford University Press.

419 Singh, M. (2020, Dec. 23). Donald Trump's latest wave of pardons includes Paul Manafort and Charles Kushner. *The Guardian.* https://www.theguardian.com/us-news/2020/dec/23/donald-trumps-latest-wave-of-pardons-includes-paul-manafort-and-charles-kunsher.

420 Fung., K. (2020, Dec. 24). Bill Barr's quote about presidential pardons resurfaces on his last day on the job. *Newsweek.* https://www.newsweek.com/bill-barrs-quote-about-presidential-pardons-resurfaces-his-last-day-job-1557145.

421   Lacey, M., & van Natta, Jr., D. (2001, February 24). Access proved vital in last-minute race for Clinton pardons. *New York Times*. https://www.nytimes.com/2001/02/24/national/access-proved-vital-in-lastminute-race-for-clinton-pardons.html.

422   L.A. Times Archives. (2001, February 21). Carter calls pardon of rich "disgraceful." *Los Angeles Times*. https://www.latimes.com/archives/la-xpm-2001-feb-21-mn-28265-story.html.

423   Clinton, W. J. (2001, February 18). My reasons for the pardons. *New York Times*. https://www.nytimes.com/2001/02/18/opinion/my-reasons-for-the-pardons.html.

424   Schweizer, P. (2016, January 17). Bill Clinton's pardon of fugitive Marc Rich continues to pay big. *New York Post*. https://nypost.com/2016/01/17/after-pardoning-criminal-marc-rich-clintons-made-millions-off-friends/.

425   Glass, A. (2018, December 24). *Bush pardons Iran-Contra felons, Dec. 24 1992*. Politico. https://www.politico.com/story/2018/12/24/bush-pardons-iran-contra-felons-dec-24-1992-1072042.

426   S. Rep. No. 216 Report of the congressional committees investigating the Iran- Contra Affair: with supplemental, minority, and additional views (1987). https://archive.org/details/reportofcongress87unit/page/n5/mode/2up.

427   Pincus, W., & Lardner, Jr., G. (1993, Jan. 16). Diary says Bush knew "details" of Iran arms deal. *Washington Post*. https://www.washingtonpost.com/archive/politics/1993/01/16/diary-says-bush-knew-details-of-iran-arms-deal/76f48355-f10c-417b-847f-6e0539cf7ff7/.

428   Fauer, A. & Haberman, M. (2024, January 19). Trump claims immunity extends even to acts that 'cross the line.' *New York Times*. https://www.nytimes.com/2024/01/19/us/politics/trump-immunity.html#:~:text=Trump%20said%20that%20presidents%20%E2%80%9Cmust,in%20another%20social%20media%20post.

429   ABC News. (2019, Mar. 24). *Read: Barr's letter to Congress on the Mueller report*. ABC News. https://abcnews.go.com/Politics/mueller-report-read-entire-letter-attorney-general-william/story?id=61911530.

430 Marimow, A. E. (2020, Jan. 30). A president "is not above the law," Trump lawyer asserts in battling back criticism of his impeachment defense. *Washington Post*. https://www.washingtonpost.com/ local/legal-issues/a-president-is-not-above-the-law-trump- lawyer-asserts-in-batting-back-criticism-of-his-impeachment- defense/2020/01/30/7b9b06ce-438f-11ea-b5fc-eefa848cde99_story.html.

431 Vogel, K. P., & Confessore, N. (2021, March 26). Using connections to Trump, Dershowitz became force in clemency grants. *New York Times*. https://www.nytimes.com/2021/02/08/us/politics/dershowitz-trump- pardons-clemency.html.

432 Schmidt, M. S., & Vogel, K. P. (2021, March 21). Prospect of pardons in final days fuels market to buy access to Trump. *New York Times*. https://www.nytimes.com/2021/01/17/us/politics/trump-pardons. html?action=click&module=RelatedLinks&pgtype=Article.

3   Reforming the Pardon Power

433 *Schick v. Reed*, 419 U.S. 256, 266 (1974).

434 *Ex parte Garland*, 71 U.S. 333, 380 (1866).

435 Colgate Love, M. (2020). *50-State Comparison: Pardon Policy & Practice*. Restoration of Rights Project. https://ccresourcecenter.org/ state-restoration-profiles/50-state-comparisoncharacteristics-of-pardon- authorities-2/.

436 Garland, M. (2021, June 14). *Statement from Attorney General Merrick B. Garland*. U.S. Department of Justice, Office of Public Affairs. https://www. justice.gov/opa/pr/statement-attorney-general-merrick-b-garland.

437 Colgate Love, M. (2020). *50-State Comparison: Pardon Policy & Practice*. Restoration of Rights Project. https://ccresourcecenter.org/ state-restoration-profiles/50-state-comparisoncharacteristics-of-pardon- authorities-2/.

438 *Records of the Office of the Pardon Attorney*. (n.d.). National Archives. https://www.archives.gov/research/guide-fed-records/groups/204. html#204.1.

439 *Connecticut Bd. of Pardons v. Dumschat*, 452 U.S. 458, 467 (1981).

440 Office of the Pardon Attorney. (2023, May 15). *Frequently asked questions*. U.S. Department of Justice. https://www.justice.gov/pardon/ frequently-asked-questions#:~:text=Show%20If%20the%20President%20 denies,so%20in%20a%20given%20case.

441 Colgate Love, M. (2002). The Pardon Paradox: Lessons of Clinton's Last Pardons, *Capital University Law Review 31*(2), 185, 193.

442 Novak, A. (2016). *Comparative Executive Clemency: The Constitutional Pardon Power and the Prerogative of Mercy in Global Perspective*. Routledge.

443 Baker, P. (2018, April 13). Trump pardons Scooter Libby in a case that mirrors his own. *New York Times*. https://www.nytimes.com/2018/04/13/ us/politics/trump-pardon-scooter-libby.html?smid=nytcore-ios-share&refe rringSource=articleShare.

444 Office of the Pardon Attorney. (2023, May 1). *Clemency Statistics*. U.S. Department of Justice. https://www.justice.gov/pardon/clemency-statistics.

445 Registration of lobbyists, 2 U.S.C. § 1603.

446 Merle, R. (2018, April 25). Mulvaney discloses "hierarchy" for meeting with lobbyists, saying some would be seen only if they paid. *Washington Post*. https://www.washingtonpost.com/news/business/wp/2018/04/25/mick- mulvaney-faces-backlash-after-telling-bankers-if-you-were-a-lobbyist-who- never-gave-us-money-i-didnt-talk-to-you/.

447 *Notable Grants of Clemency*. (n.d.). Death Penalty Information Center. https://deathpenaltyinfo.org/facts-and-research/clemency/ notable-grants-of-clemency.

448 Christopher, B. (2020, June 23). *Jerry Brown—most forgiving governor in modern California history*. CalMatters. https://calmatters. org/politics/2018/12/governor-jerrry-brown-pardon-record- number/#:~:text=Jerry%20Brown%20issued%20his%20regular,issued%20 143%20pardons%20this%20week.

Conclusion

449 Hamilton, A. (1788, March 25). *The Federalist* No. 74. National Archives. https://founders.archives.gov/documents/Hamilton/01-04-02-0226.

450 *Full transcript: Read Kristen Welker's interview with Trump.* NBC News. https://www.nbcnews.com/meet-the-press/transcripts/full-transcript-read-meet-the-press-kristen-welker-interview-trump-rcna104778 (last visited October 28, 2023).

451 *Morrison v. Olson*, 487 U.S. 654, 671 (1988).

About the Author

Kim Wehle is an author, practicing lawyer, tenured law professor, on-air legal contributor for ABC News. An expert in the separation of powers, she is a former Assistant U.S. Attorney and Associate Independent Counsel in the Whitewater Investigation. Kim comments about the law on numerous news outlets, including CBS News, MSNBC, CNN, BBC, and NPR, FoxNews, and C-SPAN, and writes for Politico, The Atlantic, The Bulwark, The Hill, and Newsweek. Kim is passionate about breaking down complex legal concepts into everyday language so that we all can better understand the basic civics underlying our complex political environment.

The three prior works in her legal expert series include *How to Think Like a Lawyer—and Why: A Common-Sense Guide to Everyday Dilemmas*, *How to Read The Constitution—and Why*, and *What You Need to Know About Voting—and Why*.

Made in the USA
Monee, IL
12 November 2024

69899892R00187